Lucky Stars:

Janet Gaynor and Charles Farrell

by Sarah Baker

Lucky Stars:

Janet Gaynor and Charles Farrell

by Sarah Baker

BearManor Media
2009

Lucky Stars

© 2009 Sarah Baker

For information, address:

BearManor Media
P. O. Box 71426
Albany, GA   31708

bearmanormedia.com

Cover design by John Teehan

Typesetting and layout by John Teehan

Published in the USA by BearManor Media

ISBN—1-59393-468-8

Table of Contents

Preface

When I was in college, a friend of mine who knew I was a classic movie buff started lending me her collection of silent films, hoping to spark my interest. It worked. Until then the only silent film I had seen was *Wings*, and I had marveled at Wellman's acrobatic flight sequences, and fallen a little in love with Buddy Rogers and Clara Bow. But I did not become a silent film fanatic until my friend lent me her copy of *7ᵗʰ Heaven*. Like most audiences who had seen Charles Farrell as Chico and Janet Gaynor as Diane, I was completely enraptured. Their chemistry seemed too real to be mere acting. Wondering if it could be some sort of fluke, I borrowed my friend's copies of *Street Angel* and *Sunny Side Up*. It was no accident. Even in an early talkie like *Sunny Side Up*, where they were forced to sing and dance and play one-dimensional characters, the Farrell/Gaynor magic was still there.

At the time I was researching my documentary on silent film star Olive Thomas, who started in pictures about ten years before Farrell and Gaynor and died before they ever made it to Hollywood. As I worked on Ollie, I kept my eye out for material on Farrell and Gaynor. I figured that two stars that gained such an iconic status and enjoyed such long, profitable careers must have miles of ink devoted to them. Sadly, this was not the case. About Charles Farrell, who had been first a matinee idol, then a television star, and the man who created Palm Springs as a desert playground for the stars, there was absolutely nothing. About Janet Gaynor, who was the finest actress of her time and winner of the first Best Actress Academy Award, and who continued acting in film, radio, theater and television well into her twilight years, there was not much more.

All historians love a challenge, and after I finished work on Olive Thomas, I was delighted to delve into Charlie and Janet's lives and careers.

They both lived rich, full, productive lives and accomplished much. I hope that the recent release of several of their films to DVD by 20th Century-Fox will reignite the public's passion for Farrell and Gaynor. I hope this book will help restore them to their rightful place in cinema history.

This work could not have been accomplished without the help of several individuals, libraries, and archives that rallied to the cause:

Massachusetts: Thanks to Cheryl MacDonald, Charles Farrell's relatives Belle Lundstedt and Shirley Seaward (Massachusetts by way of California), local historians Betty Cottrell and Lynda Ames, and Boston University archivist Diane Gallagher.

Maine: Thanks to Katherine LeBlanc, the Skowhegan Public Library; Jeff Quinn, the Lakewood Theatre.

Philadelphia: Thanks to Jamaal Abdul-Alim, Gina LoBiondo and the Germantown Historical Society.

Chicago: Thanks to Kyle Norwood.

Florida: Thanks to Ann Flotte, of Melbourne, Florida, who lived in Janet's childhood home away from home and furnished the information about her winters there.

California: Thanks to Robin Gaynor Adrian; Paul Gregory; Daniel Selznick; Frank Bogert; Gale Storm; Ned Comstock, Cinema Library, University of Southern California; Jeri Vogelsang, the Palm Springs Historical Society; Sally Presley Rippingale; Pat Atkinson; Bruce Fessier, *The Desert Sun*; David F. Miller, 20th Century-Fox Legal Department; Lauren Buisson and Julie Garwood, the 20th Century-Fox Archives at UCLA; Jonathon Auxier, the Warner Brothers Archives at the University of Southern California; William Malin, The Historic Masquers Club; John Fritsche; Sean McCourt and the San Francisco Public Library; Madeline McEntyre and Jim Yuschenkoff, the *USS Hornet* Museum at Alameda.

Nevada: Thanks to Angela Haag and the Central Nevada Historical Society.

Texas: Thanks to Steve Wilson, Harry Ransom Center at the University of Texas at Austin; the interlibrary loan staff at The University of Texas at Arlington; Millie Fain of the Arlington Public Library; and my friends Heidi Parish, Elaine Hellmund, Lisa Lewis, Brittany Lee, and Nicole New, who all volunteered their time and energies to the project.

Special thanks to Stephen O'Brien for sharing some of his research on Charles Farrell with me and acting as a sounding board. I would also like to thank authors Connie Billips, Eve Golden, and David Menefee, who offered their support and encouragement. Director Allison Anders has been a constant champion of all my projects, and I sincerely hope I can repay all the favors some day. I also owe a debt of gratitude to Deborah Ann Smith, who edited every chapter and tried so valiantly to take me out of my passive voice.

This book would not have happened without the support and encouragement of my husband Zach, who has always been my "accountability buddy." This book is dedicated to Zach and our daughter Olivia. Finally, I wish to thank Sheran Johle for introducing me to Charlie and Janet and loaning me their films. Without her love of silent film, I would have never met any of these wonderful people, including Charlie, Janet and Olive.

– Sarah Baker
Arlington, Texas
June 28, 2008

Foreword

Something remarkable took hold of me as a seventeen year-old girl: I discovered silent movies. They offered to me, a mid-century girl, a long-dead romance and beauty in cinema and I was smitten with dreamy lust for silver screen movie stars, their loves and lore. In particular, Olive Thomas: Ziegfeld Follies Girl, silent screen star, flapper, and centerpiece of a remarkable life story, which I managed to assemble from a ragged collection of library books (kept long past the due dates). I loved to stare at her photographs, my imagination in high gear, enchanted and be-witched by her obvious beauty, endearing smirk and, no matter her ex-pression, always a hint of mischief from under the brim of a straw hat. She made an indelible impression.

Unlike other teenage obsessions, my passion for Olive stayed strong, and it is how I came to meet my friend Sarah Baker, producer and screen-writer for the documentary film, *Olive Thomas: Everybody's Sweetheart*. Like me, Sarah became enamored of silent movies as a teenager, fasci-nated by the onscreen drama, but wonderfully drawn to the real-life drama off the set and behind very private doors.

Sarah and I are close, kindred spirits.

A long-time fan of Janet Gaynor's performances in *A Star Is Born* and *Sunrise*, I wasn't aware of her fragile brilliance and the power of her exquis-ite on-screen partnership with Charles Farrell until I was editing my own film, *Grace Of My Heart*, with three-time Oscar winning editor Thelma Schoonmaker (and editor Jimmy Kwei). I was given a rare opportunity to work with this power editing team by my executive producer on the film (and the second mentor in my career) Martin Scorsese. From the begin-ning of our work together, Marty insisted that I discover the personal, inner core of my inspiration, my true creative self. And one day he dragged me from the editing room to watch the work of a particular director.

"Frank Borzage," he said, "He won the first Academy Award for directing and made over a hundred movies, but his name is not on the tip of anyone's tongue. He wasn't an intellectual, he was a romantic. And his films reflect the mysticism of lovers destined to be together." I was enthralled, "Wow, that sounds like MY GUY!!!" He said, "I know he's your guy, that's why I'm introducing him to you!"

Soon enough, I'm sitting beside Martin Scorsese in his private screening room at Cappa watching a newly restored print of Borzage's *Living on Velvet*. Exquisite! Then I was taken back to Thelma's editing room where I was treated to scenes from Borzage's *7th Heaven* and *Street Angel* on the flatbed. Amazing shimmering footage and, yes, just what Doctor S. had ordered!

Turns out Marty and Thelma didn't have all this amazing footage just lying around the editing room. After spending the day editing my film, *Grace of My Heart*, Thelma spent the night editing the documentary film, *A Personal Journey with Martin Scorsese Through American Movies*, in which Marty discusses, at length, numerous scenes from *7th Heaven* and *Street Angel*. I was reminded of Janet Gaynor's own life when by day she worked for Murnau on *Sunrise* and by night with Borzage on *7th Heaven*. That my life intersected with this documentary, Marty and Thelma, Gaynor and Farrell, and Borzage, is beyond coincidence for me; it is perhaps one of the most relevant and "holy" educations of my life.

Marty spent much valuable, selfless time educating me on this man's vision and hosting marathon private screenings of Borzage's work; I'm eternally grateful. Thelma was no less the benevolent instructor. Already a fan of the work of Gaynor and Farrell, Thelma taught me to recognize and appreciate the emotional honesty in the performances of both actors. "Look at her — she's swooning!" And together we were awed by a moment when Janet, standing on tip-toes, eyes consumed with passion, reaches for Charles, big and brawny, but as delicate as an angel as he sweeps petite Janet off her feet and into his arms with a kiss. *That* is true love!

Although I had gained an entirely new appreciation for silent-era cinema, my crash-course education in silent-era film and even my deep regard for these actors was frozen on the silver screen. I could carry these images in my heart and head, and hopefully into my work, but where had they breathed, lived and loved while navigating the first generation of international fame? Why is it so hard for us to truly imagine the lives of the silent-era stars? Is it because we don't hear them speak? If I watch Jane

Fonda in *Cat Ballou*, made in 1965, I can well imagine her life on the set between takes and off the set, too; no problem picturing Jane driving home, having dinner at a fancy restaurant (but preferring to smoke rather than eat), lying in a big bed in a big house near a big ocean. But silent stars, no matter how much we know about them, often remain entombed on that silver screen or etched on a postcard or ephemera from the past.

Incredibly, even though I live in Los Angeles and walk the very sidewalks the early Hollywood stars walked and see the same hills and splash in the same ocean, rarely do their personal days and nights come alive for me. As a fan of the silent era, you often feel like a ghost hunter on a frustrating quest to sense a glimpse of what life was like in the gardens and patios, on the terraces and balconies, up and down the walkways and driveways, and yes, deep inside the hearts and minds of those once here and so alive, but now scarcely in evidence, their histories scattered to the four winds and, it so often seems, forever gone.

But, like the old saying, *it ain't necessarily so*. Thanks to Sarah Baker, the silent era speaks, and with much grace, wit and charm, in *Lucky Stars*. At last I can travel back across the decades and feel the elusive pulse of two very real hearts, Janet Gaynor and Charles Farrell, their lives now as real and tangible for me as that of...Jane Fonda!

When Sarah Baker writes about Charles Farrell taking up residence at the Hollywood Athletic Club, I can honestly and authentically feel his presence within those walls, which, by coincidence, I could by no means feel or imagine in that same blaring with hip-hop venue during a premiere after-party I recently attended. I learned that chasing ghosts in what was the Hollywood Athletic Club or any other historic early Hollywood haunt to find the past was futile. Sarah Baker gave it to me on the page and it leapt into my imagination: there is Farrell walking down the stairs to go to the gym, to play a game of pool before dressing for a getaway dinner at the beach with Janet.

And I don't need to get in my car and drive to Mound Street to find the modest house where Janet lived with her mother and sister. It exists, fully realized, in the pages of *Lucky Stars*. And besides, even if still standing, it's likely studded with Direct TV dishes and other 21st Century amenities, sure to blow the illusion of my era-otic adventure. Within the pages of Sarah's book, I can feel Janet's warm bath at the end of a long day's work, not an iconic glamorous Hollywood bubble bath, but a much-needed muscle-soothing soak before preparing herself for the next day's work. And underneath, I can appreciate the unspoken texture of these women living together, the ambitious mother, and her heartbroken resentful sister who longed desperately for the (near accidental) movie career of her younger sister.

Sarah's skill authenticates my imaginary journeys into the lives and loves of silver screen and golden era Hollywood. No longer are these people mere wax figures or one-dimensional faces in faded photographs, alive only on the screen, these long-silent stars have become real, almost like friends. And the greatest gift of all to me from *Lucky Stars* is a deepening in the education of this filmmaker.

As the sun sets behind the Los Feliz hills, two young lucky stars are watching the same sunset. They stand together, laugh, swoon a little, and take a deep breath, the same as I, before heading out to dinner.

Thank you, Sarah.

– Allison Anders
Los Angeles, Ca

Introduction

"There can never be a Janet Gaynor and Charles Farrell love team again," Janet Gaynor declared to *Look* magazine in 1970, and she was right. From their first iconic pairing in *7th Heaven* through another eleven films, they were indivisible. Though both worked with other actors in other films, in the minds and hearts of their adoring public, they were as one. So utterly complete was their pairing that in the 1970s—nearly four decades after their onscreen partnership ended—every mention of Gaynor in the press merited a mention of Farrell, and vice-versa.

To their contemporary critics and to everyone who followed, Gaynor and Farrell almost defied categorization. People speak of them as the all-American couple, but the most memorable characters they played were foreign: French, Italian, or if American, so alienated from their surroundings they were almost outcasts. Charlie is described as brawny and handsome, yet he moved with a dancer's grace and his characters were always capable of great tenderness. Janet is constantly portrayed as a waif needing rescue, but she never waited for Prince Charming to save her. Transformed instead by profound love, Janet liberated herself—and her hero, too.

Their chemistry was sparked in reality, when they fell in love on the set of *7th Heaven*, and was transferred to the screen, setting them apart in the pantheon of film couples. Farrell and Gaynor reminded 1920s audiences of first love; not in a childish or cloying way, but of passion, innocence, and longing. They brought out what was best in the audience: the nobility, depth, and spirituality that come with true love. Critic John Belton called this, "a strange, fascinating mixture of spiritual purity and physical attractiveness…a total ignorance of the state of sin," which bridged the gap between Jazz Age lust and pre-war abstinence.

1

Farrell and Gaynor carried on their secret romance from 1927 until the spring of 1929, when Farrell begged Gaynor to marry him. Gaynor refused, and married attorney Lydell Peck instead. Their breakup hit Charlie particularly hard. The following Christmas, his mother Estelle died. Those two strong women had been the core of his life. When Farrell lost them both, he was left without a compass. He married actress Virginia Valli in 1931, but as Frank Bogert, Charlie's close friend recalled, Valli was more of a mother figure than lover. Farrell spent the rest of his life bobbing from love affair to love affair, searching in vain for the same combination of mother and lover that he had in Janet Gaynor.

Eventually, Gaynor and Farrell were able to maintain a mellow friendship. They reunited in 1957 for the Lux Radio Theatre broadcast of *7th Heaven*, and remained friendly neighbors when Janet moved to Palm Springs with Paul Gregory. Gaynor lived a rich, full life devoted to painting, theatre, and friends, and Farrell leaned on her for support often. After Virginia Valli died, Farrell became reclusive and would not make public appearances unless Gaynor was at his side.

In their finest roles, Farrell and Gaynor played characters who were "human souls made great through love and adversity."[1] Their on-screen partnership brought out the best in each other—and in the audience. This partnership extended into their private lives, as their early romance and subsequent friendship lasted until Gaynor's death in 1984. With her characteristic insight, Janet Gaynor summed it up best: "We were not realistic and were far too idealistic for these times. We were romantic and beautiful and innocent."

This is their story.

Chapter One
A Very Remarkable Fellow

"There's no need of being down in this world. Set your mind upon climbing, and climb you will."

— John Golden, *7th Heaven*

August 9, 1900 was a balmy, pleasant summer day with what the *Boston Globe* called "fresh, northeasterly winds." The temperature was in the 80s, but Estelle Carew Farrell, who had been having labor pains all day, was concerned that her newborn would not be warm enough. She sent her husband, David, to the Sanfords, who also rented a room in the Fuller Tavern Annex. The Sanfords had a register cut in their floor that allowed the heat from the kitchen to rise into their room. As none of the other upstairs rooms were heated, so it was that Charles David Farrell, matinee idol, was born in his neighbors' bedroom that night.

Farrell, the man who became synonymous with Hollywood glamour and leisure, was born into a working-class family. Like thousands of other American families at the turn of the century, his had upwardly mobile aspirations. His father, David Henry, was a first generation American, born just after his parents emigrated from Ireland in 1870. Charlie's grandfather, John Henry, became a fireman on the railroads in Fayville, Massachusetts. His wife, Julia Ann, stayed home with the entire Farrell brood, which included six children and two boarders.

Charles' mother, Estelle Carew, was from a smaller family that hailed from the industrial town of Lynn. Her father, William E. Carew, had served in the 15th New Hampshire Infantry, Company K, during the Civil War. He settled in to work at one of Lynn's infamous shoe factories after

Charlie's birthplace in Walpole.

being mustered out as a Sergeant in 1863. Estelle's mother, Vicey, was born in Nova Scotia of English-Canadian parents and immigrated to Massachusetts in 1864. She stayed home with Estelle and Estelle's sister, Edith, who was seven years younger. Estelle possessed an artistic streak and, when work permitted after her marriage, helped stage local theatrical productions and sang in the Congregational Church Choir. Estelle's parents may have separated sometime prior to 1890, for Vicey is shown in the Lynn, MA directory as the sole occupant of her home. According to the 1900 and 1910 census records, William was living alone, earning a living as a house painter. In 1910, Vicey is shown living with the Farrells in Walpole. By 1920, William was listed as an occupant in the New Hampshire Soldiers' Home, and Vicey was living on his soldier's pension in Lynn. There is no record of either Vicey or William in the 1930 census.

David and Estelle married on March 2, 1897, in Mansfield, Massachusetts. They began their married life as the Gilded Age of robber barons gave way to the Progressive Era. This time in American history belonged to reformers, movers, and changers. This was the era of Upton Sinclair's searing indictment of the meat-packing industry, *The Jungle,* which brought about massive changes in food handling and packaging. This period also belonged to women like Jane Addams, Mother Jones, and Margaret Sanger, who risked their personal safety to assure a better quality of life for the poor and immigrants. David, as the child of Irish immigrants, witnessed the exploitation of his family and friends first-hand. Estelle, as the daughter of a factory worker, knew the exhausting and dangerous conditions her father worked in daily. They had a driving need to improve their lot for their own sakes, and for their children. Theirs was also an era that idolized the American dream of success through hard work, pluck, and courage. Another Massachusetts native, Horatio Alger, Jr., published 135 dime novels that exemplified the rags-to-respectability dreams of that generation. In *Paul the Peddler; or the Fortunes of a Young Street Merchant* (1871), the hero is told that "Many successful men have begun as low down; with energy and industry much may be accomplished." Following a similar philosophy, David and Estelle moved to Walpole to start their own lives.

Detail from Farrell family Bible, showing David and Estelle's wedding date.

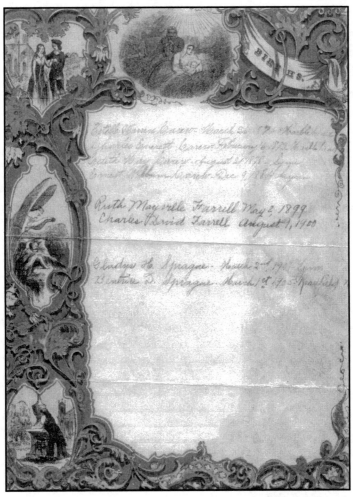

Farrell family Bible, showing Charlie and Ruth's birthdates.

Walpole, Massachusetts is a small inland town, known as the half-way point between Boston and Providence, Rhode Island. It began as part of Dedham, but split in 1724 to form its own community. The Neponset River provided ample water power for mills, and Walpole developed into an industrial community. Walpole began to grow considerably after the Revolutionary War, and experienced its largest population boom between 1900 and 1920, when 3,000 residents were added to census records. While it was an industrial town, it was much smaller than Lynn and boasted only two elementary schools, making it a much friendlier place to raise children.

The little Farrell family contributed to the rise in Walpole's population. Estelle, David, and Charlie's big sister Ruth, who was a year old at the time of his birth, lived in a back room in the Annex to the Fuller Tavern at 1885 Washington Street. The Fuller was known for its hospitality to travelers journeying between Providence and Boston. David worked as a streetcar conductor, a dirty and sometimes dangerous job. A contemporary of David's who also worked as a conductor, had this to say about his career:

No form of labor, however difficult, is harder than working on a street car…A conductor's lot is never entirely a happy one. During the summer he risks his life every time he goes to collect fares along the edge of the foot board on either side of the car. He is liable to collide with a brick pile or a lime kiln at any time; and, when it occurs, he is either killed or laid up for repairs. In the winter time he is on the back platform, half frozen…Being a single man, I was not affected by the loss of home life. I boarded with a conductor's family, and the sacrifices he had to make were really disheartening. He hardly knew his own children, and certainly did not have a chance to enjoy the society of his wife.[2]

By the time the 1910 census was taken, David had renounced the hazardous life of a street car conductor and become an entrepreneur. He had established a small restaurant in the street level of the Bird Hall Building, in the heart of East Walpole. In addition to working as a waitress in the restaurant, Estelle now ran a boarding house from their home on Rhoades Avenue, which housed six lodgers in addition to the Farrell family and Vicey Carew. Everyone in the family was expected to work and work hard. When Charlie came home from school in the afternoon, he was greeted with a sink full of dirty dishes and his father's command to

Charlie as a boy in Walpole.

"Peel those spuds, son!" Eventually David expanded his business to include a cigar stand in the Triangle Building across the street and a makeshift movie theater that took over the top floor of the Bird Hall Building. Silent films were screened in the theater, and Charlie was responsible for preparing the theatre for the shows and sweeping up afterwards, in between duties at the restaurant. In a later interview, Farrell remembered:

> Even in those surroundings, I knew I was going to be a great motion picture actor. I never sold a ticket to the theater but what I looked the customer in the eye and said to myself, "Some day that person will be going to the theater to see Charlie Farrell."[3]

Charlie and Ruth had to help out at the restaurant and theatre while staying in school and maintaining good grades. In this, the Farrells differed from many at the turn of the century whose children left school permanently and assumed low-paying jobs to contribute to the family coffers. Charlie and Ruth attended the Boyden Elementary School, Bird Elementary School, and finally Walpole High School.[4] (Years later, Charlie was inducted into the Walpole High School Hall of Fame.) A local vaude-villian named James Brooks Bailey taught Charlie to play the trumpet, a skill that helped him land an extra part in Hollywood several years later.[5] While Charlie dreamed of a career on the silver screen, his parents planned for him to attend college. David and Estelle were steadily ascending to middle-class respectability; they had gone from renting a room to owning a boarding house, and from working as wage slaves to owning several small businesses. Sending their only son to college was the culmination of the American Dream; the grandchild of immigrants and factory workers was achieving something they never thought possible.

Charlie's drive to enter show business was a direct affront to his parents' ambition. He dreamed not of becoming a stage actor—which, though bad enough, might have had some tinge of cachet—but a film actor, the lowest of the low. Mary Pickford, who reigned supreme over the silent era and helped create the motion picture industry, entered movies in 1909 to supplement the Pickford income. As a stage-trained actress it was quite a comedown, as she remembered: "those despised, cheap, loath-some motion picture studios. It was beneath my dignity as an artist, which I most certainly considered myself at the time."[6]   David wanted Charlie to become a dentist, a solid, upright career, one that would earn his son the title of "Doctor." Father and son argued endlessly until Estelle, ever the peacemaker, suggested a compromise—that Charlie would attend Boston University and earn a business degree.

To earn additional income for his tuition, Charlie worked at Hollingsworth and Vose, a paper company that still exists in Walpole today. When he entered Boston University in the fall of 1918, he used his childhood training in the restaurant to secure a job as a busboy at Walton's Cafeteria across from the College of Business Administration. He worked his way up to counter-man and then got a job as captain of waiters at Ginter's Restaurant on Boylston Street. Henry Fine, a classmate, recalled that "the struggle to put himself through college, with no financial assistance from his family, engaged most of his spare time and energy."[7] While it is likely that David and Estelle contributed what they could, the impetus to pay for college fell squarely on Charlie. His parents were committed to keeping their businesses afloat, and releasing Charlie from those obligations to pursue college was their part of the sacrifice.

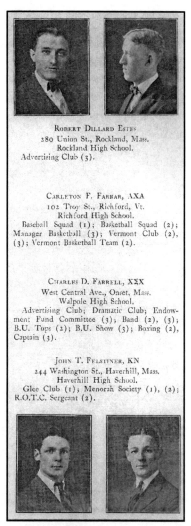

ROBERT DILLARD ESTES
280 Union St., Rockland, Mass.
Rockland High School.
Advertising Club (3).

CARLETON F. FARRAR, AXA
102 Troy St., Richford, Vt.
Richford High School.
Baseball Squad (1); Basketball Squad (2); Manager Basketball (3); Vermont Club (2), (3); Vermont Basketball Team (2).

CHARLES D. FARRELL, XΣX
West Central Ave., Onset, Mass.
Walpole High School.
Advertising Club; Dramatic Club; Endowment Fund Committee (3); Band (2), (3); B.U. Tops (2); B.U. Show (3); Boxing (2), Captain (3).

JOHN T. FELSTINER, KN
244 Washington St., Haverhill, Mass.
Haverhill High School.
Glee Club (1); Menorah Society (1), (2); R.O.T.C. Sergeant (2).

Charlie in the 1923 Boston University Yearbook.

Charlie did not confine himself to all work and no play, however. He took on a number of extracurricular activities, including Advertising Club, the Endowment Fund Committee, and the University Band, in which he, of course, played coronet. He pledged Chi Sigma Chi, "not one of the intercollegiate bodies and merely a local fraternity. Several of his friends were already members and the fraternity as a whole seemed to him to offer the largest number of congenial associations. The other considerations [such as advantageous social connections] meant nothing to him."[8] In keeping with the letter of his compromise with his parents, if not the spirit, he also participated in the Dramatic Club. Charlie also probably spent much of his spare income and time in the movie houses and vaudeville theatres in the theatre district, conveniently located within a few miles of campus. During one breathless season, Boston hosted Fred and Adele Astaire in *The Bunch and Judy*, Ed Wynn in *The Perfect Fool*, as well as traveling productions of the *Ziegfeld Follies* and *Greenwich Village Follies*. Charlie also caught all the movies starring his favorite actors: Mary Pickford, Douglas Fairbanks, and Harold Lloyd.

Charlie was naturally athletic and participated on the football and fencing teams. He tried out for the swimming team but was not selected. Fine felt that "the fact that the team was forced to practise [sic] and workout in the Y.M.C.A. tank, at some distance from the college, at times when Charlie was busy earning the money to put himself through school, undoubtedly had something to do with his failure. But it was a keen disappointment to him."[9] Charlie's greatest athletic prowess was in the boxing ring—he was on the Boxing Team his entire tenure at BU and served as Team Captain for the last two years. Charlie beat fellow classmate Mickey Cochrane (later the catcher for the Philadelphia Athletics and player-manager of the Detroit Tigers) to capture

Charlie as captain of the Boxing Team.

the school championship, and Cochrane was so mortified that he refused to speak to Charlie the rest of the term. Once Cochrane was established in his baseball career he challenged Charlie to a rematch, which Charlie politely declined. The two were able to maintain a cordial friendship thereafter.

Henry Fine recalled another moment in Charlie's academic career when his boxing skills landed him in trouble. Charlie made the mistake of cracking a joke during a lecture in Applied Psychology, given by a professor who was "recognized as one of the most brilliant and unconventional lecturers in his field." When the class broke up, the professor looked at Farrell and offered to punch the offender in the nose, if he had the courage to make himself known. Charlie turned white and remained silent; the professor resumed his lecture. The professor was known as a good amateur boxer and Charlie's refusal to fight him branded him "yellow" by his classmates. Fine recalled that:

> Two days later, Farrell was boxing a fraternity brother at the Union, when the prof. walked in and seated himself in the front row. Without appearing to see him, Charlie maneuvered his opponent to a spot directly in front of the mentor, jabbed him in the face and finally, with a quick blow, sent him backward into the prof's lap. Finally the professor got up and left. The next day, when Charlie entered his class, the prof. greeted him with a cordial, "Hello, Charlie." No other reference was ever made to what happened, but everyone knew it was the professor's way of closing the incident.[10]

Meanwhile, with Charlie safely enrolled at BU, his family moved to Onset Bay on Cape Cod. Onset began as a summer meeting campsite for the Spiritualist movement, but evolved into a "Mecca for entertainment," according to Lynda Ames, a research librarian in Onset. The Farrells got good business from the movie theatre trade—Ames recalls that "It was like Fourth of July all summer in Onset"—so they established a vaudeville and movie theatre: the New Onset.

David was an astute businessman who saw how easily money could be made from motion pictures; after all, patrons came in, saw a show, and left without actually carrying any products out with them. Those same patrons returned as soon as the program changed. Unlike the

Onset Ave. showing New Onset Theatre, Onset, Mass.

The New Onset Theatre, Onset Bay, MA. Courtesy of the Wareham Free Library.

restaurant business, where customers could simply decide to cook at home, the theater provided a unique experience that could not be duplicated by oneself. No dishes to wash, no food to order, no potatoes to peel, and owning a theatre carried with it a little bit of stardust, a little snob appeal.

Charlie's sister, Ruth, who was a gifted pianist, provided accompaniment to all the movies—a task that required improvisation and timing, since few films arrived at small-town theatres with their own prewritten scores. Estelle took the tickets while David ran the reels. Since Charlie was interested in motion pictures anyway and was obtaining his business degree, David expected that Charlie would graduate and then take over the latest family venture. At last, David and Estelle reached their goal; middle-class respectability and a steady income were theirs. As soon as Charlie graduated, he would return with his degree and take up the reins and Estelle and David could take a well-deserved break. Meanwhile, Ruth left home to study at the New England Conservatory of Music. It was all right for Ruth to pursue her artistic ambitions; after all, her talent directly benefited the Farrell family theatres. Ruth would also give up her musical career once she found the right man to marry; hopefully someone who could bring further ambition and drive to the family business.

Charlie (top row, fifth from right) with the Business Administration Class, 1923.

Henry Fine recalled that Charlie never spoke of his acting ambition except once, and was "greeted with a chorus of hoots and jeers. Charlie laughed the matter off, but that was the last time he ever referred to actors or Hollywood while he was in college." In the spring of 1922, Charlie was placed on academic probation. He made it through by the skin of his teeth and returned to Onset where he worked in the Farrell theatres and ran a tour boat out on the Bay. According to Lynda Ames, Charlie was "always dressed in white pants and hat and looked the part, drop dead gorgeous and he didn't have trouble getting the ladies to buy tickets." His charisma and presence attracted the attention of a local theatre troupe playing at the Temple Theatre (not a Farrell-owned attraction), and Little Billy, an actor with the troupe, offered Charlie a job as his manager. Charlie accepted, choosing a shot at show business over graduation. Charlie's reasons for leaving BU were simple: if he became a businessman, he would throw away his chance of becoming an actor. It particularly galled Charlie that his father had chosen to make money from the very business Charlie was denied. David was smart and knew that there was money to be made from motion pictures, but actors—unless they were highly successful—led a hand-to-mouth existence. This was exactly the kind of financial instability from which the Farrells had struggled to free themselves.

Little Billy, in a newspaper clipping, circa 1930. Courtesy of the Historic Masquers Club, www.masquersclub.org.

Little Billy was a "midget" vaudeville star who had already enjoyed quite a bit of success by the time he came to Onset. His beginnings were humble; as a five-year-old, he had been left behind by his mother, a prostitute, in a raid on a Lynn, Massachusetts cathouse and subsequently adopted by vaudeville stars Jimmy and Jere Grady (the raid had been conducted by a relative of the Gradys). When they discovered that the child could sing and dance, they incorporated him into their act.[11]   He appeared in the *George M. Cohan Revues* of 1916 and 1918 as well as countless other shows that toured the country—and even a few that made it to Broadway. Today he is probably best known as the Magistrate of Munchkinland from *The Wizard of Oz* (1939). Little Billy was Charlie's last chance to get his foot in the door of show business. When Billy offered him a job as his property manager and business advisor, Charlie left home without a backward glance. When interviewed in 1976, Charlie had the buffer of fifty years' success, and was able to proclaim flippantly, "I just did what I wanted."[12]   However, his decision was a monumental slap in the face to his parents, particularly his father. For four years thereafter, David refused to speak to his son.

Vaudeville was the most popular form of entertainment at the turn of the century. It began as a rough kind of amusement enjoyed by mostly male audiences in saloons and beer gardens, but by the early 1920s had cleaned up its act and become, with few exceptions, family-friendly. Moving pictures began to challenge vaudeville's popularity, and by the time Charlie went on the road with Little Billy, most vaudeville houses, including the

Farrells', had converted to "vaude-film" formats—vaudeville and movies shared the bill and the stage. The business was controlled by a series of monopolies which were responsible for booking the talent in their theatres. In the east, vaudeville was controlled by the Keith Circuit; in the West, it was controlled by the Orpheum. In other areas of the country, smaller companies brokered a peace with the larger monopolies.[13] The Interstate Theatre chain, which owned theatres in Arkansas, Louisiana, Oklahoma, and Texas, negotiated a peace with the Orpheum and Keith circuits[14], which is how Little Billy ended up playing at the Majestic Theatre in Fort Worth, Texas that summer.

There are two versions, both recounted by Farrell over the years, of how he ended up leaving Little Billy and coming to Hollywood. In both versions, the two had an argument:

> I had to help him dress and I got to be his guardian, sort of. I used to go around with him. He was a little fellow, you know. He was temperamental. One day he got tough with me and I walked out on him. He said, "Fix that window," and I said, "Wait a minute, I'm not your valet. He said, "Oh yes you are," and I said "The hell I am," and walked out.[15]

The difference between the two stories is exactly where the falling-out occurred. In some versions, Farrell stated that they were playing in Fort Worth, and since he was halfway to Hollywood already, decided to come out and risk his luck. In other versions, Farrell recounted that the act broke up in Los Angeles, and since he was already in Hollywood, decided to stay. The first version makes the best story; it's much more romantic to imagine Farrell with nothing left to lose, hopping a train and heading west to pursue his dream. It is also unusual that Charlie should have picked Fort Worth out of a hat; after all, it would have been simpler to say "Texas" or at least mention Dallas, which was the bigger and richer town of the two at the time. The second version is the more realistic of the two, and it makes sense that Charlie would have hung in there, tolerating Little Billy's tantrums, until he made his final goal.

But wherever the argument occurred, the end result was the same: Charles Farrell made it to Hollywood. He remembered his first day there clearly, even fifty years later:

Oh, I loved it when I first came out...It was the most beautiful day I'd ever seen...Hollywood and Vine – Vine Street was overgrown with trees. There was one restaurant, one little restaurant and the studio. That's about all that was on Vine Street.[16]

The Hollywood Charlie saw that picturesque day in 1923 was very different from what it had been ten years before, and what it would become ten years later. The motion picture industry was growing and thriving, having moved from the East Coast to the sunshine and open fields of

California. Film was gaining prestige as a legitimate art form, and was also overtaking vaudeville as the preferred form of entertainment for the masses. Movie studios were growing in size, gathering power and esteem, but the studio system that took hold in the 1930s and remained firmly in place through the advent of television had not coalesced. Hollywood was, at this particular moment, still very much in its infancy. Screenwriter Anita Loos recalled that most of the actors were just beginning to move out of the rustic Hollywood Hotel into palatial estates in Beverly Hills. Loos herself always knew that it was time to head back to New York whenever the dresses in Hollywood stores began to look chic.

Charlie arrived in Hollywood with $18 in his pocket, courtesy of his gig with Little Billy, but he knew no one and had no practical acting experience. He did, however, know how to swim, ride a horse, and dance—all in-

Charlie wearing his tuxedo, indispensible attire for a "dress extra."
Photograph by Max Munn Autrey.

dispensable talents for an extra. Charlie owned a nice collegiate wardrobe (extras had to provide their own costumes); he was handsome and tall, and these attributes, plus his other skills, put him above the ranks of hundreds who were also seeking work. He began rooming with Richard Van Mattimore, who was known professionally as Richard Arlen. Richard had been in Hollywood since 1920 and knew the ropes; he took Charlie under his wing and took him along on the rounds of the casting offices. Central Casting Corporation was not formed until 1926, which meant that hopeful extras had to make the studio rounds every day in search of work. Charlie recalled his lean days as an extra:

> And then I went around on what they call on spec, hooking trucks, rides, it was expensive to go round you know in those days, and getting out to Culver City was very expensive…that was about 34 cents I think. [I made] anywhere from 3 ½ [dollars] to 7 1/2, I worked for 7 ½ mostly, sometimes I got $10.00, a few times I rode horseback for $3.00 cause I wanted to ride a horse.[17]

The full extent of Charlie's extra work may never be known. He worked wherever and whenever he was offered a bit, often in crowd scenes that render him impossible to distinguish—assuming the film even exists today. In the 1970s he recalled working with Gloria Swanson, Reginald Denny, Mary Pickford, and director King Vidor, but he could not recall the names of the films in which he had appeared. A 1925-vintage blurb in the *Los Angeles Times* mentioned that he had appeared in Pickford's *Dorothy Vernon of Haddon Hall*, while the Internet Movie Database places him in an undetermined bit in Pickford's *Rosita*. Both films were made by United Artists, one right after the other in 1923-1924; and, it is possible that Charlie worked in both. Other possible Charlie sightings include a bit in *The Cheat* (1923) starring Pola Negri; as part of a teeming Parisian mob scene in Lon Chaney's *The Hunchback of Notre Dame* (1923); as a dancer in a nightclub for Chaplin's *A Woman of Paris* (1923); and in Douglas Fairbanks' *The Thief of Bagdad* (1924). He played an Israelite slave in Cecil B. DeMille's *The Ten Commandments*, and in those days before PA systems and microphones, earned an extra $3 a day rounding up the crowds of extras by riding out on horseback and sounding his coronet. He got another bit in one of DeMille's studies of Jazz Age marriage, *The Golden Bed* (1925). Charlie also worked with one of his favorite actors, Harold Lloyd, in *The Freshman.* Lloyd gave Charlie one of his first bits, as a bell-ringer in the "Fall Frolic" scene. It was a showy little part that came at a crucial moment of the film, thus giving Charlie quite a bit of exposure. Charlie was forever grateful and recalled, "Harold Lloyd gave me a lot of bits. He was wonderful to me."[18]

Despite this slew of extra parts, Charlie was living the hand-to-mouth existence his parents despised, and had not landed a studio contract which would ensure steady work and a possible shot at stardom. Estelle was beside herself with worry, certain that everyone in Hollywood was a dope fiend, and she begged her son to come home. She even ventured to California to check on Charlie; but, he refused to leave with her, saying, "If I went back with you, Mother, and later heard of one of my friends succeeding, I'd feel that if I had stayed, I too might have had a break, and I'd feel mad with myself for having left, mad with you for having persuaded me, and mad with everybody else."[19] Going back to Onset meant meekly surrendering to his father and reclaiming the family business. Times were hard, but Charlie was not about to admit failure.

Chapter Two

Lolly

"She realized now that she was good at her work and that she could support herself, no matter what happened."
— John Dos Passos, *The 42ⁿᵈ Parallel*

Janet Gaynor always insisted that her career as an actress started by accident, that she was prodded into her chosen craft by her mother and stepfather. She had talent, and her favorite game as a child was to sit in front of a long mirror in her mother's bedroom, mimicking the actresses she had seen at the Manheim Theatre. She spent hours absorbed in her own reflection, acting entire plays she had studied or portraying her favorite actresses, Mary Pickford and Norma Talmadge. Her only audience was her own image, and occasionally, her mother, who would pop up behind her and scold, "Don't you ever get tired of looking at yourself? Do you want to become a vain peacock?"[20] Eventually her mother realized that her daughter's gift for mimicry could be turned into a lucrative career. To fully understand Janet Gaynor's story, it is important to take a step back and look at the mother who had, as Anita Loos described another famous stage mother, "all the impact of a force of nature."[21]

Laura Josephine Buhl was born in March, 1877, the youngest of nine children. Her father Max had been born in Württemberg, Germany, and her mother Rose was born in Baden, Germany. They had immigrated to the United States in 1852 and settled in Germantown, the close-knit community of Scotch, Dutch, English, and of course, German immigrants in Philadelphia. Germantown was ... "an important section of a big city. But it [was] far more than that. With its many churches, libraries, and schools, public and private, its homes and gardens, its business and industrial areas,

19

The playacting begins: Janet at six years old, 1912.

Courtesy of Gina LoBiondo.

it is a distinct community. It has a culture, a personality, and an atmosphere of its own."[22] It was a placid village, a town of churches, a place that prided itself on piety, welfare, and education.

Laura's father Max worked as a cabinet maker, and Laura's older brothers and sisters went to school until the age of 10, when they all went to work in the cotton or hosiery mills in Philadelphia. The Buhls all lived in the same home in Germantown, even second-eldest daughter Lavinia, who was twenty at the time the 1880 census was taken. While education was prized in Germantown, the Buhls—like most immigrant families—had to choose endurance over intellectual betterment. They pulled together for the common goal of survival.

The 1890 federal census was destroyed in a fire in 1921, so it is impossible to catch a glimpse of Laura's life at thirteen. But we can assume she followed the same pattern as her older siblings: school until the age of ten, then work in the factories. By the time the 1900 census was taken, the Buhl family had scattered. After Max died, the older siblings left home and started families of their own. Her older brothers William and George moved to Chicago and opened a laundry business. Only Laura and her sister Augusta, three years older and closest to Laura in the family line, remained with Rose. They boarded with a family called the Strouds in Germantown, and Augusta and Laura worked in a hosiery factory.

Germantown was well-established as a mill town, and was known as the "first distinctly manufacturing town in Pennsylvania," [23] home of the first paper mill in the United States. The Buhl girls worked as loopers in one of the many hosiery mills, responsible for sewing the toes on socks. They were given the finished sock, minus the toe, which they placed on a complicated machine that used several small needles entwined with a spider's web of thread. The toe was attached by machine so that it appeared it had all been knitted of a piece. This was skilled factory labor, for it took a great deal of patience and training to attach the sock properly to the machine, so the toe was knitted smoothly. Like all factory labor, however, it was tedious and repetitive. Loopers were paid not by the hour or week, but by the number of stockings completed. A skilled looper, which Laura certainly was after thirteen years' practice, could expect to bring home between $2 and $3 per week.

Nothing would have changed the tedium and drudgery of Laura's life at this point, except that on September 4, 1901, she married a man named Frank Gainer. Frank was nearly ten years' her senior and worked

Laura Augusta as an infant with older sister Helen, circa 1907.
Courtesy of Gina LoBiondo.

as a paperhanger. In marrying Frank, Laura escaped the grind of the factory, and even moved up the social ladder a rung. For while Frank was still a laborer, his trade took training and skill and required membership in the Brotherhood of Painters, Decorators, and Paperhangers of America, a labor union. Wallpaper was highly popular in the Victorian era and continued to be so even into the 1920s, which is known in the trade as "The Golden Age of Wallpaper." During the Depression, Frank could earn as much as $10 a day. Naturally, his salary enabled Laura to quit her job in the hosiery mill and establish a small home at 34 Wister Street in Germantown. By the time Laura Augusta—affectionately nicknamed Lolly and later called Janet—was born, the Gainer household had moved down the block to 50 Wister Street and included Helen Rose, her older sister by four years. Her Grandmother Rose and Aunt Augusta crowded into the tiny home as well. Later, the Gainer ménage moved to Pomona Street, and it was in that house that the family remained until 1914.

Frank Gainer is a faded figure in the Janet Gaynor story. Except for one lonely interview he gave to *New Movie Magazine* in 1931, he is absent from all stories of her life. But it was from Frank that Janet got her talent for mimicry, for he earned extra cash by getting bit parts at the Lubin film studio. (Another Lubin actor, Frank Borzage, went on to direct Janet in two of the films that would earn her the Academy Award.) In his only interview, Frank Gainer recalled:

> Since then [Janet] often has told me that she thinks she inherited her desire for acting from me. On her last visit here she asked me if I remembered when I used to teach her tricks on the horizontal bar, and how I used to laugh at her, or get angry at her, depending upon my mood, when she mimicked me.[24]

He also took part in many benefit theatricals and sang lyric tenor in a neighborhood quartet. He taught Janet the songs he sang in the quartet, "then we would spend hours going over the songs together. Of course, I never dreamed then that she would become famous. We just did it because it seemed like fun."[25]

Janet called her hometown, "a city of brick and marble, that was my childhood impression of Philadelphia. A city of broad avenues and many libraries. The Benjamin Franklin library. A friendly city." [26] Janet (and presumably her sister Helen) attended the A. C. Harmer Combined School for Girls on East Haines Street. Germantown's population swelled by 45% between 1900 and 1910, but remained a quiet and dignified part of Philadelphia. Several newspapers flourished, recounting the day's news to hungry readers: Germantown had its fair share of suicides, shootings, and jewel robberies. These colorful incidents were interspersed with news about the Orphans' Asylum receiving

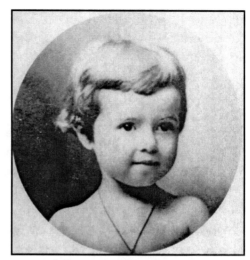

Lolly as a toddler, circa 1908.
Courtesy of Gina LoBiondo.

much-needed funding; a group of tradesmen creating a booster club to encourage higher sales; and advertisements for the new Pierce-Arrow automobile dealership. Germantown was a pleasant place to live, a good place to rear children, and a place where tradition, worth, and uplift reigned supreme. But Laura Buhl, as John Dos Passos' character Janey felt, "there was a great throbbing arclighted world somewhere outside and that only living in [Germantown] with where everything was so poky and old-fashioned...kept her from breaking into it." [27]

Their lives had settled into the groove of "We work to eat to get the strength to work to eat to get the strength to work to eat to get the strength to work to eat to get the strength to work," described by Dos Passos. Frank had his occasional Lubin bit or amateur theatrics to lighten his load, but Laura wanted out. They bickered constantly and the household was often tense and morose. Her parents were sadly mismatched: Laura was bright and ambitious, and Frank for all his artistic ambitions, was happy with his lot in life. (In 1931 Frank was still living in Germantown, still working as a paperhanger, and still boarding with his nephew and his family.) Laura had always lived her life for others: she curtailed her education to earn money for her family and delayed marriage until she was well into her twenties. When Rose died and Augusta left the Gainer household to start her own life, the tensions in the household were magnified. Laura had married Frank to escape the drudgery of factory labor but found fresh, unpaid toil in caring for a growing family. In 1914, the bickering finally ended when they filed for divorce.

Divorce is often thought of as a modern institution, made popular by the sexual revolution of the 1960s. However, Glenda Riley's landmark *Divorce: an American Tradition* reveals that attitudes towards happiness in marriage had changed at the turn of the century: "by the end of the first decade of the 20th century, divorce appeared to be everywhere; it also seemed to have garnered widespread support. Progressives had joined with feminists and others in calling for the freedom of choice to stay in a marriage or leave it." [28] In the teens, divorce law was decided by each individual state and the Western states were more lax in their marriage statutes, contributing to what some critics feared was a "divorce mill" culture. The Gainers' divorce decree has not surfaced as of this writing, but it was probably granted in Pennsylvania. Pennsylvania divorce laws were not codified until the 1930s, which makes it difficult to ascertain on what grounds a particular divorce was granted. However, we do know that divorce was granted in cases of adultery and desertion or abandonment, and husbands or wives could sue each other on those grounds. It is possible that Laura left Frank and he sued her on grounds of desertion; for Janet recalled in a later interview that her mother received the final decree after they were long established in their new home.

Although we do not know on what exact legal grounds the divorce was granted, we do know that Laura was unhappy enough in her marriage to Frank to choose the freedom of divorce over the financial and social security of marriage. Not only did she want freedom from Frank, she chose to leave her hometown and take her two small daughters with her to Chicago, where her brothers had established a thriving laundry business. Janet described Laura as having, "a good deal of pioneer blood in her veins. She has always been so game about embarking on new and uncharted enterprises." [29] They settled in Uptown, which was about as different culturally from Germantown as can be imagined. Janet fondly remembered the libraries of Philadelphia, but her new home was described by Sarah Bernhardt as "the pulse of America." Uptown was known for its fabulous entertainment district, where notorious gangsters like Al Capone, John Dillinger, and Machine Gun Jack McGurn frequented the ballrooms, theatres, and nightclubs. These nightclubs were home to the burgeoning jazz scene, which made the Twenties roar.

Janet around the time of her parents' divorce. Courtesy of Gina LoBiondo.

The three women settled in a brick apartment building located at 4149 Kenmore Avenue, three miles from Laura's brother George and his family, and five miles from Laura's brother William and his wife, Tillie. Their neighbors included real estate agents, decorators, and engineers—working-to-middle-class people who were educated and artistic. Janet's principal fear at this time was leaving the "friendly city" of Philadelphia for the "noisy, dirty, depressed city" of Chicago. She called her parents' divorce "the first tragedy of my life," adding, "I recall it only dimly now, except for the feeling that some awful thing had made its appearance in our lives." [30] The divorce was a mixed blessing for Janet, as she came to realize in time. On one hand, she had an affectionate relationship with Frank and missed him keenly. Her security blankets—her family, the familiarity of her friendly city—were yanked out from under her. On the other hand, the constant squabbling between her miserable parents ended. She began to like Chicago when she saw the "lovely lake, framed with trees and green grass and blue, blue sky...I emotionally accepted this city as my new home." [31] This mixed lot of goodness and sorrow forever changed young Janet. Growing up so quickly and losing out on girlhood opened her eyes, gave her a gravity and maturity far beyond her years. Irene Mayer Selznick, one of her dearest friends from Hollywood, remembered Janet as "deep without being complicated—and ever so wise. As she grew, essentially she remained the same, because she had absolute authenticity." [32] That authenticity was born out of the ashes of her parents' divorce.

Laura found a job in an office, while Janet and Helen went to school and explored their new home. Janet recalled "school, play, small pleasures...the fairyland aspect of Michigan Boulevard...the joys of Clarendon Beach...the ghostly thrills of the cemetery near where the North Shore elevated tracks ran. Helen and I would steal away from the

Janet at Clarendon Beach, Cook County, Illinois. Courtesy of Gina LoBiondo.

house on gray afternoons to walk, or run wildly, among the somber tombstones."[33] The Essanay Film Manufacturing Company was located just a few short blocks from the Gainer home, and it is possible that when Janet and Helen roamed their neighborhood, they peeked in at the red brick building on Argyle Street, known as the "House of Comedy Hits." Essanay was founded in 1907 by George K. Spoor and G.M. Anderson (later known as the screen's first cowboy star, "Broncho Billy"). Their roster of stars included matinee idol Francis X. Bushman, his leading lady Beverly Bayne, Gloria Swanson, and Charles Farrell's future wife, Virginia Valli. In 1915, Essanay briefly engaged the services of a brilliant young comedian named Charlie Chaplin for a series of fast-paced farces featuring his Little Tramp character. Essanay was also famous for its slapstick comedies featuring Ben Turpin, Max Linder, and Wallace Beery (in drag) as "Sweedie, the Swedish Maid."

In Uptown's fresh, vibrant atmosphere, Janet moved beyond her girlish playacting in front of a mirror. She established herself as an "elocutionist," keeping her neighbors in stitches with her imitations of an elderly woman and her cat that lived on their block, and Koenig, who kept the corner grocery store. Her favorite recitation piece was "Bonjour, Mademoiselle." She tagged along with Helen to the Great Lakes Naval Training Station, where both sisters gave recitations to the soldiers as part of their wartime volunteer work. Janet and Helen also knitted socks, mittens, and sweaters for soldiers while Laura made surgical garments at the Ladies' Aid of their Presbyterian church.

An attack of influenza left Janet "weak and listless," so Aunt Tillie began taking her to Melbourne, Florida every winter. They stayed in a rambling white house while Janet attended Melbourne High School. Those winters in Melbourne were the closest thing Janet ever had to an idyllic American girlhood. She went to dances at the Melbourne Golf and Country Club, escorted by a young man named Delbert Thompson, and dated another young man named Cecil Powell. She swam in the pool at the Bahama Beach Club, played basketball, and played ukulele when a group of her friends gathered around to sing. Her best friend was Jane Hedges, who remembered Janet as a "beautiful girl with a lovely speaking voice...popular with the young people and a very good student in school...but she never particularly aspired to be an actress."[34] During one of her winters in Melbourne, she was chosen to perform in "Fascinating Fanny Brown," the class play. Janet had a character role as a "queru-

lous old lady...it tickled me to death, not because of the dramatic possi-
bilities it offered, but because it gave me the privilege of staying up every
school night of the month until ten o'clock." [35]   In the spring and summer, Janet joined Helen at Lake View High School in Chicago. Janet
despised that school: "I hated the indifference with which Latin, algebra,
history were passed out. I was always glad when the winter months took
me to Florida, where I studied the same lessons under the influence of
balmy beaches and azure skies and waving palm fronds." [36]

During one winter in Melbourne, Janet received letters from her
mother that mentioned Harry C. Jones rather too frequently. Some sources
call Harry a private detective—and he may have done a little snooping at
some time—but he was primarily a mining man. He lived in Berkeley,
California, and had diverse mining interests in Tonopah, Nevada, where
a huge silver rush had taken place during the teens. He was described as a
mine operator in the 1910 census, and was well known and respected in
the mining community. So well known, in fact, that Governor Denver
Dickerson of Nevada appointed him delegate to the twelfth American
mining congress. Jones was also married to a young woman named Adele
Terrill. When Terrill and Jones divorced in 1919, Adele married journalist and author Benjamin de Casseres (*The Shadow-Eater, Love Letters of a
Living Poet,* and *I Dance with Nieztsche*). As Adele "Bio" De Casseres, she
wrote *The Boy of Bethlehem* (1926). Exactly how Jones met Laura Gainer
is a mystery—in interviews, Janet only mentioned him as a good friend
of her family. His spirit of adventure completely ensnared Laura; in him,
she found the perfect match for her outgoing and daring personality.

When Janet finally met "Jonesy" in person, she found the man who
became her fairy godfather, the driving spirit behind her career. "We
liked—no, that is not the word—we adored each other from the start.
He did not see a thin, spindle-legged girl with large dark eyes. He saw a
little girl who would someday electrify, so he said, the world with her
dramatic ability." [37] In the winter of 1921, while Janet was with Aunt
Tillie in Melbourne, she received another letter from her mother. Laura
wrote that they would be married in San Francisco as soon as Janet could
make the journey. "Despite my fondness for Jonesy, I had that feeling
that I was being deprived of something precious," Janet wrote nine years
later. The new family lived at 1233 First Street in San Francisco and
Janet enrolled in Polytechnic High School, where she graduated in the
spring of 1923. (Her future co-star George O'Brien was an alumnus.)

Janet at Polytechnic High School, 1923. Courtesy of Gina LoBiondo.

She worked at Frank More's Shop on Geary Street, with a starting salary of $18 a week. She began in payroll, and then worked her way up to the "adjustment department," where she answered calls from irate customers for $20 a week. For a brief time she worked as an usherette at the Castro Theatre. "No one ever told me that I had nice eyes. That I should be in pictures. Only Jonesy, at home, said that." [38]

For Jonesy, with his gambler's intuition, took a look at the three Gainer women and backed Janet to be a great actress. Jonesy was a prospector "with his dreams of wealth when this mine or that yielded its treasure…he lived in a tomorrow bright with promise," and the next gold mine he dreamed about was Janet Gaynor, Famous Star. Janet felt that he was silly, saying, "One must be very beautiful to be an actress. Look at Helen, she is beautiful. She should be an actress."[39] In fact, Helen wanted to be an actress—in all interviews and articles written once Janet became a star, Janet insisted that of the two sisters, Helen had wanted the career while Janet wanted to go to secretarial school. Janet had always enjoyed acting as an amusing game, nothing more. Despite Jonesy's great plans, Janet enrolled in the Hollywood Secretarial School while Helen went the rounds of the casting offices.

One day Janet tagged along with Helen to the Hal Roach Studio, probably as a lark, and probably to prove Jonesy wrong so he would leave her to her secretarial career. Helen, in a charitable move she almost certainly later regretted, made her sister up for the camera, "covered the tan freckles, rouged my lips, darkened my brows. I was tremendously thrilled, and equally embarrassed." After that, Janet was bitten by the acting bug, but still unsure that she could be a success. "The superiority of the other extras simply floored me. So suave, so elegant, so unperturbed. I was quite miserable. Really too self-conscious of my defects." [40]

As soon as Janet began the rounds of the casting offices, Jonesy and Laura (whom Janet always called "Gaynor") devoted themselves to her new career. Jonesy changed her name from Lolly to Janet, because Janet could not be diminutized, and changed Gainer to Gaynor because he felt it would look better on a marquee. Janet was unsure she could be a success, but her parents were supremely confident. Between the two of them, they had Laura's pioneering spirit and Jonesy's gambling instincts, making them the ultimate stage parents. They placed all their eggs in one basket, to Helen's detriment. "Her older sister Helen was prettier, but it wasn't Helen upon whom [Jonesy] concentrated. It wasn't to place Helen in pictures that he moved the family to Hollywood. It was to make Janet the Sarah Bernhardt of the movies," Ruth Biery, a writer for *Modern Screen Magazine,* wrote in 1934. This decided split between the sisters, spelled out in candid detail in a fan magazine, was devastating to both, particularly to Helen. The "something precious" Janet lost once her mother married Jonesy was her relationship with her sister, and the last traces of her girlhood.

Chapter Three
Lucky Breaks

"I've worked as an extra, but I haven't had a real chance yet. I expect to get one soon. All I ask is a chance...Luck is just hard work, they say, and I am willing to work as hard as anybody."
– Nathaniel West, *The Day of the Locust*

Hollywood, 1925: A typical day for an extra meant making the rounds of the casting offices at the major studios until a job appeared. More often than not, nothing materialized, which meant trudging back home in failure, only to start the process over the next day. Janet met with failure often during her searches—she was shy and so small she had to stand on tiptoe to be seen by casting directors through their office windows. She would "walk elegantly away, hoping to convey my utter nonchalance to these terrifying men." At home, she was pampered by Laura, who removed Janet's slippers and made her a fortifying cup of tea, and given a pep talk by Jonesy, who said, "That's all right, Lolly. Wait. Your time will arrive. You have talent. Patience is what you need." As though they were grooming a thoroughbred for the Derby, Laura and Jonesy coddled and coached Janet, giving her the courage to face each day with fresh hope.

Charlie had no family waiting to reassure him when he returned to his cheap flat each day, just his roommate Richard Arlen, who was given to complaining vociferously that he hadn't been given a proper break in Hollywood since his arrival in 1923. Charlie had sent Estelle back home in tears, his father wouldn't speak to him, and only his stubborn refusal to

The Two Lauras, early 1920s.

accept failure kept him in Hollywood. When he landed a part, he loved the work, so he knew he had made the right choice. With the boundless optimism that carried him to Hollywood, Charlie set his sights high. Naturally, he developed a crush on one of Hollywood's most sophisticated stars, Virginia Valli. Valli was under contract to Universal and had just starred in *The Pleasure Garden*, Alfred Hitchcock's debut feature film. She was also married to Demerest Lamson, a shadowy figure who apparently managed a few actors. Charlie worshipped Virginia from afar during these days as an extra.

The film studios sprawled across the San Fernando Valley, meaning that—then, as now—transportation was a major issue for people seeking work. Central Casting was not established until a year later, so hopeful extras had to seek out the casting offices at each studio. Charlie solved this by hitching rides—the streetcar was too expensive—until he saved up enough for a used flivver that he shared with Arlen. Janet bummed rides with fellow extras Clark Gable and Fay Wray. Wray became Janet's closest friend in these early years; both girls found work often at Hal Roach's Studio as bathing beauties. Hal Roach's stars included Harold Lloyd, Will Rogers, Charley Chase, and Laurel and Hardy, and pretty girls were in demand as foils for those comedians. Eventually Wray signed a six month contract at Hal Roach, which meant no more trudging the studio rounds. Wray remembered that Roach gave all the girls beaded handbags at Christmas. "It was really nice to be 'in the movies' at the Hal Roach studio. The salary I got made it possible to rent a better house," [41] Wray recalled in her memoirs. Molly Thompson, an actress and casting scout at Hal Roach, took a liking to Janet and helped her get extra work, but she was never put under contract.

Janet appeared with her friend Clark Gable as an extra in Clara Bow's *The Plastic Age*. Later she got extra work in a series of comedies starring actress Alberta Vaughn. The director, Wesley Ruggles, took Janet aside and told her she definitely "had something," which, Janet reported,

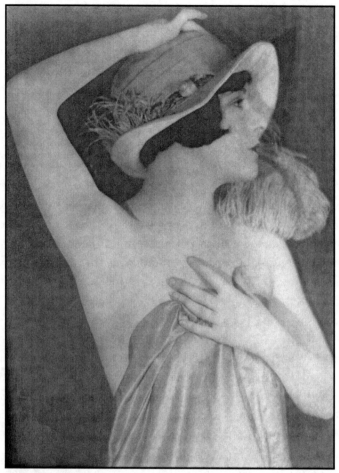

Virginia Valli in the 1920s. Photograph by Edwin Bower Hesser.

only Jonesy believed. In July 1925 she journeyed south to Lompoc, California, to appear in a two-reel drama called *Faith,* produced by the Catholic Motion Picture Guild of America. As if a message from above, filming was interrupted by an earthquake which sent the small film crew scurrying back to Los Angeles. Later that month, Janet was set to appear as an extra at Hal Roach when she received a phone call from Fred Datig, casting director at Universal, offering a lead. "Oh, Mr. Datig! I *can't*! Oh, I can't. Isn't it too bad? I've just promised Mrs. Thompson at Hal Roach that I will do extra work tomorrow. Oh, isn't it a shame?" [42] Datig laughed and assured Janet that he could "fix it up"—and with that, Janet received her first break. She reported to work on August 2, as the leading lady for Pee Wee Holmes and Ben Corbett, who were Western comedians.

Universal made its bread and butter from these Westerns, and from inexpensive melodramas and serials. Studio head Carl Laemmle was extremely cautious, and refused to take on debt to finance his pictures. These "quickies" made the income that allowed the studio to splurge on its stars, especially Lon Chaney and director Erich von Stroheim. At the time that Janet joined Universal, Laemmle's appointed head of production, Irving Thalberg, had just been lured away by Louis B. Mayer. With Thalberg's departure, much of the gloss left Universal.

Janet's first day on the set was an embarrassing one—she was flustered and teary when she learned she had to ride a horse, something she had never really done before. Dozens of cowboys on the set milled around her, hats in hands, each one only too happy to offer her private lessons. The disturbance shut down filming and director Vin Moore had to round up his straying herd with the sarcastic reminder that they were supposed to be making a picture, not conducting a riding academy. Janet learned to ride when the cameras were idle. It was a skill she needed, for she was offered the female lead in five more Holmes-Corbett Westerns:

> Heretofore they had changed leading women with each picture, but they liked my work. I received fifty dollars a week, and the days I did not work in my Western comedies, I worked as an extra on some Laura La Plante pictures and others. I was not under definite contract, but I was in stock. So was Fay Wray.[43]

Wray joined Universal when her contract with Hal Roach expired, and she and Janet shared a dressing room. Wray recalled, "If there was such a thing as a makeup department, we knew nothing of it. We put on our own greasepaint, making our faces very light, our mouths very dark...this helped our faces register in the long shots." Westerns were shot outdoors in full sunlight, so the girls had to be at the set and ready as soon as the sun came up. Reflectors were used to angle the sunlight onto a scene, and Wray remembered them as "a literal pain. Leading ladies who had to look up adoringly at tall cowboys had a struggle just keeping their eyes open." But despite the discomforts of filming, both actresses knew they were moving upward and onward. Wray recalled her contract implying a great future, with a salary that gradually increased over time, "so that if you looked at the amount set down for the final year, you could feel all that great potential."[44]

Charlie was convinced that he had potential, and in early 1925, he received his first big break. In *Wings of Youth* (Fox, 1925), described by the *Los Angeles Times* as "a story of modern youth and the method by which one mother achieved success for her children in spite of the so-called jazz tendencies of today," Charlie played Ted Spaulding, a flapper's beau. His turn in the film brought him to the attention of Warner Bros. An item in the *Los Angeles Times*, dated May 23, 1925, read: "Another young sheik has been added to the movies. His name is Charles Farrell, a young fellow of only a little over a year's experience in Hollywood, who was signed to a long-term contract with Warner Bros. yesterday." The article noted that Charlie had appeared as an extra in Warner Bros.' crime drama *On Thin Ice*, and had a part in *The Wife Who Wasn't Wanted*, which was "so good it resulted in his contract."

Warner Bros. had been established in 1923 by the four brothers Warner, and by 1925 it was still a fledgling studio. Their status as newcomers to the Hollywood scene made Warners more willing to take chances and try out new technologies, for they faced stiff competition from the larger studios in town. Charlie probably liked this quality about his new studio; their confidence and rough-and-ready approach to filmmaking echoed his own personality. Charlie had reason to be optimistic, for after signing his contract with Warner Bros., he finally met the woman of his Hollywood dreams. He met Virginia Valli at a house party, and she allowed him

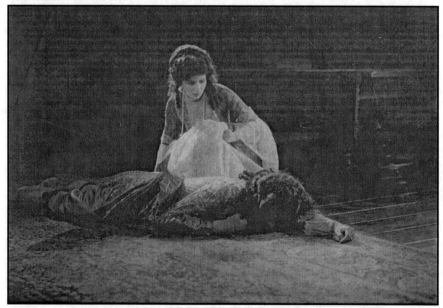

Virginia Valli in *A Lady of Quality*, Universal Pictures, 1924.

to drive her home in his cheap car. He was ecstatic about her—so excited that he rolled on the floor when telling Richard Arlen about his evening.

It was quite a coup for Charlie. Virginia Valli was one of Universal's biggest stars, soon to be lured to Fox Films. Virginia was older than Charlie by about five years (an eternity in Hollywood time, especially back then), and had started her career with Essanay around the time Charlie started college. She was still married to Lamson but they lived apart in an arrangement the *Los Angeles Times* dubbed "a marriage with variations." Virginia was possessed of an aloof, reserved personality and a regal beauty, which combined to make her an enigma to the press. In an extraordinary interview, published in 1922, journalist William Foster Elliott described her:

> She is a nice girl; she is thoughtful and reserved…Miss Valli's attitude was not the intensely personal, almost physical sense of natural forces that makes for "red-blooded" literature and plays. She was a nice girl in a drawing room, talking over with polite detachment some experiences that were not part of her.[45]

Virginia was unlike any woman Charlie had met before, and he was smitten. She became the embodiment of what he wanted from Holly-

Charlie in *The Love Hour*, 1925.

wood—all the fame and glamour he had desired since he was a little boy changing the reels in the family theatre. He was more determined than ever to become a success.

Charlie's first role under his new contract was supporting character Kid Lewis in *The Love Hour*, but the star of the picture was a suave matinee idol named Huntley Gordon. When filming wrapped on *Love Hour*, Charlie journeyed to Victorville, California, to start filming with Warner's biggest star—a German shepherd named Rin-Tin-Tin, also dubbed "The Mortgage Lifter" by Jack Warner. The Rinty films were made cheaply and turned out huge profits; hence, Rinty's reputation as the dog that saved Warner Bros. from bankruptcy. Rin-Tin-Tin was a star in every sense of the word: at the height of his fame, he received 10,000 fan letters a week, earned $6,000 a month, and had his own chauffer and valet. Charlie's 1925 contract with Warner's has not yet surfaced, but it is likely that Charlie was earning a mere pittance compared to Rin-Tin-Tin, and certainly shared none of those perks. While Rinty dined on T-bone steaks, Charlie ate sandwiches.

The film was called *The Clash of the Wolves,* and rounding out the human cast was June Marlowe, best known as "Miss Crabtree" of the *Our Gang* series. Charlie played a young borax prospector named Dave Weston, who must win the heart of the wealthy rancher's daughter (Marlowe), save his claim from claim-jumpers, and rehabilitate Lobo (Rin-Tin-Tin), whom he found injured and dying of thirst in the desert. Charlie had a lifelong affinity for animals and his affection for his canine lead is palpable. The best Rin-Tin-Tin films were crowd-pleasers with "a little comedy, a little romance, a little sentiment, and a lot of danger and action," [46] and *Clash* was no exception. The final scenes with Rinty, Charlie, and the unscrupulous claim-jumper are thrilling, showcasing not only Rinty's acrobatic finesse, but Charlie's all-or-nothing approach to fights and daring stunts.

Clash of the Wolves was the last picture Charlie did for Warner Bros. Despite the *Los Angeles Times* report that he had been signed to a long-term contract, he worked at Warner's for only a few months, and did only two films for which he received any kind of credit. It is possible that "long term" was just an exaggeration and Charlie only signed a two-picture deal, and when his option was up, Warners chose not to renew. Another likely scenario is that Charlie, at the end of the option, demanded more money in his new contract. Unhappily for Charlie, Jack Warner was notoriously

Lobby card for *Clash of the Wolves*, 1925. Courtesy of Tim Lussier, SilentsAreGolden.com.

tight-fisted with his actors and resented their demands for perks; he was also infamous for firing actors on the spot. (Rinty was no exception— "The Mortgage Lifter" was fired in 1929.) Whether he had a long-term contract and was fired, or if he had a two-picture contract and finished his work, the end result was the same: Charlie was without a studio.

Charlie's last picture for 1925 was a lead role in a two-reel comedy called *The Gosh-Darn Mortgage*, produced by Mack Sennett of Keystone Cops fame, and directed by Eddie Cline, director of Buster Keaton's most imaginative shorts (*One Week, The Balloonatic*, and *Cops,* to name a few). When Sennett saw the rough cut, he yelled, "Who's that tall kid who can't act? Get rid of him!" With that, Charlie's career at Sennett ended as quickly as it began. Indeed, it appeared that Charlie's entire film career had skidded off the tracks. For the winter of 1925-1926, Charlie was out of work. He still roomed with Arlen, turning a sympathetic ear to Arlen's constant complaints. While Arlen hadn't received a real chance, Charlie had, and from all perspectives, he had blown it. Those months without work forever scarred Charlie. He was never so audaciously sure of himself again.

When Janet was not required on the set, either of her own pictures or as an extra in others, she posed for publicity photographs. Fay Wray recalled posing as Kiki, as a farm girl, and as an athlete poised for the starting gun. "Young reporters from the newspapers stopped by occasionally," Wray added. "Their friendly kindness got some of these pictures printed." One such reporter was Herbert Moulton, the drama critic for the *Los Angeles Times*. Janet remembered Moulton as a "sweet, a darling boy," in a 1929 interview. She began dating Moulton, attending theatrical openings, sitting beside him as he covered plays and pictures. At night, as he typed out his reviews in the newspaper office, Janet perched on his desk and sifted through his stacks of publicity photos. As she studied each one, she analyzed how she might have posed. She cast a sharp eye

Publicity photograph of Janet, circa 1926.

over each actress, predicting who would make good. Janet and Moulton often went on double dates with Fay Wray and Moulton's friend, journalist Whitney Williams. Moulton and Williams also got the girls jobs as Renaissance pages at the Writer's Club, "Which demanded only that we stand at each side of the proscenium arch, looking pretty." [47]

In November of 1925, Janet's option with Universal came up and it seemed likely that she would be picked up again. But around that same time, she received a call from Fox Films—they were looking for a second lead for their film, *The Johnstown Flood*. Fox was formed by William Fox in 1913 and it was one of the biggest film studios in America. Fox was also developing a reputation for producing sensitive, artistic films, which intrigued Janet. She did a few tests with director Irving Cummings and was offered a one-shot deal: she could have the role of Anna Burger in *The Johnstown Flood* or, if they chose someone else, a lead role in a comedy. Janet gave up her $50/week salary for the chance to try her dramatic wings. After all, if she was going to be an actress, she was going to go for the parts that intrigued her; otherwise, why bother? With that, she left Universal and its silver nitrate range behind.

The Johnstown Flood was a fictionalized account of the disaster that struck Johnstown, Pennsylvania in 1889. Janet had a pivotal role as Anna Burger, who gives her life to warn the town about the break in the dam and save the man (George O'Brien) she loves, even as he is marrying another woman (Florence Gilbert). *The Johnstown Flood* was an intersection of fresh, undiscovered talent and stars on the wane: Janet's friend Clark Gable had a few bit parts in the film, and a newcomer named Jane Peters (later known as Carole Lombard) was an extra. Florence Lawrence, one of the first movie stars in motion picture history, had a brief bit as well. Of her work, Janet recalled:

> I shall never forget how hard I tried to do well. I would tremble so before I went into a scene that the property boy would grip me tightly by the arms, lest my trembling show on the screen…We worked in water most of the time. Irving Cummings was a prince. Nevertheless, I went into each scene super-charged with emotion…I was constantly at the highest pitch. I would come out of the scene hysterical, and go home, quite spent, to go immediately to bed. [48]

Janet's complete devotion to the role, even at the risk of her own health, paid off in spades. On November 12, 1925 she signed her first contract with Fox, the studio that would be her home for the next decade. She signed for a six-month period, with options coming up in alternating Mays and Novembers. Her starting salary was $100/week, increasing slowly over the four-year terms of the contract. As originally forecast, Janet would earn $500 per week at the end of her contact in May, 1930. Fox agreed to furnish her costumes for all her parts and sufficient lodging if she was required to film on location. As was typical for a beginner's contract, there were no clauses indicating time allotted for vacations or sick leave, or the number of hours she worked per day, or if she would be paid overtime. As with any contract player, Janet was expected to show up and work hard until the boss called a wrap. Even so, her salary was double what she earned at Universal and there were no cowboy pictures on her horizon. Signing with Fox proved to be the single-best career decision Janet Gaynor ever made.

On the brink of fame: Janet in 1926.

Rounding out 1925 on a high, Janet was nominated as a WAMPAS Baby Star of 1926. Herbert Moulton and Whitney Williams secured Janet's nomination along with Fay Wray's, a Christmas gift that boosted them into the limelight. The Western Association of Motion Picture Advertisers sponsored the contest, which they used to promote young actresses who were on the verge of true stardom, and it was a highly prestigious honor. Thirteen girls were selected with two alternates in case anyone dropped out. Being a WAMPAS Baby Star was the Hollywood equivalent of being a debutante. The annual contest ended with a "WAMPAS Frolic," which presented the young women to the press. The nominees were feted and honored at several events throughout the winter of 1925-1926; including being master showman Sid Grauman's honored guests at a screening of *The Big Parade*. Either because of the publicity or out of sheer luck, most WAMPAS Baby Stars did go on to achieve great fame. Janet's class of 1926 was especially strong: along with Janet and Fay Wray, the other honorees included Mary Astor, Dolores Del Rio, Joan Crawford, Marceline Day, and Dolores Costello. Previous honorees included Colleen Moore, Laura La Plante, Clara Bow, and Bessie Love.

The WAMPAS Frolic was a huge social event, one in which "Los Angeles vies with Deauville and Biarritz," according to the *Los Angeles Times*. The gowns worn by the WAMPAS Baby Star nominees as well as the stars attending the event received as much press coverage as the Oscar's "red carpet" receives today. Janet originally chose a "magenta-colored gown of duvetyn with self-toned embroidery in rope silk." [49] However, in the society columns after the ball, her gown was described as "pale yellow chiffon over silver cloth, her frock so girlish she seemed only 13." [50] Wray recalled that the studio made her special gown of "rose-colored taffeta trimmed with rhinestones" and set her up with director William Seiter as her escort. "It was an awesome moment when William Seiter arrived at my house in a limousine," Wray recalled. "I was speechless and remained that way." [51] Among the attendees was the ever-chic Virginia Valli in an "ankle-length pink taffeta Lanvin number embroidered in pearls and a pink rosette."

The evening began with a three-hour long theatrical show, supervised by Sid Grauman, with matinee idol, Lew Cody, acting as master of ceremonies. Among the eight presentations were "The City of Mecca," a ballet by Theodore Kosloff and Mlle. Fredova; "A Night on the River Volga," presented by Cecil B. DeMille; and "Ballet des Enfants," a spe-

From *Sandy*: Charlie in background, with David Torrence, Madge Bellamy, and Bardson Bard.

cial toe dance performed by fifty ballerinas under the age of eight. The presentation of the WAMPAS Baby Stars was made "in an unusual setting, representing the drawing-room of Colleen Moore's home, with Colleen herself acting as hostess for the thirteen girls whom the publicity men have selected for the honor this year." [52] After the theatrical entertainment concluded, the party continued at the Shrine Civic Auditorium. Nearly 7,000 people attended the Frolic, which netted $45,000—

most of which was donated to the Motion Picture Relief Fund. Naturally the newsreel cameras were on hand to film portions of the event to be shown in theatres around the world.

Hollywood is the land of second chances (and thirds, and fourths), and Charlie's second chance at stardom came packaged with a flapper who danced the Charleston on a table. The film was *Sandy*, a "story of the modern girl and her attempt to free herself from traditional restraints."[53] The leading lady was Madge Bellamy, one of Fox's rising stars that happened to be Fox vice-president Winnie Sheehan's mistress. Charlie played her first love, Timmy. The *Los Angeles Times* noted that "Charles Farrell, who is Sandy's first love, gives a well-balanced performance." [54] Based on his work in *Sandy*, Charlie was offered a contract at Fox, and he signed on January 30, 1926. Like Janet, he was offered a six-month contract with options for renewal at six-month intervals.   He started out at a higher salary—$125 per week—and by December 1930 he was expected to earn $600 per week. Except for "character" or "costume" roles, Charlie provided his own clothes for his films. He played a small role in the comedy *A Trip to Chinatown*, but Fox had no plans to star him in any upcoming films. Charlie was summoned to Lasky-Paramount to audition for James Cruze's film, *Old Ironsides*. During the audition, Charlie was asked by Cruze if he would be afraid to climb the rigging of an old sailing vessel. "No," Charlie replied. "I was born near Cape Cod and used to dive off the riggings of ships in the harbor when I was a kid." That answer sealed his fate: the character in the film was supposed to be from Cape Cod. Paramount obtained a two-picture loan for Charles Farrell, and by March 1926, Charlie was on location in Catalina Island.

Old Ironsides was the epic story of the *U.S.S. Constitution's* Battle of Tripoli Harbor in 1804. In the film, Charlie plays a naïve young lad (jestingly called "The Commodore") who is unwittingly shanghaied by two scruffy sailors (played by Wallace Beery and George Bancroft) aboard the *Esther*, a merchant ship. He falls in love with a young woman on the ship (Esther Ralston). When the *Esther* is taken over by pirates, *Old Ironsides* comes to the rescue. Although he is enslaved by the pirates and shackled together with his shipmates (Bancroft, Beery, and heavyweight champion George Godfrey, who played The Cook), Farrell helps save the day and the woman he loves. The film was historically accurate down to the smallest details, for Cruze had begun preparations for the picture half a year before filming began. The crew members plundered the Congressional Library and the Naval Archives and came up with the original plans for the *Constitution*, and retrofit nearly eighteen boats to comply with 1804 standards. Each ship was fitted with a radio so that Cruze could direct the action sequences from shore. Twenty-two cameramen were commandeered, and several of their cameras were fitted with a special mechanism to hold the cameras steady while simultaneously photographing the roll of the sea. Cruze decided to film in "Magnascope," an early widescreen process that brought the battle scenes to life. Catalina Island itself was transformed into "Camp Cruze," a city that included its own post office, general store, and hospital. The main cast stayed at Hill House on Catalina Island.

Lean and hungry, Charlie gives his all for *Old Ironsides*.

Old Ironsides was a huge film in every sense of the word, and as the romantic lead, Charlie was given a real chance at stardom. He threw himself into a part that seemed tailor-made just for him—his athletic prowess was showcased in his many stunts: as he climbed up and down rigging with ease, jumped off decks into the ocean, and swam while shackled to three cast mates. He peeled potatoes in the ship's galley, in homage to the days of "Peel those spuds, son!" in his father's restaurant. "The Commodore" marked the birth of the Charles Farrell brand of hero, a characterization unique to Farrell that he brought to all of his roles, particularly in his later work with Frank Borzage. As played by Charles Farrell, the romantic hero was naïve, tender, and innocent—but also virile and brave. For example, when "The Commodore" comes to rescue the girl, who is being held captive by pirates, he swims to the deck of the *Esther* and, still chained to his shipmates, climbs up to the railing. Reassuring her that she will be saved, he bends down and kisses the top of her foot— a sweet and humble gesture, when many other heroes, fettered or not, would have found a way to sweep her into their arms.

Farrell and Esther Ralston got along very well—Charlie called Esther "Lady" and "Mah Honey"—but there was no romance between them as Ralston was married to George Webb, who accompanied her to Catalina and was on hand for every shot. For modesty's sake, Esther chose to wear long bloomers under her gown, but was asked to remove them for one memorable scene:

> Leonora, my hairdresser, came to me and said, "Mr. Cruze wants the bloomers off for the next scene. He wants to photograph you at the wheel with the wind blowing against your dress and outlining your figure. It's for the big scene with you and Charley [sic] Farrell." It must have been an effective scene, for in later years, men particularly were to remember and comment on that figure-revealing scene from *Old Ironsides*. [55]

Old Ironsides was more than just a love story between "The Commodore" and Esther; it was primarily an action film with thrilling battle scenes. As could be expected from a film with a cast of thousands (Richard Arlen, Boris Karloff, and Gary Cooper were among the extras) and scenes on board antique sailing vessels, problems arose constantly. Cruze unwittingly blew up the entire cast and crew's lunch one day, which had been stored on the pirates' ship. On another occasion, the *Esther* was left to drift when the tugboat that was supposed to bring her back to shore ran out of gas. Esther Ralston recalled:

> As night came on, I began to worry about what George [Webb] would think when we hadn't returned and wondered what steps he would take to rescue us. Charley [sic] came into the cabin with a plate of flapjacks for me. Since there was no food on board and everyone by this time was dying of hunger, Charley

The Commodore steers the *Esther*.

had foraged around and discovered an old box of stale flour and mixed it with some water from a barrel on deck, then cooked the mess on an oil stove. I thanked him, but as hungry as I was, decided to forego the flapjacks.[56]

Caught in the midst of a storm, and without radio communication, the *Esther* drifted for hours until a warship spotted her and turned a big spotlight on her. One of the cameramen scuttled to the top of the mast and tied a few rags to the top, then lit them on fire. The warship spotted the blaze and sent a speedboat to the rescue. Sometime near dawn, the *Esther* was towed into harbor.

The cast was also plagued with injuries. On the first day of filming, Esther Ralston was being helped aboard when her foot caught in her long skirts. She fell onto the deck and sprained her ankle, then fainted. She was laid up for a week, unable to stand or walk. For the filming of the battle scene between *Old Ironsides* and the pirate ship, the masts of *Old Ironsides* were strapped with dynamite charges. James Cruze had the trigger nearby and the stunt coordinator was to pull the trigger when Cruze gave the signal. Charles Barton, who was the property man, recalled that the stunt, though carefully choreographed, did not go off as planned:

> As soon as the men on the rigging came down and cleared the area, the charge was to go off. Jim made a sudden move while the men were still up there, and the special effects man thought it was the signal. He hit the button. The mast[s] blew off with all these men still on it…Duke [Kahanamoku] and my brother—I don't know how many people they saved by picking them up and laying them on the floating spars. [57]

Six men were thrown from the rigging, and one of them died en route to the hospital. Charlie also sustained injuries during filming. Like Janet in *The Johnstown Flood*, he was determined to do well, even at the risk of his own health. He performed virtually all of his own stunts and at one point in production, cracked two ribs and burst an eardrum. He was out of filming for a few weeks until he healed. It is not known whether that accident happened during the botched battle scene that killed one man and injured several others, or during one of the other countless moments in the film that Charlie put life and limb on the line for fame. In later years, Charlie's friends commented that he was hard of hearing, and it is possible that his eardrum never properly healed from this accident.

Despite the accidents, the injuries, and the discomforts of location filming, the end result was a rip-roaring action adventure yarn that received high praise from the critics when it opened the following February, and it holds up excellently today. *Photoplay* led the way, declaring "It is a glorious story of a glorious achievement…gorgeous comedy…played with salty gusto by Beery, Bancroft, and Godfrey…Also on the honor roll are Charles Farrell, a newcomer, and Esther Ralston." [58] Perhaps the most satisfying homage came from Charlie's former BU classmates, who bought out the entire orchestra section of the Tremont Theater when *Old Ironsides* was shown in Boston. As Charlie took Esther in his arms during the "bloomerless" love scene, one of them called out, "The lucky so-and-so mugging a gorgeous dame like that! And it wasn't so long ago he was slinging hash at Walton's." [59]

There was no doubt that Charlie had done well, and Paramount was so pleased they were ready to star him in another epic film. Commenting on Charlie's good fortune, Whitney Williams wrote, "Lady Luck must be Charles Farrell's middle name. The ink on his contract with Fox was scarcely dry when Lasky borrowed him for the lead role in 'Old Ironsides,' one of the largest productions ever filmed. Five months ago Farrell wondered where he could find his next meal. He's made now, his career settled for good, unless something unforeseen shows up." [60]

While Charlie had one role that kick-started his career, Janet was taken under Winnie Sheehan's wing. He carefully nurtured her career along, giving her small parts under good directors. *Variety* called Sheehan "the backbone of Fox ever since he joined nearly 20 years ago," and he possessed a rare instinct of the motion picture business that proved highly lucrative to Fox. Born in Buffalo, New York, in 1883, Sheehan was the son of Irish immigrants. He served in the Spanish-American War and later began his career as a newspaperman, working for the *Buffalo Courier* and the *New York Evening World*. After that, he served as Secretary to the Fire Commissioner and Secretary to the Police Commissioner in New York City. When he joined Fox in 1914, Sheehan organized several foreign film exchanges that eventually became 40% of Fox's income; he also organized the Fox News and Fox Education Departments.

Madge Bellamy, who was his mistress for a brief time during her career at Fox, remembered Sheehan as "rather stout with broad shoulders and large, light blue eyes. He had been a policeman and knew gangsters like Dutch Schultz very well. He loved to tell ribald jokes and loved my being offended by them." [61] Janet referred to Sheehan as "one of my greatest friends," in an interview in 1958, adding:

> He was absolutely wonderful to me, because he gave me very good advice. He also handled all my pictures. I could go in and discuss anything with him. Of course, he was very Irish and had an Irish humor and also an Irish temper. But we always got on extremely well. I've heard he could be almost as concentrated an enemy. But I never saw that side of him. I only saw a very charming and generous side. [62]

Did Sheehan take more than professional interest in Gaynor? After all, he had fresh flowers delivered to her daily, and once she became a star, he made sure she had the best bungalow on the lot. Some fan magazines hinted that he was in love with her; but, if that was the case, the feelings

Janet with a host of admiring studio executives on the set of *The Midnight Kiss*.
Courtesy of Gina LoBiondo.

Janet and co-star Richard Walling, *The Midnight Kiss*. Courtesy of Gina LoBiondo.

were not reciprocated. Laura Gaynor was her daughter's watchdog and chaperone; she accompanied Janet on location and to the set, keeping Janet safe and unsullied. Janet was easy prey—after all, hadn't she nearly passed up a lead role because she had promised to be an extra at Hal Roach's studio? Laura kept close to Janet, ensuring that her dreams for her daughter did not become a nightmare. Janet slowly ascended the ladder of fame by working hard in front of the camera; she was not one to cheat a shortcut with the casting couch. Moreover, in October she became engaged to her "sweet, darling boy," Herbert Moulton. The wedding date was set for June 1927.

Her first film under her new contract was *The Shamrock Handicap*, a horseracing film directed by John Ford. Janet played a "dainty little daughter of a poverty-stricken but proud old Irish lord," in the first Ford film to feature a distinctively Irish motif. "I think the only reason I even remember it—because it certainly was not very memorable for me—was that John Ford made it," Janet recalled. [63] Then she played in another Ford picture, *The Blue Eagle*, co-starring George O'Brien from *The Johnstown Flood*. Irving Cummings, her favorite Fox director, starred her in *The Midnight Kiss,* adapted from the stage play *Pigs* by John Golden. In the film, Janet played Mildred Hastings, who saves her boyfriend's business from going under by selling his father's pigs at $1 each. None of this was exactly star-making material.

But Janet's luck changed when she was cast as Catherine in *The Return of Peter Grimm*, directed by Victor Schertzinger and based on the David Belasco stage production. The film is a supernatural drama, in which Peter Grimm, a family patriarch who has just passed away, returns to Earth to right the wrongs in his family. As Catherine, who was forced into marriage with Grimm's malicious nephew, Frederick, Janet gave a lovely, haunting performance. Singled out for high praise by the *Los Angeles Times,* "she discloses a consummate artistry in the taxing emotional scene at the death of Peter. And she is radiantly beautiful in the old-fashioned wedding gown which she wears in the latter sequences of the picture." [64] Peter's death scene was the first time Janet showed her uncanny ability to laugh through tears, a trademark that became known throughout Hollywood as "doing a Gaynor." Unbeknownst to Janet, director Frank Borzage was lurking behind the scenes, watching her performance. What he saw was the only actress who could bring to life an iconic role, as Diane in *7th Heaven*. Janet Gaynor did not know it at the time, but based on her performance in *Peter Grimm,* she was about to be given the biggest chance of her career.

Chapter Four

7th Heaven

"Sometimes I feel I could reach up and touch a star!"
— Chico in *7th Heaven*

She was as "open, as sun-loving, as joyous as a flower—and, like a flower, frail and crushed by the first blow…expose her to the storms of the world and one trembled at the thought of what might happen."[65] No role was more coveted than that of Diane, the Parisian street waif, in the movie adaptation of *7th Heaven*. Hollywood began buzzing about possible casting choices as early as July 1924, when Fox acquired the movie rights to the tune of $155,000. Fox then committed $1 million to the film's budget. In doing so, Fox actually outbid Mary Pickford, who wanted to play Diane and star her husband, Douglas Fairbanks, as Chico, the "very remarkable fellow" who rescues Diane and is transformed by her love. It was one of the few times Pickford failed to get what she wanted. Every actress in Hollywood, obscure or well-known, vied for the part, including Joan Crawford, Blanche Sweet, and Dolores Costello. The man who made the final choice was Frank Borzage, a director who had shown great sensitivity with pictures such as *Humoresque*, *Lazybones*, and *Secrets*, and thus was entrusted with bringing the film to life. According to Borzage biographer Herve Dumont, *7th Heaven* was not assigned a director until April of 1926, when Borzage was finally approached by Sheehan himself. Sheehan then pressed Borzage to select his girlfriend, Madge Bellamy. However, Borzage and Madge Bellamy did not get along on the set of *Lazybones*:

Borzage and I quarreled over the little matter of my fingernails.
In the picture I played a poor white-trash girl. Every morning,

Frank Borzage, the man behind the magic.

he would inspect my nails to see if they were dirty enough. They never were, so he had mud rubbed in them. I did not think that the camera was close enough to catch this detail and took it as an insult. This was to prove a great disaster for me as he refused to have me for the role [of Diane].[66]

When Borzage had lurked secretly behind the scenes of *The Return of Peter Grimm,* he observed the only actress who could bring Diane to life. He insisted that Janet Gaynor, and no one else, play Diane.

To further ensure Fox's status as the most artistic studio in the business, Sheehan and William Fox began a deliberate campaign to bring prestige pictures to the studio. Accordingly, Sheehan imported F.W.

Murnau, the esteemed German director who filmed the legendary *Noseferatu* in 1922 and *The Last Laugh* with Emil Jannings in 1924, a film that caused a furor because it was completely done in pantomime, with no intertitles. Sheehan enticed Murnau to Fox with the promise that he could choose his own films, and Murnau chose an adaptation of Hermann Sudermann's novella *Die Riese nach Tilsit*. It is a simple story of a man who, fascinated by a vamp from the city, plots to kill his wife and run away with the temptress. In Murnau's hands, it became *Sunrise: a Song of Two Humans*, an allegory for good versus evil, the quiet country life versus the madly spinning world of the city.

Sheehan allowed Borzage to cast Gaynor as Diane, and then requested that Murnau use Gaynor as Indre, the betrayed wife in *Sunrise*. Murnau had not heard of Janet Gaynor and preferred Lois Moran or Camilla Horn for the role, but Sheehan prevailed. Sheehan foresaw that Murnau's perfectionism was the ideal boot camp for Gaynor, who described herself as "absolutely untrained." She remembered Murnau would take "twenty or thirty takes of the smallest scene. I must say this wasn't because of me, but because there'd be a glimmer of light on the wrong bulrush or something equally small. But it was wonderful training." Later she described working for Murnau as equivalent to spending a year in drama school.[67]

The *Los Angeles Times* noted that Janet had won the two finest screen roles of the year, adding, "These roles were sought by some of the most celebrated actresses of our time."[68] Gossip columnist Louella Parsons was aghast at Fox's decision to cast an unknown like Gaynor in two of the most highly desired parts of the year, and aired her views in her column, which was read throughout the nation. Janet recalled, "Columnists wrote articles and said that they just hoped Fox knew what they were doing, to put this unknown, inexperienced little girl in this very dramatic part."[69] She went into both roles with a lot to prove; in fact, it would not be wrong to say her performances would either make or break her career.

Charlie was still working out his two-picture loan to Paramount. He received such fantastic notices for his work in *Old Ironsides* that Paramount tried to buy him out from Fox. Fox and Sheehan both realized they had lent a potential superstar out to a rival, and refused to sell Charlie's contract. They promised instead that he would be starred in a world-class film upon his return to the studio. Meanwhile, Charlie was set to star in William Wellman's *Wings*:

So when I got *Wings* they were all—everybody on Paramount was sore as hell...See I was to do *Wings* first because I had done *Old Ironsides* with Paramount and I was scheduled for *Wings*, and then Wellman was not a big director on the lot then, but Fleming—Victor Fleming—was the big one. And he wanted me for a picture that started a couple months earlier [*The Rough Riders*].[70]

Legend has it that Charlie learned about Fox's intention to film *7th Heaven* and went straight to Borzage to try and convince him to cast Richard Arlen as Chico. According to the story, Borzage was so impressed with Charlie's earnestness and naïveté that he promptly cast Charlie in the role instead. The truth is, Fox determined to cast Charlie in the role as soon as Paramount tried to buy out his contract. It was the biggest plum they could offer, the only way they could keep Charlie from defecting to Paramount. Although it appears that the legend of Borzage sizing Charlie up and pronouncing him the perfect Chico is mere publicity fodder; the truth is Charlie was perfect for the role. Chico was described as "broad-shouldered, high-chested, mightily good-looking," possessing a "philosophy of his own making...audacious, square-fronted, challenging." [71] Borzage had seen his work in *Old Ironsides*: Charlie's interpretation of "The Commodore" was tender, sincere, brave, and naïve—all integral characteristics for the character of Chico. Charlie did, however, help Arlen land a coveted role:

Now Dick Arlen never tells this; he was my roommate at the time, and he'd been under contract for several years to Paramount; they'd never given him a damn thing, and he was so emotional about it. So when I had to be sent to Texas to do *Rough Riders* I went to Billy Wellman. Now, he's never, never mentioned this. I heard Dick and he and I were good friends, but Dick always liked to build himself up a little bit. So I heard him say "I got it over – I got *Wings* over Charlie Farrell." And this guy said "You mean to say you got it over Charlie?" He said "Yes." I got Billy Wellman to give him a test, and he gave him a test, he did a wonderful test. Billy gave him the job. Buddy Rogers was already in it. And then we were together down in Texas, *Rough Riders* and *Wings*.[72]

Filming on *7ᵗʰ Heaven* was supposed to begin the summer of 1926, but Murnau's arrival in August changed that, and *Sunrise* was given preferential treatment. Since *Rough Riders* began filming before *Wings*, Charlie would finish around the time that *7ᵗʰ Heaven* commenced filming at Fox. This serendipitous bit of scheduling worked out best for everyone: Charlie got *Rough Riders* and *7ᵗʰ Heaven*; Arlen got *Wings*, a role that finally catapulted him to stardom and made him stop whining and start bragging; and Janet got her boot camp training with F. W. Murnau. Farrell was on location, shooting *The Rough Riders* in San Antonio, Texas, when he heard that he had been given the role.

The Rough Riders is an historical drama about Teddy Roosevelt's famous cavalry regiment and its charge up San Juan Hill. Farrell and his friend Charles Emmett Mack played the leads, and Mary Astor played the love interest. Filming took several months to complete, as Texas weather did not cooperate, and more than once Fleming thought of taking the company back to Hollywood. Astor recalled that after weeks of not being able to film due to rainy conditions, they filmed twenty scenes in one day when the sun came out. During their downtime, Astor remembers being "lionized, partied, dated almost to death. The Texans were justly noted for their hospitality, and never a night passed without something to do." [73]

Charlie and co-star Charles Emmett Mack in *The Rough Riders*, Paramount, 1927.

Wings director William Wellman remembered that the cast and crew of both films made salacious use of their leisure time:

> We stayed at the Saint Anthony Hotel and were there for nine months. I know that was the correct time because the elevator operators were girls and they all became pregnant. They were replaced by old men, and the company's hunting grounds were barren. Victor Fleming was making *The Rough Riders* at the same time and was staying at the same hotel. San Antonio became the Armageddon of a magnificent sexual Donnybrook. The town was lousy with movie people, and if you think that contributes to a state of tranquility, you don't know your motion picture ABCs.[74]

Love was definitely in the air in San Antonio. Mary Astor pined for her fiancé in Los Angeles, Clara Bow got engaged to Victor Fleming,

Charlie, Joby, and Richard Arlen.

and Charlie and Richard both fell head over heels for Jobyna Ralston, also appearing in *Wings*. Joby, as her friends called her, was a Victorian Valentine come to life, a beautiful girl with masses of curly hair (at a time when bobbing was the rage) and large dreamy eyes. She had a sweet Southern accent and spoke with a charming lisp that made men feel protective of her.

Joby had been Harold Lloyd's leading lady after Mildred Harris retired to marry Lloyd, and was in *The Freshman* when Charlie was just a bit player. Charlie had admired her from afar, but in the end, Joby chose Richard. She was the wedge that began driving Arlen and Farrell apart, but the final blow to their friendship was Arlen's refusal to thank Charlie or give him any credit for his part in *Wings:*

> But anyway that's water under the bridge, but I always could never understand why Dick wouldn't come out and say—say that, you know. Well, fellows are kind of funny about that. I don't know why Dick—because I did a hell of a lot for Dick, he lived and roomed with me and I've done an awful lot for him, but he—he wouldn't—I don't know why he wouldn't admit it. I think he would, I'd think he'd been very proud. I'd have been very proud if anybody done anything for me like that.[75]

Charlie contented himself with flirtations with the local girls, including one local girl named Connie. Connie kept a scrapbook of the filming in San Antonio, dutifully clipping and pasting any article she could find about the stars of *Wings* and *Rough Riders*, but her heart belonged to Charlie Farrell. He signed her scrapbook many times: "Love and kisses from Charlie," and there are pictures throughout her scrapbook of the two of them together. Charlie and the rest of the cast stayed on through the fall, and finally went home when filming wrapped in Los Angeles in November 1926.

Although filming on *Sunrise* officially ended January 20, 1927, there were a few difficult scenes that required extra work. Gaynor recalled that "At noon [on January 24] I took off my blonde wig [from *Sunrise*] and had my lunch and let my hair hang down and put on a little old black dress, and went on as the waif in *Seventh Heaven*. No preparation, no nothing. You just changed character with lunch, and at that I started on my way to success… [To go from Murnau] to Frank Borzage was almost

Charlie as Chico and Janet as Diane in *7th Heaven*, Fox, 1927.

enough contrast for a lifetime. Murnau was all mental, Borzage totally romantic—all heart. It was another lovely and valuable experience." [76]

7th Heaven is a love story between a waif and the young man who saves her from her abusive sister. They are parted by WWI, but remain with each other in spirit by returning to each other at the same time daily and repeating their declaration of love, "Chico—Diane—Heaven!" The overriding themes of *7th Heaven* are courage and faith—courage in the face of war and gained through love, and faith's ability to heal and regenerate.

One of the most iconic scenes in the film is the wedding scene in which Chico and Diane conduct their own impromptu ceremony as Chico is about to leave for the war. This scene makes extraordinary use of Borzage's "discreet but effective eroticism" [77] and neatly juxtaposes the chaotic prepa-

rations for war outside with the tender intimacy between the two characters inside. When Chico sees Diane in her wedding gown, he is overcome
by love, fear, and sadness—all three emotions managing to register simultaneously on Farrell's face. It is then that he is finally able to say the three
words that mean so much—"I love you." This is followed by, "I am afraid!"

At first, Farrell sits in a chair, pressing Gaynor against him—almost
as if he is willing the strength from her small body into him. At this
moment, Diane is the courageous one, the leader, while Chico cowers in
fear. She begs him to "always look up," saying, "Look what you've made
of me!" Chico then lifts Diane up and carries her around the apartment,
and for sixty full seconds there are no intertitles and no cuts as Farrell
and Gaynor kiss repeatedly. This stops only when Farrell leans breath-
lessly against a pillar, Gaynor lying limply across his chest, and Borzage

The iconic wedding scene from *7th Heaven*, Fox, 1927.

cuts immediately to the soldiers marching out in the street. They realize they have no time for a proper wedding and perform an impromptu ceremony with the medallions Père Chevillon (the local priest) gave Chico at the beginning of the film. Overcome with emotion, Chico vows to give "*Le Bon Dieu*" one last chance. As they say their vows, Borzage cuts to the chaos on the streets outside. The soundtrack effectively underscores this interruption, as the love theme is drowned out by the sounds of military bands and marching feet.

The final scene is perhaps the best known and most referenced of the entire film. Diane has just learned that Chico died, and sits in a state of shock as the sounds of frenzied celebration drift in through the opened windows—the Armistice has been declared. Again, in an intimate moment, war breaks through. Her three friends, Mme. Gobin, Col. Brissac, and Pere Chevillion, rush to the window to celebrate, leaving Diane alone with her grief. She wildly questions her faith in God. She hysterically berates Père Chevillon. Brissac takes advantage of the moment to persuade Diane to marry him. This time, Diane is almost defeated: "I am right at the beginning again," reads the subtitle.

Meanwhile, Chico—who is alive, but blinded—pushes his way through the frantic crowds on the street and finds his way home to Diane. He stumbles up the seven flights of stairs, calling her name. Diane hears him before any of the others do. As he flings open the door, the clock strikes eleven; the others are awestruck—Diane simply embraces him. "You saved me," one can lip-read Farrell saying, and the title continues, "I've been hit by every shell made, but Chico will never die!" Chico is blinded, but his eyes are still full of his vision of Diane as they parted. Diane promises to be his eyes, but Chico, reverting to his cocky reassurance, says, "Nothing can keep Chico blind for long!" This final scene is infused with a sense of holiness, as the light streams in from the left, gently illuminating the lovers as they kneel on the floor.

Modern critics often deride Borzage for being too sentimental, and point out *7th Heaven*, its final scene in particular, as being melodramatic in the extreme. But as critic John Belton explains, "Chico's miraculous return to life is no lapse in narrative continuity but an illustration of the transcendent nature of love in Borzage's work. Chico and Diane's love defies not only time and space but also mortality." [78] Carli Elinor, who conducted the orchestra at the world premiere of *7th Heaven* simply called this final scene, "the greatest love scene Hollywood has ever filmed." [79]

The chemistry between the two leads, and the rapport they shared with Borzage created a rare, indefinable screen magic. Gaynor described the atmosphere Borzage cultivated on the set:

Frank Borzage was marvelous. He was dear and he was soft and he was really a great contrast to Murnau. And yet I responded to Murnau, too. But with Frank you responded more with your heart. He would talk to me during a scene and he loved it—which was really exciting as an actress, to have this happen to you. We would rehearse a scene up to a point and then it was supposed to be cut, but when we'd really get into it...you'd keep it going. For Charlie and for me, it was more like home than home. We just couldn't wait to be there at nine o'clock, and we left at whenever...I was terribly tired, but I loved it and couldn't wait to get back in the morning.[80]

According to Dumont, Borzage often worked independently of the shooting script, paring down or elaborating as he felt suited his central

Glowing stars: Janet and Charlie are instantly famous at the Los Angeles premiere of *7th Heaven*.

storyline. Given his method of encouraging improvisation in his actors, and the fact that *7ᵗʰ Heaven* had only a quarter of the intertitles originally planned, it is safe to assume that Farrell and Gaynor improvised a great many of their scenes together, particularly the wedding scene. This is why *7ᵗʰ Heaven* is such a seductive film. What we see on the screen is in fact, Janet and Charlie playing out their love affair. From the first day they met on the set, they had fallen in love.

Although both denied this in print for most of their lives, Janet finally confessed in a 1976 interview with Rex Reed, "We were lovers. In fact, Charlie was my first big love affair in Hollywood." [81] She attended the premiere of *7ᵗʰ Heaven* on Herbert Moulton's arm, attired in a chiffon gown "in an apricot shade, made bouffant as to its skirt and further adorned with floral petals of pastel shades…and a wrap of the same fluffy material trimmed with peach colored fox fur." [82] Her entire family attended the premiere that night, even Helen. A journalist for the *Boston Globe* described the festive opening night activities:

> Overhead fireworks played in the starlit sky, where rockets burst into cloud like angels and dropped their wings below…Motors purred and cameras clicked as the notables arrived under the sputtering Kliegs. As the broadcaster called their names, the enormous crowds that "rush the ropes" on first nights in Hollywood surged forward for a closer look.[83]

In this carnival atmosphere, Charlie fielded questions from reporters while standing over Janet, to protect her from being crushed by well-wishers. Afterwards, Janet maintained a standing date with him to see the film every Monday night. Although Farrell and Gaynor desperately tried to keep their dates secret, a line of cars one city block long snaked around behind them, following them wherever they went. By October of 1927, Janet publicly broke her engagement to Herbert Moulton, stating that they were "too young to marry." Moulton made no public acknowledgement that the engagement had been broken until Janet admitted so in print. [84]

Charlie never actually ended his relationship with Virginia Valli the way Gaynor called off her engagement to Moulton. He cultivated her friendship instead. There was no trace of Valli at the premiere of *7ᵗʰ Heaven*. Farrell entertained Victor Fleming, Hedda Hopper, Julanne Johnston, Richard Arlen and Jobyna Ralston (still his friends at this point), Mervyn

LeRoy and his fiancée, Edna Murphy.[85] Charlie had started to develop a reputation for being a playboy: he enjoyed playing the field and he developed crushes easily, always convincing himself that he was in love. But there was something about his relationship with Janet Gaynor, something that elevated it above the usual flirtations and dalliances. Janet and Charlie were strongly attracted to each other physically, but there was something more—he respected her. He desired her good opinion. For the first time in his life, Charlie was deeply in love and it brought out his best intentions.

Fox was so pleased with *7th Heaven* that it was released before *Sunrise*, with much fanfare and publicity. *Heaven* was a box office smash, grossing $1,750,000 during its first run. Alfred Kuttner, critic for the *National Board of Review*, wrote, "Janet Gaynor as Diane and Charles Farrell as Chico...made the shameless, frank appeal of youth and beauty which dissolves the strictures of the old in warm memories and evokes the helpless rapture of the young. They were graceful with the grace of beautiful animals. This Chico was shy as a young man might be shy, and Diane's shyness was a trembling sweet thing to see. None of them acted shyness." [86] *New York Reviews* singled out Farrell's performance, calling it "a performance free from self-consciousness and grimace, a piece of work quite out of the ordinary." [87]

Paramount took advantage of the *7th Heaven* furor to release *The Rough Riders* in June. Farrell's performance was singled out for high praise by the *Los Angeles Times*: "I am inclined to give first honors to Charles Farrell as the New York boy. I can imagine no one else in the role—just the right amount of deviltry tempered with the ability to understand wonderful heroism in another. In one brief year, this young man has almost scaled to the pinnacle of film fame. *The Rough Riders* will undoubtedly carry him further on his way." [88]

Janet used the stellar notices she was receiving for her work in *7th Heaven* to demand a salary raise. At the time, she was earning $300 per week. Her attorney, Milton Cohen, sent the following plea to Alfred Wright, Fox's legal counsel:

> I desire in a spirit of fairness to call your attention to the fact that Miss Gaynor is receiving a very small compensation, and is unable to maintain herself in the way that she should considering the caliber of the work she is performing...she feels that the company should reconsider the compensation being paid her

and give her an equitable allowance. There are stars on the lot who I believe do not measure up to her artistic ability but are receiving a great deal more money.[89]

The letter closed with the threat that Janet had signed her original contract when she was underage,[90] and would break the contract once she came of age in October, unless her salary increased. This was the first of many battles Janet had with the studio, as she insisted on artistic integrity and adequate compensation for her work. The legal battle lasted months and got quite nasty, as Wright dug around in Janet's family closet to determine her true date of birth. The answer came from the principal of her old alma mater, Polytechnic High School in San Francisco. Mr. Addicott supplied the attorney with Janet's true date of birth—and in closing, as if pleading Janet's case, added, "She did excellent work here." The mudslinging got so intense that Cohen appealed directly to William Fox that "Mr. Wurtzel [Sol Wurtzel, head of West Coast production] has seen fit to make this a personal matter and considers something ulterior was done, and has even gone so far as to inform persons that he would not desire any persons,

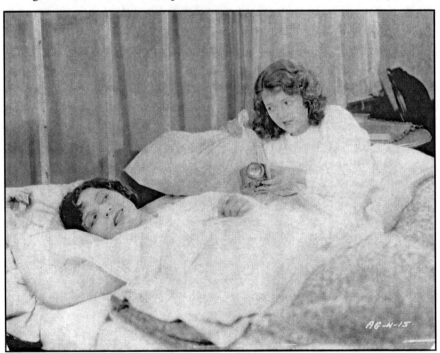

Janet with co-star Doris Lloyd in *Two Girls Wanted*, Fox, 1927.
Courtesy of Gina LoBiondo.

Still from *Fazil*, Fox, 1928. Charlie, as Prince Fazil, is on far left.

either artists or directors, coming through my office." As the legal brawl continued, Janet was assigned to *Two Girls Wanted*, a thin comedy that was an artistic comedown from her two previous films.

Two Girls Wanted, described by critic Muriel Babcock as "good-natured hokum," is the story of two sisters who set out to make good in the big city. Subsequently, Gaynor has trouble landing any jobs, and after a stint as an errand boy (in drag) and a stenographer, she is cast as a maid. In this role, she "rescues a handsome young man from 'shanghai' efforts of business opposition and helps him put over a big deal." [91] This was the kind of silly comedy that Gaynor rebelled against once talkies came into vogue, and her assignment to this picture was obviously a way to put Gaynor and "the caliber of her artistic ability" in their respective places.

While Gaynor worked on *Two Girls Wanted*, Farrell began filming *Fazil* June 5, under the direction of Howard Hawks. *Fazil* is a fable about an Arabian price who marries a liberated Frenchwoman, Fabienne (Greta Nissen), but their marriage cannot withstand the clash of cultures. "East is east, west is west and never the twain shall meet," and after Fazil and Fabienne make disastrous attempts at domesticity, the only way out is a suicide pact. *Fazil* was designed to cash in on the Valentino "sheik" craze, but Farrell—

who had played in two historical epics and was currently a smash as a French lover—was uncomfortable in the part. Hawks had to work hard to get his stars to relax and exude the necessary heat for their roles, according to biographer Todd McCarthy: "Before one of the lovemaking scenes, Hawks told both Farrell and Nissen privately that the other was very shy and that they would have to do something provocative to bring the scene to life. 'Well, they were two of the busiest beavers you've ever seen in all your life,' Hawks chuckled." [92] Hawks' white lie paid off—*Fazil* is one of the most frankly erotic of all Farrell's films, second only to *The River* (1929).

While Gaynor was at work on the set of *Two Girls Wanted*, she received word that Jonesy had died suddenly of heart failure. Farrell was

Charlie and Greta Nissen in *Fazil*, Fox, 1928.

on the set of *Fazil* when he heard about the tragedy. He rushed to the Gaynor home in full sheik costume to comfort Janet and pay his respects to her family. The funeral was on a Friday, and the following Monday Janet was at work, giving an interview to *Photoplay* magazine writer Ruth Lieber Biery. The interview, "Janet's Jonesy," is Janet's homage to the gambler who took a chance and made her a star. Laura was her manager and chaperone, Jonesy had been her cheerleader. Between the two of them, they formed the mind and the heart of Gaynor's career:

> You see, I really am just what 'Jonesy' and mother have made me. Why, 'Jonesy' taught me everything I know. I haven't dared grieve for his death, for fear he would return and say, 'Is this the result of what I have taught you?' You see, 'Jonesy' was such a big success in business. He was a philosopher and he wrote poetry. And he just made me be an actress.

Losing Jonesy's unwavering support just as her career took flight came as a terrible shock to Gaynor. For the rest of her life, Janet always gave Jonesy primary credit for her career.

Charlie had family matters to deal with that August, too—the prodigal son made his triumphal visit home after finally making good in Hollywood. He had not seen his family in three years and only after the success of *7th Heaven* did he feel confident that he could return home and, as he put it, "show the old man." Mayme Ober Peak, who covered the gala premiere of *7th Heaven* for the *Boston Globe*, recalled him shouting above the din of reporters and admirers: "Give my love to Boston and say I'm coming home this summer!" Charlie's success made his career acceptable to David; their long war finally ended. The Farrell family rift was so well known that his trip made all the newspapers. Afterwards, the locals joked that the Farrells were the first family to ever have a theater where the father ran the projector, the sister played the piano, and the son was in the movie.

In September, Janet's option came up and her contract was renewed. The months of legal wrangling paid off—her salary was bumped from the projected $500 per week to $1,000 per week. Charlie never campaigned for a raise and was making $300 per week until the end of the year, when he too was bumped to $1,000 per week. This difference in salary is indicative of how very different Janet and Charlie were in terms of temperament and their approaches to their careers. Charlie had just completed three star turns in three big pictures and a rival studio had tried to buy out his contract. If he had wanted to, he could have hired a lawyer and insisted on an immediate salary raise. He had just as much right to demand more money as Janet had. But Janet was the one who fought, and Charlie, if not content, was quiet. That lean winter of 1925 had scarred Charlie deeply and he was not eager to fall out with a studio again. On the other hand, Janet had been thrust into her career by her parents, and while she enjoyed the work, she was also removed enough to regard her career coolly. She had always had her family backing her, and this gave her the confidence to demand her worth from the studio.

In the meantime, when Farrell returned from Massachusetts in September, and with all salary disputes settled, Sheehan gave the green light for the next Borzage/Gaynor/Farrell project, *Street Angel*. Filming began that month. Once again, on the surface it appears to be merely a love story, but the beginning title set the tone for the film, and could be used as Borzage's motto for all of his films: "Everywhere…in every town, in every street…we pass, unknowing, human souls made great by love and adversity." The story was set in Naples. Janet played Angela, a poor young woman who attempts to prostitute herself to pay for her dying mother's medication, and is subsequently sent to jail. Charlie played Gino, an itinerant artist who falls for Angela as she is on the run from the police, working in a traveling circus.

Although Angela is able to elude the police for a while, she is eventually discovered on the very eve of her wedding to Gino. Although the sergeant tries to take her away immediately, Angela convinces him to let her have one last hour with Gino. While Gino innocently celebrates their good fortune and talks of marriage and children, Angela joins in the laughter, all the while keeping a tearful eye on the window, where the sergeant lurks. When Angela pretends to go to bed, but is actually taken away by the police, she whistles "O Sole Mio" to Gino, a particularly effective use of Fox's new Movietone sound-on-film system. Gaynor remembered this new innovation:

> When we were to go to the preview, Mr. Borzage said there was going to be a surprise. I couldn't imagine what it was, because I had seen the daily rushes each day and I'd seen a rough cut. We got to the preview, and all through the picture, Charlie and I whistled to each other. This sounds very strange, I know, but in the picture it

Janet as Angela in *Street Angel*, Fox, 1928.

wasn't strange. I remember it vividly: the first time, I was standing at the top of a stair, and whistled, and the sound came out, and I actually whistled, I just couldn't believe it...They had added someone else's whistle—certainly not mine—because I can't whistle.[93]

When Gino finds that Angela is gone, he looks for her in the streets. An astonishing tracking shot follows him as he searches, picking up and passing others on the street, reinforcing Gino's sense of isolation and the underlying sense that he is just one of those "human souls" now facing adversity. When it finally dawns on him that Angela has deserted him, Farrell as Gino grows taller and more angular—his boyish innocence dissipates as fear, confusion, and finally, bitter anger take its place. He loses his inspiration and with it, a commission for a career-making mural.

Street Angel has been called one of Borzage's most Expressionistic films. The lighting and cinematography created a sense of "despair, sordidness, and indifference,"[94] only relieved by Angela's transcendent glow. The final chase scene at the wharves is a Borzagian masterpiece. We follow Gino from behind as he picks up and drops several girls. He is a stark black

Janet and Charlie in a still from *Street Angel*, Fox, 1928.

figure, his fedora brim sharp as a knife. Angela is shown in ethereal profile, glimmering through the mist. As the darkness deepens, Gino must strike a match, the brief spark illuminating each woman's face. As Gino approaches from the left, Angela stumbles in from the right, and as they literally run into each other mid-screen, her head remains bowed. When his match illuminates her face, Borzage focuses on Gaynor's lovely eyes, full of love and tenderness—then on Farrell's, which glitter first with disbelief, then hatred. It is a moment that sends chills down the collective spine of the audience, a memorable melding of the Gaynor-Farrell chemistry, Ernest Palmer's cinematography, and Borzage's vision.

Of all the Farrell/Gaynor films, *Street Angel* is the one in which Farrell and Gaynor are most evenly matched in terms of characterization and performance. Reviewing the film, *Film Daily* said, "Janet Gaynor again proves she is a great actress. Farrell maintains a balance between arrogance and congeniality without sacrificing masculine appeal." [95]

During the filming of *Street Angel*, *Sunrise* had debuted to critical acclaim, with the *Los Angeles Times* stating, "Janet Gaynor actually gives a more shimmering performance than in *7th Heaven* though the casual picture-goer will deny this because of the greater appeal of Diane to the popular imagination." [96] Diane launched Janet's career, and she was forever grateful. For good luck, Gaynor wore a pair of shabby black slippers from *7th Heaven* in at least one scene in every subsequent picture. Her stellar performances in *7th Heaven*, *Street Angel*, and *Sunrise* earned her reputation as one of the finest actresses of her time.

Farrell took a lucky charm from *7th Heaven*, too, but his was less tangible than Gaynor's shoes. In that film, in *Street Angel*, and in four more to come, Farrell developed a mentorship with director Frank Borzage. Between the two of them, they created a kind of mythical character: handsome, innocent, naïve, pure, but with a sinister, morose vein deep within. More than any other actor, Farrell was able to embody the

Janet with her lucky shoes. Photograph by Max Munn Autrey. Courtesy of Gina LoBiondo.

"soul made great through love and adversity," so essential to Borzage's work. From 1927-1932, Borzage made thirteen films for Fox, half of which starred Farrell, and a quarter of which starred Farrell and Gaynor. Borzage used Farrell more than any other actor in his career. Farrell reciprocated by doing his best work under Borzage's direction.

In 1927, Gaynor and Farrell went from obscurity to fame. They became stars. They made good for their families. Both had suffered the loss of a loved one—Farrell lost good friend and *Rough Riders* co-star Charles Emmett Mack in a car accident that March, and Gaynor lost her beloved Jonesy. And in the heady but unsteady world of Hollywood, they found each other.

Chapter Five

Fame

"The fans are young and the new stars are young. Youth calls to youth and the hand that cranks the camera rules the world."
– Ruth Waterbury, *Photoplay,* November 1927

Janet and Charlie were on top of the world, and tops at the box office at a time when Hollywood was a giddy and glamorous place to be. They had achieved the kind of wealth and fame their families never expected. They were no longer tied to workaday jobs, selling shoes or slinging hash, or even toiling anonymously on a movie set, hoping to be discovered. Going from obscurity to fame in a short time had an unsettling affect on many stars, who retaliated by "Going Hollywood": building enormous mansions filled with servants, buying outrageously expensive cars, or searching for a spouse among the impoverished nobility of Europe. Screenwriter Anita Loos watched the antics of her peers with glee, and wrote, "To place in the limelight a great number of people who would be chambermaids and chauffeurs, give them unlimited power and instant wealth, is bound to produce a lively and diverting result." [97] So how did Charlie and Janet adjust to their newfound fame? Neither "went Hollywood." They remained resolutely normal kids.

Janet lived with Laura in a small stucco house in the Hollywood Hills, at 2709 Mound Street. When Janet finished work, she went home to rest and to prepare herself for the next day's performance. Although she had learned to conserve her emotion, rather than going at each take 110% as she had for *The Johnstown Flood,* movie-making was still an exhausting experience. Charlie and she were required to work six days a week, each day until the director dismissed them. Janet, whose constitution was weakened by her childhood bout of influenza, felt the workload

77

Newspaper photo of Janet and Laura, late 1920s.

keenly. Laura took care of her, pampering and catering to Janet's every need when she was not required on the set. After Jonesy's death, Laura and Janet became inseparable, in a relationship that wasn't "merely mother-daughter devotion… [but] a rare comradeship." Laura continued to act as her daughter's agent, a position she had taken on in the early Universal days, and Janet remarked, "It is fun to have her for my best friend and to have her back of me in each step, each problem, and every little triumph of my career. It has developed a perfect understanding between us."

While Janet's close relationship with Laura helped her career and personal life, it was extremely difficult on Helen, who was deeply bitter over Janet's success. Helen was neither the first nor the last person to lose out on a Hollywood career to a favored sibling; for example, Baby Peggy Montgomery, one of the biggest child stars of the silent era, had an older sister named Louise who did not make it in pictures. In telling of Louise's resentment, Montgomery (now known as Diana Serra Cary) could just have easily been describing Helen:

> Louise was marinating in a brine of resentment against me. I had not only replaced her in Father's affections, I was her eternal jailer, blocking all her efforts to forge an identity of her own.

Worse still, as the acknowledged breadwinner, I was the one on whom both parents focused their full attention. She knew it wasn't my fault; at times she even felt sorry for me: this in turn curdled into self-hatred when she realized she was jealous and envious of her baby sister who was every bit as helpless as herself.[98]

It is impossible not to feel sympathy for Helen, who despite her desire for the career, saw her family's support and devotion go to her younger sister, someone who didn't even want to be an actress. Having her stepfather declare Janet the actress of the family was downright devastating. Only someone with a very strong sense of self could congratulate her sister and continue on her chosen path, or choose a different career and give up the dream altogether. On November 20, 1925, Helen married a young man, Daryl Brown, who lived around the corner from the Gaynors at 1625 Cherokee Street. On the marriage license, he listed his occupation as "chauffeur," tellingly; Helen listed hers as "stenographer." In all likelihood, the marriage was Helen's stab at independence; the only way she could free herself from the crushing guilt and anger that she must have felt at home. Shortly after her marriage, she changed her name to Hilary (sometimes spelled "Hillary"), perhaps as an attempt to establish a stage name. If she continued to look for a job in motion pictures, she had no success. So she turned to the bottle for solace. Paul Gregory, Janet's third husband who knew her in later years, said, "Hilary was really a very nice lady. And it was sad, you see, if you understand, it was Hilary that wanted to be the movie star. And of course, Hilary never, ever got over it." [99]

Janet lost her sister to fame, but began a friendship with Irene Mayer, daughter of MGM President Louis B. Mayer, that was an approximation of sisterhood. Irene and her sister Edie had been rivals almost since birth, a stormy relationship that was, in some ways, encouraged by their father. Irene was lonely and felt like an outcast in Hollywood, and Janet was sideswiped by fame and the loss of her sister. They became best friends from the moment they met. Irene recalled:

Janet Gaynor showed up in my life at just the right moment, as though scheduled. It's pathetic that this was the first time I'd ever confided in anyone; I was a late starter right down the line. I remember sitting with her on the sand facing the ocean, hidden by our sea wall. She was the one to whom I confessed my feeling about David [Selznick]. She never let me feel ridiculous when I asked her about dating etiquette, those fine points which came naturally to other girls as they grew up. I learned to trust friends beginning with Janet.[100]

Irene added that even Louis B. trusted Janet:

My father, who disapproved of us having actress friends ("They're not after you, they're after me," among other failings), couldn't fault her. She wore low heels, no makeup and was the symbol of wholesomeness. Moreover she had a long-term contract with Fox...and she was number one at the box office. She didn't need my father.[101]

Because of her friendship with Janet, Irene Mayer felt more self-assured when dating young David Selznick, and called Janet "the first star who gave glamour to simplicity, and niceness a new definition." Out of admiration Fay Wray imitated Janet, even down to her speech: "She never said 'because' but always 'on account of.' I found that fun to imitate and later it would be copied from me for the character Nikki in John Monk Saunders' *Single Lady*." [102]

In contrast to Janet, Charlie's family life had improved. The rift between Charlie and David had healed, Ruth and Estelle were doing well, and the family business had certainly improved due to Charlie's celebrity. In 1928 David expanded his business, acquiring the license to the Pasttime Theater on Union Avenue, which backed up to his New Onset Theater on Onset Avenue.

David, Estelle, and Ruth also invested in "summer cottage" properties that were near White Island. For the time being, the Farrells stayed happily in Onset, and Charlie lived at the Hollywood Athletic Club. It was the perfect lodging for his bachelor lifestyle—at home, he could box, swim, or play tennis to his heart's content. Charlie always had a robust constitution and he loved the athletic life. Far from being tired at the end of the day, Charlie looked forward to sports as a way to blow off steam.

Living at the Athletic Club, well-liked by everyone, Charlie's life began to resemble his college days, when he spent more time on athletics and his fraternity duties than on studying. He was gregarious, the life of the many parties he attended. While Janet had a few intimate friends who spoke of her in glowing terms, Charlie was (superficially at least) friends with everyone. He was a natural addition to the weekend parties at San Simeon, the lavish California estate of publishing magnate William Randolph Hearst and his mistress, actress Marion Davies. Charlie en-

The Pasttime Theatre, Onset Bay, MA. Courtesy of the Wareham Free Library

joyed playing tennis with Hearst on the superb courts.

Janet and Charlie were fundamentally different in their interests and tastes, but opposites attract, and of course, spending long hours together, playing in some of the most romantic films ever made, certainly added fuel to the fire. Charlie was attracted to Janet's wry sense of humor, and what Fay Wray described as "an elfin wisdom about her, as though she might know certain charming secrets." Her gravity and sincerity were healthy antidotes to his often excessive ego. Janet was attracted to his virility and fun-loving nature; he took her outside of herself.

There are many reasons why they chose to keep their romance a secret. In their sudden rush to fame both lost all their privacy, which meant that every little thing they did made the gossip columns. Janet particularly valued discretion in her personal life, and to have the details of her first "real love affair" splashed across newspapers would have been mortifying. It may have been, too, that they purposely kept their romance a secret so as not to have the studio meddle in their offscreen lives. The studio system was taking shape by the late 1920s and studios were beginning to regulate stars' personal lives. (Anyone doubting the power studios wielded over their stars' love lives should look at the doomed love affair of Nelson Eddy and Jeanette MacDonald, or William Haines' forced retirement from MGM because he lived openly with his lover, Jimmy Shields.) Had Fox and Sheehan known about the romance, they would have either cashed in on the affair, or worse, meddled with them in the hopes that the two would save their attraction for the cameras. Sheehan, who felt more than businesslike about Janet, might have interfered simply from jealousy. Their secret romance meant happiness as well as continued employement.

Douglas Fairbanks, Jr. was one of the few people who knew about their affair. He became friends with Charlie and Janet while he was at Fox making *Is Zat So?* (1927), and remembered:

> We three were so chummy that I became their "beard," the cover-up for their secret romance. I would drive them out to a little rundown, wooden house well south of Los Angeles, near the sea. I'd leave them there and go sailing or swimming until [it was] time to collect them and then we'd all have a bit of dinner.[103]

This indicates that Janet even went so far as to keep her relationship a secret from Laura, who would have been absolutely dismayed at how far the affair had progressed. Those stolen moments in a rundown shack were the first time that Janet slipped her mother's leash and did exactly what she wanted. For his part, Doug Jr. recalled that he had been going through an agonizingly poetic phase, which he dropped once he met Charlie and Janet: "I was periodically saved from this sophomoric behavior by work and companions. I made friends with Charles Farrell and Janet Gaynor...that palship helped...I began to drop some of my aesthetic affectations and return more or less to normal."

While Charlie and Janet remained lovers offscreen, they did not do another picture together in 1928. Fox capitalized on their popularity by splitting the team up, and starring them with other actors. For the first part of 1928, Charlie worked on *The Red Dance* (also called *The Red Dancer of Moscow*), with director Raoul Walsh. Walsh had been acting and directing practically since the birth of the film industry; one of his first parts was as John Wilkes Booth in *The Birth of a Nation* (1915). Before he began work on *Red Dance*, Walsh had directed and starred in *Sadie Thompson* with Gloria Swanson, one of the most famous, most glamorous stars of the silent era. Walsh had established a reputation for "fast-moving, romantic, and hard-hitting films," [104] and *The Red Dance* had the necessary elements for a Walshian epic. Set against the backdrop of the Russian Revolution of 1917, Charlie played Prince Eugen, who becomes romantically involved with peasant Tasia (played by WAMPAS graduate Dolores Del Rio). Tasia saves him from death at the hands of the Revolution, and the two fly away to freedom in an airplane.

Reviews of the film were decidedly mixed when it debuted later that year. *Motion Picture Classic* pronounced, "The Russian Revolution turns

The peasant girl and the prince, *The Red Dance*, Fox, 1928.

out to be a topsy-turvy, harum-scarum, hit-and-miss affair as revealed in *The Red Dance*...The trouble is too much picture." While Charlie and the stunningly gorgeous Del Rio made an extremely attractive couple, the chemistry he had generated with Gaynor simply wasn't there. "Del Rio has a chance to look picturesque and act with a fair amount of feeling," read a review in *Motion Picture Classic*, "...As for Charles Farrell, he wears his uniform well and his quick stride is all to the military." [105]

Dolores Del Rio and Charlie in a scene from *The Red Dance*, Fox, 1928.

Another reviewer wrote, "Strange it seems that Charles Farrell cannot be given a boost—has so frequently deserved one. His addition to the film is not that which he has made to others." [106] This same review declared that Dolores Del Rio was *the* star of the film. Director Walsh may have considered it a turkey too, for although his direction is dramatic and the photography gorgeous, he never mentioned it in any of his later interviews.

While Charlie was up to his boots in fake snow and Russian peasants, Janet began working with F. W. Murnau on what is certainly one of the most eagerly sought-after "lost" silent films: *4 Devils*. Janet played Marion, part of a circus act ("The 4 Devils") who nearly loses her man (Charles Morton) to a vamp (Mary Duncan). Janet had already learned some basic balancing tricks from Frank Gainer when she was a girl, but underwent weeks of training with the Flying Cardonas. Alfredo Cardona helped Janet with her trapeze act. She recalled that the pedestal she had to land on was less than a foot wide, but she felt secure knowing Cardona was there to help her. Murnau, a stickler for realism, employed nearly 8,000 extras for the circus customers, completely changing the audience for each "performance." He insisted that it would not do for the film's audience to recognize the same extras in each scene. Janet recalled one scene the crowd of extras would not quickly forget:

> There was one scene that was supposed to be the scene where we fell, towards the end [of the film]. Murnau had the camera on a dolly, but it was high in the tent, and he was photographing the other people, the spectators. He did not tell them what they were seeing, only that they were seeing people doing an aerial stunt. Then at a given moment the camera came shooting down this trap at full speed. People fell back, women fainted—it was absolute pandemonium—because they thought that the camera was loose and was coming down upon them. Of course, this was the reaction he wanted. That's the way he directed it.[107]

Janet, who had regarded Murnau as a great master on *Sunrise*, quickly grew disenchanted with his sadistic directing technique, especially when one particular stunt could have killed her. During this sequence, Charles Morton was supposed to hang upside-down with his legs around Janet while she hung on the trapeze. Alfredo Cardona told Murnau the stunt was simply unfeasible: "No woman can hold her weight and a man's weight with her hands. This is impossible. I can't do that, no one can do that." Murnau devised a wire harness, set up in a leather pair of shorts for Gaynor to wear, and attached to the trapeze. Once Janet was rigged and Morton was on the trapeze, his weight was still almost too much for her to bear:

> It pulled at me so I was nearly cut in two with this leather harness. They let us go, up in the middle of the circus tent…it was as high as a real circus tent. And I was in absolute agony with this weight, and there I was wired, and I couldn't move, and he was swinging. I was stretched out there and of course I screamed and I cried and I was almost hysterical. Finally they cut us down and I said, "Mr. Murnau, you didn't tell me anything!" He said, "You did just what I wanted you to do. You were in agony, and that's what I wanted." [108]

Sheet music for the love theme from *4 Devils*, Fox, 1928. Janet and co-star Charles Morton.

Janet was furious with Murnau; she did not need to suffer abject cruelty to give a convincing performance. Of that moment, she later said, "I didn't think anything with my mind...I think it's much better when you know what you're doing, and you project emotion, but it must never get out of control."

Janet spent 1928 training for, filming, and recovering from *4 Devils*. Still secretly seeing Charlie, she was also being rushed by a young San Francisco man named Jesse Lydell Peck. He was tall and handsome, well-traveled, and from a deep-rooted Oakland family. He was born July 7, 1899 in Oakland; his father, James, was a lawyer and his mother, Emma, stayed at home. The Peck family had a well-established law firm in Eastbay (Peck, Bunker and Peck), of which Lydell's older brother Charles was a junior member. In 1918, when he was a student at Washington and Lee University, Lydell joined the Army and served in WWI. Upon his return, he followed in his father's and brother's footsteps and became an attorney. In 1927, Peck saw Janet in *7ᵗʰ Heaven* and was instantly smitten. While entertaining Fox director William K. Howard in the Peck family home, Lydell pressed for an introduction.

Their thoroughly modern courtship prompted a flurry of newspaper blurbs—Peck sent love letters via telegram and flew down to Los Angeles just to squire Janet to parties. On May 15, Janet left on a cruise to New York, and Peck flew down just to see her off at the docks. When she returned to San Francisco in late June, he was on hand to meet her. The press speculated that they were already secretly engaged, but Janet stalled them with a pat denial, "I am taking my career seriously and will devote all my time to it. Of course, I expect to get married some day, but not very soon." [109]

Lydell was attractive to Janet because he represented everything that was not Hollywood. He had a stable, respectable career as an attorney far removed from the motion picture business. His family was well established and had nothing whatever to do with movies. Lydell seemed like the perfect, self-fulfilled man, and Janet, who had never wanted her career in the first place, was intrigued by the possibility of life with Lydell. If she married him, she could leave pictures, have the life she wanted, still care for her mother, and perhaps heal the rift with Helen. She had already proved herself in her career for Jonesy's sake; surely she could quit when she was still on top. For his part, Lydell wooed with a vengeance, and Janet was swept off her feet.

Meanwhile, Charlie renewed his interest in Virginia Valli, who had recently divorced the shadowy Demerest Lamson. Now completely free of her husband, Valli could be seen with Charlie—and she was. As often as gossip columns mentioned Janet and Lydell, they mentioned Charlie and Virginia. If Janet was attracted to Lydell because of his anti-Hollywood qualities, Charlie desired Virginia for precisely the opposite reason—she was his Hollywood ideal. Ever since he had seen her while he was just an extra on the Universal lot, she represented the unattainable. He wanted his career, he wanted fame, and he wanted every part of the Hollywood success story. Yet he wanted Janet Gaynor, too. This fundamental difference—desiring or rejecting Hollywood and fame—between Charlie and Janet spelled trouble.

Wooing with a vengeance: Lydell Peck and Janet are caught by the camera's glare.

There was one other cloud lurking on the horizon: talking pictures. *7ᵗʰ Heaven* had been one of the highest-grossing films of 1927; another was *The Jazz Singer*, which incorporated spoken dialogue and singing into what is essentially a silent film. Released by Charlie's former studio, Warner Bros., *The Jazz Singer* was a sensation and prompted the beginning of a revolution. The whistling added to *Street Angel* was the tip of the iceberg. Fox had patented its own method of adding synchronized sound to pictures known as Movietone. The Movietone method recorded sound onto the variable-density optical track of the same strip of film used to record images. This method ensured correct synchronization, unlike the Vitaphone method, which required that the sound be recorded onto 78-rpm discs, spun in synch to the film. (The film *Singin' in the Rain* owes quite a few of its biggest laughs to pointing out the failings of the Vitaphone system.)

To stay abreast of the competition, Fox ordered that the last two reels of *4 Devils* be reshot, with sound added. Janet recalled that the cast was ordered back to the set, which had been covered in felt to absorb all extraneous sound, and the camera was placed in a soundproof box. All the familiar sounds of the camera grinding, of mood music being played by the studio orchestra, the director whispering commands, were replaced by a terrible silence. The entire cast felt confused and unnatural, Janet recalled:

> Finally we did a scene…we did it the best we could. You must remember we'd had no kind of training at all. These were just our natural voices. Of course, the next day we heard it, and you know how everyone is shocked to hear his own voice for the first time…I thought, this is too awful, because I didn't like the way I sounded, my voice was high, and oh, it was just horrible. Doesn't it sound awful, to think of a whole film being geared to the silent technique, and then, all of a sudden, having the last two reels in sound! But they had to do it to compete.[110]

When *4 Devils* premiered at the Gaiety Theatre in New York on October 3, it received critical praise, most of it reserved for Murnau. The *New York Times* raved:

> It is, however, the unfaltering manner in which Mr. Murnau attacks his scenes that is responsible for this picture's greatness. One forgets the actors and thinks of the characters… Miss

Gaynor's acting is effective. She portrays the little soul who loves Charles no matter what happens...But one could go through the whole list of players congratulating one after another, and they probably all know that they owe a great deal to that artist among directors, F. W. Murnau.[111]

Janet, who knew just how Murnau had coaxed those performances from his actors, was disgusted. She must have conveyed her feelings to Win Sheehan, for she never worked with Murnau again.

Janet in *Christina*, Fox, 1929.

Janet spent the last half of 1928 working on *Christina,* a role written especially for her by Tristram Tupper, an author who was frequently published in the *Saturday Evening Post* and would eventually become a screenwriter for Fox. *Christina* is the story of a young Dutch girl who cares for her blind father and creates a world of make-believe just for his benefit. She also becomes caught in a love triangle between workingman Dirk (Harry Cording) and circus performer Jan (Charles Morton). A critic for the *Los Angeles Times* called Janet's performance "natural and wholly affecting" but bemoaned the addition of sound to the film, "the talking finish seems static in comparison with the silent portion." [112] The reviewer mentioned that, when typing Charles Morton's name, he almost typed "Farrell." It was clear to Fox that the public wanted Charlie and Janet to star in another picture together, and as soon as possible.

Meanwhile, Charlie's next picture after *The Red Dance* was held up because Frank Borzage needed actress Mary Duncan and cameraman Ernest Palmer, who were both assigned to *4 Devils.* After Murnau finished principal photography on *4 Devils* in June, filming began on *The River* on Fox Hills-Westwood. *The River* was Farrell's third film with Borzage, and his first Borzage film without Janet. For years, *The River* was considered a lost film, until historians William K. Everson and Alex Gordon discovered an incomplete copy in the 20th Century Fox Archives. The first and last reels and a couple of scenes in the middle are missing from the extant copy, but were reconstructed using stills from Borzage's own collection and the finished film script housed in the UCLA archives.

Incomplete though *The River* may be, it is worth taking a moment to study, for in this film, Charlie gave the best solo performance of his career. Charlie plays Allen John Pender, a young man who has grown up in the Rockies and who builds a houseboat to seek adventure. As he drifts down the river, his progress is halted by a dam that is being constructed. He stays on at the site of the dam, becoming entangled in a love affair with Rosalee, a young woman who is the mistress of the foreman of the site, Marsden. (For a full description of the plot and Borzage's directorial technique on the film, please read Herve Dumont's excellent biography, *Frank Borzage: The Life and Times of a Hollywood Romantic.* I will confine my analysis to Farrell's performance.)

Charlie's performance of Allen John Pender is the culmination of his collaboration with Borzage, and of all his characterizations, the definitive Charles Farrell brand of hero. In the extant copy of the film, the

1928

U.S.A.

DRAME

LA FEMME AU CORBEAU
THE RIVER

RÉALISATEUR
Frank Borzage

French movie card showing scenes from *The River*, Fox, 1929.

first glimpse we get of Allen John is as he drifts down the river towards a whirlpool. This scene is also Rosalee's (Mary Duncan) introduction to him. She sits, fully clothed down to fetching high heels, on a rock on the river bank, and watches Allen John, who is completely nude, as he drifts along. He grabs onto the rock and begins to haul himself out, then upon seeing Rosalee, quickly jumps back into the river. As they talk, Allen John still clinging to the rock, he points out his houseboat with childish pride. "That's my boat!" he exclaims, trying to impress her. Rosalee is bored; she is sophisticated; and she can barely contain her laughter at his awkward situation. Allen John knows Marsden was hauled off to jail, and he asks her if she will be lonely through the winter, without a man around. "I hate men!" she exclaims, flouncing off to her cabin.

Later, they meet again, this time in her cabin. Allen John, who has been trying to catch a train out of the camp, has missed it and Rosalee, knowing that he will miss it, is expecting him. He apologizes for making her angry, hoping that even though he is a man, they can still be friends. "You don't count," she replies. "I meant that you were a boy, and I've known only men—like Marsden." The film is a dance between these two characters, the jaded woman of the world and the completely innocent, almost primeval, boy-man. Allen John tries to prove himself; Rosalee laughs at him. Allen John tries to leave the encampment, and each time is thwarted by either visiting with Rosalee or helping her with some small task. As Allen John, Charlie perfected the naïve innocence so critical to his brand of hero. He hunches his shoulders, stares down at his shoes and gives quick darting glances from under his brows. He fidgets, not knowing what to do with his hands, and hesitates before speaking. When he smiles, it is almost as if he too is laughing at himself—a half-smile that quirks the right corner of his mouth. The overall contrast with Mary Duncan, who lounges with catlike grace across tables and beds, swinging her feet, and smiling openly, is electrifying. Even though Charlie was easily a foot taller than Duncan, he is submissive to her every demand. No other actor of the silent era could have played the role with any degree of success; Charlie is able to walk the line between virility and purity without appearing ridiculous. *The River* is worth seeking out just for his performance, his penultimate expression of innocence and desire that was snuffed out with the end of the silent era.

The entire film is an exploration of seduction, one that Herve Dumont calls "the most erotic film of the silent era," and European critics, especially the French, agreed: "In all cinema, Frank Borzage's film is the one that contains the most disturbing sensuality." The most memorable scene of the entire film fortunately survives in the extant copy: Allen John has almost succumbed to frostbite, after trying to chop down trees in the driving snow to prove his manhood to Rosalee. As he lies prone and unresponsive on the bed, Rosalee—who looks more than ever like the "rag and a bone and a hank of hair" described by Kipling in "The Vampire"—slips under the covers in her negligee, pressing her body to him. While appearing like a succubus, Rosalee wills life back in to Allen John. This scene had (still has) enough erotic charge to send the gentlemen critics of *Cahiers du Cinema* into raptures decades after the fact; critic George Auriol exclaimed, "Don't take your eyes off her: she glows, burns, trembles, her teeth are dangerous, she undulates, leaps up, escapes…"

Filming on *The River* lasted until September 5, and it premiered at the Gaiety Theater in New York City on December 22. In an entertainment world now consumed by talking pictures (Dumont describes some of these, quite charitably, as "simple minded, jazzy entertainment"), no one knew quite what to do with the film. Unbeknownst to Borzage, William Fox added a Movietone musical prologue to the film, in which an "obese tenor in city clothes sings the tune of the film ("I Found Happiness When I Found You") with a soprano in an evening gown." [113] Critics and audiences alike laughed at the result. The film was released in Europe without any alterations, which may be why it was so well-received, especially in France. Fox pulled all prints from circulation in April 1929, cut out the introduction, and also cut the last fifteen minutes of the film, which they replaced with a spoken conclusion. This final mishmash was re-released as *Song of the River* (to capitalize on the movie musical fad of the late '20s-early '30s) in October 1929. And that was the ignoble end of a film containing Charles Farrell's best performance, a film considered by *La Revue du Cinema* to be, along "with the films of Keaton and Langdon, with *Flesh and the Devil* and *The Wind,* one of those rare films in which the face of love moves us by its truth." [114]

Filming on *The River* took nearly four months, and neither Charlie nor the rest of the cast and crew were given a rest upon its completion. On September 6, the day after filming wrapped on *The River*, almost the entire company was rushed to Pendleton, Oregon, to begin filming *Our Daily Bread* with F.W. Murnau. The film was, as with most of Murnau's films for Fox, an exploration of good versus evil, the city life versus the country life. Charlie played Lem Tustine, a young wheat farmer who is sent to Chicago by his puritanical father to sell the family's wheat crop. Mary Duncan played Kate, a young waitress in the city who falls for Lem and dreams of an idealized life in the country. They marry, but their happiness is threatened by Lem's father, played by David Torrence, and farmhand Mac (Richard Alexander). With Murnau, Charlie explored his dark side further, giving a slightly sinister twist to his characterization of Lem. Unable to consummate his marriage to Kate due to the interference of his family as well as Kate's reluctant horror at her bucolic dream crumbling to dust, Lem chases her around and out of their bedroom, where Mac is lying in wait. Lem is a disturbing inversion of the purity and innocence of Allen John and Chico—a fascinating, complex characterization that should have developed Charlie's range even further.

Unfortunately for everyone, studio politics intervened. Murnau and Fox fought bitterly over the ending of the film; Murnau wanted a tragic ending; Fox wanted a happy one. Fox also insisted that spoken dialogue be added to the film, and Murnau was absolutely dead set against adding any sort of spoken prologue, epilogue, or dialogue to his films. After all, he had made *The Last Laugh*, which was done completely in pantomime, and insisted that the ideal silent film needed no intertitles. He had been enticed to Fox with the promise of complete control over his films, only to find this control eroding when talking pictures invaded. Murnau furiously terminated his contract with Fox, and *Our Daily Bread* was completed by assistant directors Frank Powolny and William Tummel. By the

Charlie's new home on Toluca Lake.

time *Our Daily Bread*, now retitled *City Girl*, limped into theatres in 1930, it was a severely compromised version of Murnau's original film.

After completing three films in one year, Charlie spent the few remaining months of 1928 working on his home, "of Norman architecture...with an exceptional setting on Toluca Lake." [115] He tired of his bachelor lifestyle at the club, and was willing to make a commitment—at least to a home. Virginia took over much of the planning and interior design. Janet and he began seeing each other openly, often going out to the Montmartre nightclub. A gossip columnist painted this picture of the two of them, in 1928:

> It was good to see them together—Charlie bubbling over with boyishness, very much resembling an overgrown Saint Bernard in a Pekinese kennel, Janet like a little mother, scolding him...consoling him...reassuring him...teasing him....begging him prettily...It has been said that Charlie, rather bewildered by success and beautiful women, falls in love with all his leading ladies. Several months ago the papers carried a hysterical story of a secret marriage between him and Greta Nissen, while rumor has recently had it that he is enamored of Virginia Valli. Of course, too, Janet has come in for her share of newspaper publicity. Only a few days ago it was hinted in the press that she is engaged to Lydell Peck, a wealthy San Francisco man. [116]

He did continue seeing Virginia, and gave her a party at Mme. Helene's Tea Room on October 14. Meanwhile Janet continued her Jazz Age courtship with Lydell Peck. On Thanksgiving, while Janet dined with her family and Virginia went to the Cocoanut Grove, Charlie dined alone at the Montmartre.

Charlie had originally planned to spend Christmas playing a round of golf at the Lakeside Club with pro golfers Walter Hagen and Johnny Farrell (who had won the 1928 US Open, and was no relation to Charlie). But in the weeks leading up to Christmas, his good friend, actor Fred Thomson, was hospitalized. Thomson, a former clergyman, was married to screenwriter Frances Marion. He had starred in a number of wildly popular Westerns with his horse, Silver King. He was also a gifted athlete who had been an All-Around Champion in Track and Field before embarking on his film career. Thomson remained in the hospital for much of

Janet and Charlie dance together at a Los Angeles nightclub.

December with symptoms the doctors could not diagnose. Finally, on Christmas Day, Thomson's jaw began to set, and the doctors finally realized he had tetanus, contracted when he stepped on a rusty nail several weeks earlier. Charlie kept a constant vigil outside Thomson's hospital room, along with a group of Thomson's cowboy friends and actress Marie Dressler. The gathering was finally shooed away by Hedda Hopper, Frances Marion's good friend, that night. By midnight, Fred Thomson had died in his wife's arms. His funeral was December 28 at the Beverly Hills Community Presbyterian Church. Charlie served as pallbearer, along with Harold Lloyd, Douglas Fairbanks, and Thomson's brothers. Fred's silver coffin was covered in a blanket of yellow roses. As the simple ceremony drew to a close, Charlie and the other pallbearers rose to carry the casket out of the church. Moving towards the front of the church, the pallbearers were briefly blinded by a glorious shaft of sunlight from the opened doors.[117]

Fred Thomson's death had a profound effect on Charlie. Fred had been successful at everything he tried, was well-liked by almost everyone in Hollywood, and had been in the peak of physical and mental condition. He was married to a beautiful, accomplished woman and had two handsome sons. Despite all these things—no matter how active and healthy he had been—Fred had died too young, felled by a simple rusty nail. Seeing himself mirrored in Fred Thomson, Charlie realized that fame, career, wealth, or even good health offered no guarantees of life. Even as late as 1976, when Thomson had long faded from public memory, Charlie mentioned him in an interview:

> And I was up there all the time; I saw a picture in the paper today or yesterday of their [the Thomson's] house. I was up there all the time, 160 acres from the top of the hill. Fred Thomson? No, he died and Frances Marion died, and Harold Lloyd and his wife died, they all died. Yeah...the boy died.[118]

He also realized that the very industry, around which he had built his career, and even his identity, was undergoing fundamental changes. The very language of film was changing. He had built a career on what seemed a sure thing in 1925, only to find that he had built his foundation on shifting sand. Exhausted, scared, and lonely, Charlie turned to the one woman in whom he had complete faith.

Chapter Six

Lucky Star

"Adding sound to movies would be like putting lipstick on the Venus de Milo."

– Mary Pickford

Hollywood, 1929: Fox rang in the New Year by making Charlie and Janet, along with all its other talent, sign amended contracts. These amendments were specifically made to address the issues surrounding talking pictures. The most damning of these amendments stated that the producers now owned the "rights to the artist's voice, and all such recordations and reproductions." Although Fox had owned the rights to the actor's screen images before sound came in, this wholesale ownership of all aspects of an actor's performance added a whole new dimension, and it made Charlie and Janet wary. George Bagnall, Fox's comptroller, asked Janet and Charlie several times to sign the amended contracts, but "they decline to do so, stating that they want to think it over further." [119]

These amended contracts were the culminations of six months' work—a complete revamping of the studio to make it a major player in the talking-picture market. Beginning July 1928, Fox had poured all of its resources into creating "Fox Movietone City," an impressive, state-of-the-art sound studio. Studio workers had worked 24 hours a day, 7 days a week to create the 35 buildings that housed eight soundproof stages. The old studio stages were converted to labs and Fox's management offices moved to Westwood. [120] William Fox took the studio one step further when he began a takeover of Loew's Inc., the world's largest movie theatre chain, and its production company, Metro-Goldwyn-Mayer. Fox bought out the Loew's family's shares in the company, making Fox "the largest production and distribution enterprise in the history of film."[121] Fox Studios now had the most modern production facilities in the industry, the most theatres in the country, and the top box-office stars in the world. Small wonder Sol Wurtzel was so eager to have them sign the new contracts.

In this revolutionary climate, Charlie and Janet began work on their last silent film together, and the last of their films together with Frank Borzage, *Lucky Star*. Filming began on February 4. The screenplay was based on the short story "Three Episodes in the Life of Timothy Osborne," written by Tristram Tupper. Of all the screenwriters who worked at Fox, Tupper possessed a rare understanding of what made Janet and Charlie click onscreen. He had written *The River* for Charlie and *Christina* for Janet, and both vehicles capitalized on Charlie's naïveté and innocence and Janet's wistful, melancholy tenderness. *Lucky Star* brought all of these characteristics together, and combined with Borzage's intuitive direction, the film had all the makings of another surefire hit. But on March 24, William Fox issued a decree that from then on, all Fox productions for the English-speaking market would be made as talkies; silent films would only be released overseas, since the synchronization process was not completed for the foreign market. Filming on *Lucky Star* was immediately halted, and Charlie and Janet were bundled off to Palm Springs for a few days, for a series of concentrated voice-training sessions.

As they worked together to conquer this entirely new artistic medium, Charlie reached out to Janet and proposed marriage. He had been deeply shaken by Fred Thomson's death and the harried changes in the motion picture industry. He needed a rock, and he clung to the "deep, ever so wise, and absolutely authentic" Janet Gaynor. For her part, Janet had spent the Christmas holidays with Lydell Peck's family; as she grew closer to the Pecks she saw the end of her servitude in motion pictures. She loved Charlie and was still mightily attracted to him, but his continued relationship with Virginia Valli and his womanizing reputation sent up red flags. It does not appear that Janet ever actually accepted Charlie's proposal, but they did continue their affair throughout the filming of *Lucky Star*.

After they returned from Palm Springs and passed the "microphone test," the pair resumed filming *Lucky Star* as both a silent and talking picture. For the talking portion, Sheehan hired a dialogue director from Broadway to correct the stars' diction. Furiously, Borzage banished him from the set:

'What is this?' I said. 'You're a nice guy, but you've been a stage director, so have I when I was a kid, but I said you just move over around the side, will you? You're not gonna destroy the naturalness of these kids.' So we finished the picture like that.[122]

Filming on both versions wrapped on April 20, 1929. As with all films made during this period of transition from silents to sound, *Lucky Star* suffered from the addition of dialogue. The talking version was released with a different ending from the silent version, and Borzage historian Herve Dumont says, "The dialogue not only adds nothing, by being overexplicit it detracts from the picture, reducing the metaphoric nature of the tale." [123] When *Lucky Star* was released on July 21, critical reaction was mixed: *Variety* called it "indifferent and poor," the *New York Herald Tribune* said it was "a likeable mediocrity," but *Film Spectator* declared, "*Lucky Star* is not going to be one of the biggest box-office pictures that come from the Fox lot this year, but it will be one of the finest." [124]

For decades *Lucky Star* was considered a lost film, until Nederlands Filmmuseum discovered a complete copy of the original silent version. The Dutch intertitles were translated back into English, using the original shooting script. What emerges is the most eloquent, most fascinating

Hedwig Reicher, Janet, and Charlie in a scene from the talkie version of
Lucky Star, Fox, 1929.

film of the Borzage/Gaynor/Farrell triumvirate. It is the simple story of two outcasts who fall in love: Tim Osborne, a crippled World War I veteran who lives to repair broken things, and Mary Tucker, the distrustful, dirty child-woman. Rounding out the tiny cast are Guinn "Big Boy" Williams as Martin Wrenn, Tim's former sergeant in the Army, and the Widow Tucker (Hedwig Reicher), Mary's mother.

As Mary Tucker, Janet gives the most understated performance of her career, entirely free of any trace of histrionics or hysteria. In the beginning of the film, when Mary is fifteen, Janet is all awkward legs and arms, moving in a quick, jerky fashion. Our first glimpses of Mary show her for the black sheep she is: she waters down the milk she is going to sell and pretends that she hasn't been paid for it so she can cheat an extra dime. Later, as Mary blossoms under Tim's love and attention, Janet becomes graceful, her movements fluid. In contrast, Timothy Osborne is casual, offhand, and paternal. As Tim, Charlie lets go of some of his naïveté, instead showing us Tim's loneliness and his driving need to make broken things—everything from lamps to phonographs, and finally Mary—whole. He is always concerned with doing the job at hand and doing it right: it was in delivering water to soldiers at the front that he was badly wounded and lost the use of his legs. He cleanses Mary literally body and soul, teaching her not only to wash her hands and face properly, but also teaching her right from wrong.

In a pivotal scene that is both comic and erotic, Tim washes Mary's hair in the pond beside his house. Mary is like a child, embarrassed but also overjoyed at the attention being paid her. Meanwhile, Tim is all business, seeing only what needs to be repaired and charging ahead to mend it. After scrubbing her hair until it is so clean it nearly stands on end, he notices her filthy neck and shoulders. He immediately moves to fix the problem, not thinking until the back of her dress is almost completely undone. "How old are you, anyway?" he asks in amusement. "'Most eighteen," she replies, and everything screeches to a halt. He hastily buttons the dress, and shoos her down the river to bathe. "You do it yourself, okay?" he says; Mary is confused and flustered. She moves down the river bank and undresses, and Tim cranes his neck to watch. Tim has just realized that Mary is a woman, a desirable one at that, and the realization makes him laugh at himself.

The most poignant scene in *Lucky Star* could well be the most moving scene in the entire Gaynor-Farrell *oeuvre*. Mary has skimmed money from her mother's farm's profits to buy a pretty dress to wear to a dance and comes to Tim's house to get ready. When she emerges from his bedroom in all her finery, she has the handkerchief Tim made for her (to stop her constant nose-wiping on her sleeves) pinned over her heart. Smiling, surveying her, Tim gently unpins the handkerchief and tucks it into her belt. When he learns that she has bought the dress with stolen money, he warns her that she's "still filthy inside" if she lies to her mother. Then he tenderly ties a ribbon around her hair and encourages her to look in the mirror. Delighted at her reflection and overcome with gratitude, she throws her arms around him. Overwhelmed, Tim closes his eyes in ecstasy and embraces her, then the realization slowly dawns that he is just a cripple, confined to a wheelchair, and he can't have her. He slowly opens his eyes and drops his hands but Mary clings to him—he must finally reach up and pry her loose. The embrace lasts for nearly 45 seconds, so long that the moment feels agonizing, unbearable. She stands in front of him, gazing at him with love; he tries to break the moment by joking that she'll be late, but she remains enthralled, torn between desire to attend the dance and to stay with him. "Wish you were a-goin'," she whispers, and Tim hustles to get her moving: he hands her shoes, wraps her in his old Army jacket, and pushes her out the door.

Tim Osborne is the last of the Charles Farrell heroes, capable of being tender and naïve while still remaining virile. Apart from being just the last of the breed, Tim Osborne is also Charlie's roundest characteriza-

Janet and Charlie, two stark figures in the snow, *Lucky Star*, Fox, 1929.

tion—less of an allegory, more of a human being. After all, Tim is only somewhat pure: he does steal a glimpse of Mary as she bathes, and he exchanges blows with Wrenn early in the story, before Wrenn even becomes involved with Mary. As Tim, Charlie also gives his best physical performance, especially when Tim tries to walk for the first time after being wounded. Pigeon-toed, he slides one foot out and then another, collapsing heavily on the floor, beads of perspiration on his brow. It is a masterful piece of work, brilliantly convincing.

But the laurels went to Janet Gaynor for her role as Mary Tucker, and the *Los Angeles Times* declared, "Miss Gaynor's ability to portray convincingly the change in the character and appearance of the little farm girl further clinches her position as one of the cinema's outstanding players." [125] In fact, Janet had earned the respect and admiration of the entire industry, and ranked with dramatic heavyweights Mary Pickford and Lillian Gish. She was so highly regarded that she earned a nomination for the first Best Actress Academy Award from the Academy of Motion Picture Arts and Sciences.

The Academy was formed in May 1927, with Douglas Fairbanks acting as its first President. The Academy was created to promote harmony within the divisions of the motion picture industry and to recognize and award achievement in the making of motion pictures. In February 1929, the Academy decided to recognize several professionals for excellence in the film industry, and the Oscars were born. Janet was nominated for her work in *Sunrise, 7th Heaven*, and *Street Angel*. Her fellow nominees were Gloria Swanson for *Sadie Thompson*, and Louise Dresser for *A Ship Comes In*. Frank Borzage was nominated for Best Director for *7th Heaven*; Benjamin Glazer for the adapted screenplay for *7th Heaven*; Harry Oliver, for Interior Decoration for *7th Heaven*; and *7th Heaven* was nominated for Best Picture. Notable by his absence, Charlie was not nominated for the Best Actor award. The Best Actor nominees for that year were Richard Barthelmess for *The Noose* and *The Patent Leather Kid* and Emil Jannings for *The Way of All Flesh* and *The Last Command*.

The first Academy Awards ceremony was not the highly publicized media circus that the ceremonies became in later years; indeed, Janet garnered much more press coverage as a WAMPAS Baby Star. The winners, including Janet and Borzage, were notified three months in advance. The awards were presented at a subdued dinner at the Hollywood Roosevelt Hotel on May 16. Underscoring the casualness of the occasion, Janet wore a simple skirt and sweater set; presenter Douglas Fairbanks wore a blue blazer and white pants. Even though the event was modest by modern standards, a crowd of well-wishers and autograph hounds hung around the hotel doors, waiting for a glimpse of the stars. As Janet and Laura pulled up to the hotel, a drunken Hilary was in the crowd, waiting:

> They pulled up in the limousine, and Hilary was there on the ropes, and she hollered out, "There she is, there's my sister!" You know, it was devastating for Janet to see her sister there, hanging over the ropes, half-gassed.[126]

Recalling her Oscar win several decades later, Janet never mentioned her sister's behavior. Instead, she said, "It didn't seem like the big thrill it is today because there was no tradition behind it. We all went to the old Roosevelt Hotel, and it was a very nice small dinner party. Very nice. I accepted my Oscar, and I don't think I said anything but, 'Thank you.'" When Janet received her Oscar, she felt all that it cost her: her win further alienated two very important people in her life, her sister and Charlie. Two-hundred-and-seventy people attended the ceremony, but the one person who didn't still remained on Janet's mind, fifty years later: "All I remember is that I was very disappointed Charlie Farrell didn't come to the dinner, too." [127]

Charlie must have been deeply hurt that every aspect of *7th Heaven* was nominated for an award—except the leading man. In later years, he mentioned his exclusion only in general terms, such as, "some people thought I should have been nominated," but never directly admitted he deserved the honor. It is perplexing that Charlie was not nominated; his performances since *Old Ironsides* were uniformly excellent and reviewers had given him consistently high marks along with Janet. On the other hand, Charlie never made noises about being a great artist, whereas Janet had (via her lawyer, to Fox) immediately upon completing *7th Heaven*. Of the two nominees for Best Actor, Richard Barthelmess was a stage-trained actor who had worked closely with master director D.W. Griffith; he also happened to be one of the founders of the Academy of Motion Picture Arts and Sciences. Emil Jannings, the winner, began his career in Max Reinhardt's theatre company and later starred in Murnau's highly regarded *The Last Laugh*. These credentials alone recommended him as a serious contender. Perhaps Charlie would not have won out against these big-league thespians, but by all rights he should have received some recognition for his work.

To add further insult to injury, in a ceremony that took place a week later, only Janet was asked to leave her footprints in the forecourt of Grauman's Chinese Theatre. Emil Jannings was not included, so it was not due solely to her Oscar win; also, other famous screen couples such as Douglas Fairbanks and Mary Pickford (and later William Powell and Myrna Loy) were immortalized in cement. Fame, recognition, adulation—all things that Charlie craved and didn't get, while Janet did—may have been the driving wedge between them. The burden of fame was (and is) often too much for Hollywood couples to bear. Anita Loos, who had witnessed Mary Pickford and Doug Fairbanks' romance from its beginning, remembered exactly when it began to crack; arriving in two different parties at a premiere, Doug and Mary were separately acclaimed. "The next day at the studio," she recalled, "Doug, smoldering with anxiety, took me aside to ask, 'Do you think that Mary got more applause last night than I did?'" [128] Similarly, when Charlie refused to attend the Academy Awards dinner with her, Janet saw the handwriting on the wall.

In the ending scene of *Lucky Star,* Janet and Charlie embrace in the swirling snow, two stark black figures standing in the middle of train tracks that stretch on to the horizon. As the scene darkens and the film ends, there is a feeling that we want to see more, to see where Charlie and Janet and Frank Borzage are going to take us, what emotional heights they will scale next. In that final fadeout we witness not only the death of their silent film careers, but the death of the Borzage/Gaynor/Farrell partnership. Amid the post-Oscar tension, Janet and Charlie began *Sunny Side Up,* an all-talking, all-dancing, all-singing extravaganza. *Sunny Side Up* was directed by David Butler, who played Monsieur Gobin in *7th Heaven* and would achieve great fame in the 1930s for directing most of Shirley Temple's films. In addition to supplying the music for the film, the songwriting team of DeSylva, Brown and Henderson wrote the story and dialogue.

Sunny Side Up is the story of rich boy Jack Cromwell (Farrell), who, after fighting with his fiancée on the 4th of July, goes slumming in Yorkville, a tenement. He meets Molly Carr (Gaynor), a sweet but poor young girl, and is so wowed by her amateur performance at the neighborhood Independence Day talent show that he invites her and her friends back to Southampton to perform in a charity concert. He puts them all up in a fancy house next door to his, and of course, word gets out that Molly is being 'kept' by Jack. This leads to many misunderstandings and silly situations. At length, Jack realizes that Molly is worth ten of his fiancée,

Poor girl, rich boy: Janet and Charlie in *Sunny Side Up*, Fox, 1929.

and tries to get her to marry him. She refuses, thinking he is only trying to salvage her reputation. They are finally united when she sees him singing "If I Had a Talking Picture of You" to her portrait.

Naturally, the storyline offers many opportunities for singing and dancing, and Janet and Charlie do their best alongside veteran vaudeville performers El Brendel, Marjorie White, and Frank Richardson. Of Charlie and Janet's debut musical performances, David Butler recalled:

Janet Gaynor had a lot of guts, that girl, to sing. She had never sung in her life before. She had a little bit of a voice...We were all scared to death when Charlie Farrell, who was great, started singing…But I think the fact that sound was just coming in—I think we could get away with things like that. I think a lot of people got away with it.[129]

Butler neglected to mention that neither Charlie nor Janet received any special training for their roles. The *New York Times* excused this by mentioning that their performances didn't have to be vaudeville quality:

So far as her singing is concerned, she is not supposed to be any prima donna, but just Molly Carr of Yorkville, Manhattan, who falls in love with Jack Cromwell (Mr. Farrell), the scion of a wealthy family…Mr. Farrell's singing is possibly just what one might expect from the average young man taking a chance on singing a song at a private entertainment. His presence is, however, ingratiating and his acting and talking are natural. He may not strike one as an experienced stage actor, but one is gazing upon a motion picture comedy in which the people are not on a stage, but walking through real roads and into houses that look real and sometimes are real. So his speech and even his singing suit the part.[130]

Nor does Butler shy away from the use of accents in the film; in fact, he exploits his performers' accents to denote the differences of class. In the tenement, we hear Italian, Irish, and Bronx accents along with El Brendel's Swedish dialect shtick, and in Southampton, Charlie Farrell's thick Boston Brahmin accent fits nicely with his upper-class image. We also find out that Ruth was not the only Farrell to play piano: Charlie clearly accompanies himself in at least one number.

Sunny Side Up is not a bad film; indeed, given the technological constraints of the time, it is quite excellently done. In contrast to other circa 1929 talking pictures, the camera stays mobile and fluid. Ernest Palmer's opening boom shot takes us through the tenements of Yorkville, picking up and leaving several characters: screaming children, brawling couples, and gossiping housewives, before settling on Eric Swenson's (El Brendel's) store, the scene that introduces us to Janet. It is a neat talkie callback to his opening tracking shot of Naples in *Street Angel*. Butler also incorporates little touches, including a trick shot that makes Janet's portrait come to life and sing back to Charlie, to keep the pace of the

Charlie on piano, getting ready to accompany Janet, *Sunny Side Up*, Fox, 1929.

film lively and amusing. The dance sequences are imaginatively staged by Seymour Felix, particularly "Turn on the Heat," in which a dozen girls dressed up like Eskimos get so hot dancing that they melt the snow, and palm trees spring up in place of igloos.

But after the emotional depths Charlie and Janet had plumbed in their silent films (particularly *Lucky Star*), *Sunny Side Up* comes as a complete shock. Where *Lucky Star* is brooding and gently melancholy, *Sunny Side Up* is noisy, silly, pure entertainment. Their characters are mere stereotypes; there is no depth to the picture at all. With each of Janet and Charlie's silent films, the casts grew smaller and more intimate, forcing the focus solely on them as a couple. *Sunny Side Up* bucked this trend; it has a huge cast and gives a lot of face time to the supporting players, relegating the romance to the sidelines. In addition, whereas their silent films had been tailored to fit Charlie and Janet and their particular chemistry, beginning with *Sunny Side Up*, they were expected to conform to the material chosen for them. The difference is, while it is difficult to imagine anyone except Charlie as Chico or Tim Osborne, and Janet as Diane or Mary Tucker, anyone else could just as easily have played Molly Carr or Jack Cromwell. In fact, an entire slew of actors could have done a better job; *Sunny Side Up* was made for a screen couple like Dick Powell and Ruby Keeler.

Sunny Side Up also marked the death of the Charles Farrell brand of hero. Jack Cromwell is not called upon to tenderly nurture Molly Carr, nor is he innocent and naive; he's just supposed to sit around and be the unattainable rich boy Molly moons over. This is most apparent in the scene where Jack tries to convince Molly to marry him: "I love you. I love you more than anything else in this world. And I must have you. And I will have you!" he cries—then he seizes her and kisses her. The Charles Farrell hero never grabbed and seized, never insisted on having his way. "Go away, I tell you! Oh, go away! You've hurt me enough as it is," Molly cries, and he gives up. He gives up too easily! The Charles Farrell hero always went through a transformative baptism of fire before winning his love. "Very well, Molly. I'll go," he sighs. "But I hope you'll find out how wrong you are—before you ruin both our lives." Part of this change can be blamed on the constraints of spoken dialogue; what played out poetically on the silent screen might have sounded ridiculous if spoken aloud. Moreover, DeSylva, Brown and Henderson were more used to the rhythm of pop music than the subtle nuances of romance; their dialogue has a lot of snappy one-liners but precious few poetic flights of fancy.

When *Sunny Side Up* had its debut at the Gaiety Theatre in New York that October, critic Mordaunt Hall, writing for the *New York Times*, declared:

> It is a production which abounds in good fun, whimsical touches and brilliant staging and one in which Miss Gaynor and also Charles Farrell are called upon to sing. Miss Gaynor's voice may not be especially clear, but the sincerity with which she renders at least two of her songs is most appealing. Her performance is as fine as anything she has done on the screen.[131]

Was Hall seriously comparing Janet's performances as Diane, Angela, or Mary to her work as Molly Carr? It was a sweeping generalization that pointed out where public opinion was heading. Whereas critical reception to *Lucky Star* was decidedly mixed and it bombed at the box office, readers of the *New York Daily News* and the *Chicago Tribune* voted *Sunny Side Up* the most enjoyable production of 1929. The die was cast, and Fox was more than prepared to follow suit.

Janet and Charlie had each signed their amended contracts by the time filming wrapped on *Sunny Side Up* in September. Janet even received a $4,000 signing bonus. There is nothing in Charlie's personnel file to indicate he also received a bonus. Once again, Janet held out for money while Charlie merely accepted what Fox was willing to give him. True, he was receiving $1,750 per week to Janet's $1,250 per week, while an extra on *Sunny Side Up* would have been happy to earn $50 per week. But while he was financially solvent, Charlie's unwillingness to challenge the studio became a detriment to his career, especially once talking pictures took over.

The day after filming wrapped on *Sunny Side Up*, Janet shocked the entire nation by filing for a marriage license at the Alameda County Courthouse—with Lydell Peck. For nearly six months, Charlie had tried to convince Janet to marry him, but Lydell won out with a telegraphed proposal. Years later, Janet explained her break up with Charlie:

> I think we loved each other more than we were 'in love.' He played polo, he went to the Hearst Ranch for wild weekends with Marion Davies, he got around to the parties—he was a big, brawny, outdoors type...I was not a party girl...Charlie pressed me to marry him, but we had too many differences. In my era, you didn't live together. It just wasn't done. So I married a San Francisco businessman, Lydell Peck, just to get away from Charlie.[132]

She explained as much to her son Robin years later: "he was a great guy but let's leave it at that... she had this feeling about Charlie-'we've got to leave it the way it is.'"[133]

Some gossip magazines hinted that Janet had initially accepted Charlie, but then found out Charlie had gone to see Virginia Valli one last time. Realizing that Charlie would never give up other women, she

The happy couple: Lydell Peck and Janet in 1929.

furiously wired her acceptance to Lydell Peck. There may be a grain of truth to the story, as Janet herself implied that her marriage to Peck was completed in haste, "just to get away from Charlie." However, it seems that in marrying Lydell, Janet was also saving herself from a Hollywood marriage—she thought she was marrying a self-assured man, in no way connected with the industry.

On September 10, the day before Janet's wedding, Charlie left Hollywood on the Santa Fe Chief for the East Coast. Hounded by reporters, he tersely admitted that he and Janet had never been "actually engaged, but had several spats and reconciliations." The *Los Angeles Times* guessed that their onscreen partnership was over, too, noting that "no contemplated productions list them together." [134] The next day Janet married Lydell in a quiet ceremony in his father's home, 652 Spruce Street in Oakland. Of Janet's family, only Laura attended, and her only bridesmaid was a young woman named Alice Bergdoll. Her Hollywood friends, including Fay Wray, Irene Mayer, and Clark Gable, did not attend. Janet and Lydell then departed immediately for a honeymoon cruise to Hawaii.

On the cruise, Janet realized her mistake. "It was a disaster," she declared. Later she told her son, Robin, "By the third day she knew she had made a mistake…It was on the ship going over to Hawaii…she knew she had blown it." [135] Her third husband, Paul Gregory, explained, "She knew when she married him it wasn't going to last. And it didn't. She was just trying to find a harbor." [136] Janet and Lydell returned from their honeymoon on October 15, and set up housekeeping at 504 Palm Drive in Beverly Hills. All hopes of Lydell remaining unconnected with the film industry were dashed when he accepted a job as a writer and assistant director at Fox. Not only was Lydell in the industry, he was at Janet's home studio, where he could keep a close eye on her and any hanky-panky with Charles Farrell.

Two catastrophic events added to the chaos in their personal lives. A week after Janet's disastrous honeymoon, the stock market crashed. Soon thereafter, William Fox was sued by the U.S. Justice Department for violation of antitrust law. His acquisition of 53% of the shares of Loew's Inc. and Metro-Goldwyn-Mayer had infuriated Louis B. Mayer, who used his pull with the Justice Department to subject Fox to legal action. At the time the suit began, William Fox was recovering from a near-fatal car accident and had lost a fortune in the stock market crash. In addition, the creditors he had pumped for the funding to expand and modernize the studio began demanding nearly $50 million in payments due.

William Fox was forced to sell his shares in the studio in a hostile takeover; he lost his shares in the Loew's deal, and began a seven year descent into bankruptcy. His shares were sold to one of his creditors, Harley Clarke, who was head of a holding company that owned many gas and electrical companies in the United States and Great Britain. Win Sheehan, who had sided against William Fox, remained head of production and in April 1930, Clarke became the head of Fox Films. With bankers now running the studio, Win Sheehan announced, "The war is over and we are back in the amusement business." [137]

Sheet music from *Happy Days* featuring Charlie,
Janet and its huge cast, Fox, 1930.

At the end of 1929, Charlie and Janet were forced to appear in the ensemble musical, *Happy Days*. Dressed as babies, they sang, "We'll build a Little World of Our Own." It was a bizarre performance that perfectly distilled how Janet and Charlie were being infantilized by their own studio once talking pictures swept the industry. Next, Sol Wurtzel rushed Charlie and Janet into *High Society Blues*. It was a shameless bid to capitalize on the success of *Sunny Side Up*—another all-talking, singing, and dancing extravaganza, directed by David Butler. To spice things up, Janet played the rich girl this time. Mordaunt Hall explained the paper-thin plot in his *New York Times* review:

The ingenuous nature of this film is possibly to be excused on the ground that it is partly musical, with singing by both the principals. So as to afford a reason for this melody, Eddie Granger, impersonated by Mr. Farrell, seldom goes anywhere without his ukulele, which serves him in helping to charm Miss Divine (Miss Gaynor) and also in enticing his rival, Count Prunier, to the Granger home on the day the nobleman is to wed Miss Divine. The momentarily crafty Edward undertakes to give the Count a ukulele lesson and also to quench the Frenchman's thirst with alcoholic beverages, so that he is eventually in no condition to attend the ceremony. Then, while the Count is shouting wildly and laughing loudly, Edward elopes with Miss Divine, much to the consternation of her parents when they finally learn that she has run away with young Granger and not, as they at first presumed, with the supposedly diffident Count.[138]

Press herald from *High Society Blues,* Fox, 1930.

Janet watched a rough cut of the film in February 1930. She was absolutely livid with what she saw and sent Win Sheehan a blistering three-page letter that was part plea for artistic integrity and part diatribe against the studio. Lydell Peck, who had established himself as Janet's representative, had an obvious hand in the letter, which is written in both self-important lawyerspeak and impassioned defense:

> Never have I been so humiliated or so angry. Believe me, Mr. Butler did the best he possibly could with my part but the result is pathetic. The piece offers me nothing by way of characterization nor could I inject any into it. As far as I am concerned there is only one remedy and that is to retake my scenes with another girl in the part. I can't for the life of me understand why I was cast as an ingénue lead in a character story. I am furious—after the work I have done for the Fox Company—this then [is] my reward. Never will I put my foot on the Fox lot again until all my grievances are settled once and for all.[139]

Janet then listed her demands, beginning with the command that she see a completed script, including dialogue, before starting a film. "I am demanding protection for all time," she added. Her next claim was obviously influenced by Lydell Peck: "Right now let me just say that if there is a next picture, it will not be with Charles Farrell. I know that I am a star in my own right just as Charlie is in his, and after two or three good pictures by myself I will be happy to star with him again." Her other requirements included: shorter hours due to her health; billing in "larger type than that of the picture or any other member of the cast"; a raise to $4,000 per week, which was more than double her current salary; and finally, a cap of only three pictures per year. She closed the letter with the indication that she knew Fox was in serious trouble: "I am sure that in New York you are protecting your own interests with all the astute acumen at your command and I feel that I have the same impregnable right to safeguard my own interests with similar caution."[140]

With that, Janet planned a trip to Hawaii with Laura and left Lydell Peck behind to spar with the studio. Charlie had inadvertently booked passage on the same ship, and only realized the mistake when he saw Laura and Janet walking up the gangplank. Acting swiftly, he ordered his baggage off the ship and greeted both women with a kiss. Pretending he had just come to see Janet off, he saved her from Lydell Peck's jealousy and a flurry of rumors in the press. Meanwhile, Charlie would just have to vacation somewhere else.

Chapter Seven

Strike and Depression

"You know an awful lot of people, Liliom."
"They know me, or think they do. When you are in the public eye,
like I am, all sorts of people claim to know you."
                                        – From *Liliom* (1930)

Janet could not have picked a worse time to fight with the studio. By the time her letter reached Win Sheehan in New York, he was embroiled in a fight against William Fox, trying to keep his job and keep the company from bankruptcy. When the dust settled and Harley Clarke became studio head, Sheehan and he were only concerned with keeping the studio financially solvent. No one was particularly worried about Janet's artistic integrity. What they did care about was box-office success, and since *Sunny Side Up* and *High Society Blues* made money and *Lucky Star* did not, the pattern seemed set.

Many close to Janet blamed Lydell Peck for appointing himself her counsel and then giving her poor advice. Paul Gregory both confirmed and denied this in his analysis of their marriage:

> He *tried* to control her. [Emphasis added.] Actually, Janet was a very—I used to call her 'The Original Platinum Butterfly' because she was just as beautiful as she could be and strong as iron.[141]

This power struggle was the cause of most of their early unhappiness, but it also points out that, though Lydell did advise Janet and his voice can be heard in her letter to Sheehan, Janet had full knowledge and control over her own career and decisions. Though Peck may have egged her on, it was Janet's voice that cried out:

> My work demands all of my energy and emotion without harassment of any kind from the outside and until I can continue to work without the hindrance of other and material circumstances, I would rather not make any more pictures for the Fox Company.[142]

Moreover, Janet had been litigious from her earliest days at Fox. How many other young starlets, earning six times what they had as extras, would have had the gall to demand *more* from the studio once they had a hit film? What other actress would have brought in an attorney and threatened to break her contract, unless her demands were met? Anyone else would thank her lucky stars for what she had. Janet was different, and it was perfectly in character for her to both walk out on her contract and appoint an attorney to finish the fight. The fact that the attorney in question was also her husband only made it more convenient.

It is the timing that makes Janet's walkout suspicious. Surely Janet, who was an astute businesswoman, could see the studio's point. Given the state of things, her salary demands were downright laughable. Making a dramatic exit during such a perilous time, not only for her studio, but for the industry in general, as it adjusted to talking pictures and pulled through the dismal economy was suicidal. As Paul Gregory said, "she didn't really

Friend husband: how the press painted Lydell Peck in 1930.

like being an actress, but she got swept up in it and she thought she might as well ride on it till the end," so it is possible that Janet chose to walk out simply because she no longer liked the parts she was being given. Figuring the ride was over; she was prepared to leave everything behind. Coming on the heels of both her Oscar win (which simultaneously rewarded her good performances and further damaged her relationships with her sister and Charlie) and her marriage, which should have moved her further away

Janet in Hawaii, turning her back on Fox, 1930.

from the industry had Lydell not taken a job at the studio, Janet's walk-out was also her last-ditch effort at liberty. It also provided her a little physical freedom from Lydell, since he stayed behind to act on her behalf while she and Laura enjoyed Hawaii's soft sea breezes.

Sol Wurtzel tried to corral his wandering star by sending a series of blunt telegrams, ordering her back to the studio. He even sent her a schedule of ships returning to California. Janet's walkout was holding up production on *Liliom*, starring Charles Farrell and directed by Frank

Borzage. The film was adapted from Ferenc Molnar's play about the ill-fated love affair between Liliom, the swaggering carousel barker, and the ethereal Julie.[143] Janet was supposed to play Julie, a role made famous by stage doyenne Eva Le Gallienne. The irony of Janet's strike was that it actually cost her opportunity to play an artistic role with some depth. After several failed attempts to reach Janet, Sheehan wired Wurtzel:

> There is only one course to pursue, viz: to accept her decision that she will not work and take her off payroll, then let matters settle themselves. In the meantime there is no hurry and we will talk it over when I return. I think it is in the best interests of the Corporation and the picture *Liliom* that Borzage obtain another actress to play the lead and we will save the expense of Gaynor's salary in the meantime.[144]

At the bottom, written in Wurtzel's handwriting, is the sigh: "May be necessary to see Peck." On March 15th, Janet was officially removed from payroll.

Even without a paycheck, Janet remained staunch in her demands. On April 29, nearly a month before filming commenced on *Liliom*, Janet returned to Los Angeles to keep a promise. She was one of Irene Mayer's bridesmaids at Irene's wedding to David O. Selznick. The wedding was, by Hollywood standards, exceedingly small and simple, with Irene wearing an understated empire gown by MGM's top designer, Adrian. The wedding took place at Louis B. Mayer's home, in front of the fireplace. Of that day, Irene recalled, "Janet Gaynor, my best friend, was the only one of my bridesmaids really close to me." [145] Janet's stay in Los Angeles was brief, and not once did she set foot on the Fox lot.

Meanwhile, Frank Borzage found his Julie in stage actress Rose Hobart, who had just made good on Broadway in *Death Takes a Holiday*. Hobart was imported especially for the production and given the star treatment, which she recalled as "a blur of makeup tests, hair appointments, wardrobe sessions…more reporters and studio people, hairdressers wanting to change the color of my hair, and makeup people wanting to pluck my eyebrows." [146] When filming commenced on May 19, Hobart recalled, "I met my leading man, Charles Farrell, on the first day of shooting. I was totally unprepared for this. In theatre we rehearsed with the whole cast for a month so that by the time we came to a performance we were comfortable with each other." Charlie, squeezed between veteran stage actor Lee Tracy and

Charlie, James Marcus, and Lee Tracy in a scene from *Liliom*, Fox, 1930.

newcomer Hobart, was decidedly uncomfortable. He was nervous about his voice and delivery, especially in his scenes with Tracy, who had a distinctive, rapid-fire patter. Trying to cover his nervousness, he approached Hobart. "You New Yorkers are all so sophisticated, how do you get that way?" Hobart replied with "some crack and he turned away. I realized he was serious, and I had gotten off on the wrong foot right off the bat." [147]

Liliom is imaginatively and beautifully staged, especially in the scenes with the "celestial trains" that carry people to Nowhere or the Beyond. Despite the dazzling sets and Borzage's sensitive direction, *Liliom* is lacking something. It may be the complete absence of chemistry between Rose and Charlie, who, stemming from that first disastrous meeting, did not click off-screen or on. Rose's portrayal of Julie lacks tenderness and warmth; her voice is deadpan and her delivery wooden. Charlie's characterization of Liliom is off, too. Reviewing the film, *Theatre Magazine* said, "Charles Farrell fails completely to bring to the part of Liliom that lovable devilishness that was Joseph Schildkraut's distinction in the play. Molnar meant his audience to love Liliom; it is difficult to love the film character of Farrell's." [148] Watching the film again today, though, Charlie has all the boastful cockiness of a young boy trying to masquerade as a man. He is not lacking in devilishness, but he wants a fundamental streak of meanness that would put the character across. In the end, Farrell's Liliom comes across as whiny instead of roguish. Lee Tracy, who plays the Buzzard with his signature machine-gun panache, steals the show.

While Charlie may have been struggling at the studio, his personal life was going like gangbusters. After Janet's rejection, he threw himself into the night life. Not a week went by without some mention of Charlie in the society columns. It was almost as though he was trying to prove Janet right—that he was a player and that he would always 'get around to parties.' He dated not just Virginia Valli, but an entire constellation of young starlets, including Lois Moran and Anita Page. He escorted Moran to the gala premiere of *Sunny Side Up* and spent Christmas 1929 in her company. Together they attended an "International Fiesta" in honor of Broadway star Fay Marbe the following month. Moran was considered among the most beautiful women in Hollywood at the time, and had been an object of fascination for F. Scott Fitzgerald when he lived in the film colony a few years before. Many of Fitzgerald's biographers consider Lois the original model for Rosemary Hoyt in *Tender Is the Night*:

> Her fine forehead sloped gently up to where her hair, bordering it like an armorial shield, burst into lovelocks and waves and curlicues of ash blonde and gold. Her eyes were bright, big, clear, wet, and shining, the color of her cheeks was real, breaking close to the surface from the strong young pump of her heart. Her body hovered delicately on the last edge of childhood—she was almost eighteen, nearly complete, but the dew was still on her.[149]

By the time Moran and Charlie began dating, she had tired of Hollywood and longed to try something new. She studied dance as a child and had performed for years at the Paris National Opera before being tapped for a Hollywood career. By mid-1930 she left Hollywood for Broadway, starring in George and Ira Gershwin's musical *Of Thee I Sing* and later, its sequel *Let Them Eat Cake*. Confiding her private thoughts about Hollywood in her diary in December 1929, Lois said, "There are so painfully few good actors and actresses…Charlie Farrell has great talent in certain parts, where he can play himself, a masculine Gaynor as it were." [150] Even if Charlie questioned his own talent, and had been passed over by the Academy, the astute Lois Moran had faith in his work.

After Lois left, Charlie went back to dating Virginia Valli while also dating starlet Anita Page, who had just made a hit in *The Broadway Melody of 1929* (which won the Academy Award for Best Picture in 1930). Page abruptly broke off her relationship with Charlie:

> What happened was terrible and I made a big mistake…When we were together, I saw what looked to me to be eyebrow pencil and I thought he was using makeup. I decided I wouldn't go out with him again. Years later, however, I saw him and realized the man had the same marking there. It was just a scar.[151]

Over the years, this quote by Anita Page has been twisted and truncated by gay Hollywood historians to "prove" Charlie's supposed homosexuality. These writers deliberately cut off Page's explanation of her mistake and subsequent regret. Frank Bogert, who was Charlie's best friend from their first meeting in the late 1920s, put paid to the gay rumor when questioned by the author in 2004. "Jesus, no!" he exploded. "If anything—he was too much the other way," referring to Charlie's endless womanizing.[152]

Never missing a beat after losing out on Anita Page, Charlie attended Edith Mayer's (Irene's older sister) wedding to producer William Goetz in March of 1930 and then escorted Lady Mountbatten to a party given by Douglas Fairbanks and Mary Pickford later that same week. "Charlie was never lonely, I can tell you," Paul Gregory affirmed, "He had any pretty girl he could beckon, you know, he could get." [153] But despite his outward appearance of devil-may-care happiness, the party scene began to pall. Charlie moved his entire family from Onset Bay to live in his newly completed home in Toluca Lake. By the end of April, Estelle and David, Ruth and her husband Harry Jelliff, and their three-year-old son Charles Farrell Jelliff, were ensconced in the $30,000 mansion.[154] It was a cheerful but decidedly more upscale version of the old Farrell boarding houses of his childhood. In 1932, long after the Farrells had all moved out, Charlie rented out the house to a young contract player named Bette Davis and her mother Ruthie, who were both delighted by the house's "true Yankee style…a model of the *Mayflower* perched on the fireplace mantel, near a lamp whose shade had been stenciled with a map of Massachusetts. Outside, weeping willows drooped over a private lake, where mute swans regularly glided past."[155]

While Charlie finished *Liliom* that summer, Janet remained obstinately off-salary. In June, Fox prepared a "Digest of Demands of Janet Gaynor," in final response to her letter to Win Sheehan. The digest settled the studio's position on Janet's strike and answered all of her demands. In short, the studio's position was "the contract gives us the right to cast her in any pictures and in any parts which we desire." Of her demand not to be teamed with Charlie, the studio noted, "The members of the cast are not subject to her control under her contract." Of her salary demand, the studio simply said, "She is now getting $2,000 per week when on the payroll." Of billing and limits on the number of pictures per year, Fox noted that there were no such requirements in her contract. The only issue on which Fox was prepared to budge was on her working hours: "the contract does not limit her to any hours of work but we are willing to agree that there shall not be more than 8 hours per day, or 48 hours per week while she is working."[156] The digest was compiled into Fox's official answer, and delivered to Lydell Peck. On July 9, the press was informed that Fox refused to change Janet's contract, which left the ball squarely in her court. In addition, Fox forced Max Factor to pull an entire advertising campaign featuring Gaynor, stating that such a campaign was signed without the company's knowledge and went against their publicity policy. Fox dogged the Max Factor Company mercilessly, making sure that every scrap of paper featuring Janet was pulled immediately. By 1931, every drugstore in the country had been given orders to dispose of any displays featuring Gaynor.

After the press received notice, Janet took a trip to her friendly city, Philadelphia, to see her father once more. She had seen him only once or twice since her parents' divorce. It was almost as if, during this crisis, she needed to get in touch with her roots to figure out her future. The prodigal daughter arrived at 1372 Gillingham Street, where her father was living with his nephew Ralph Gainer and his family. A screaming police escort heralded Janet's arrival, and two burly bodyguards broke through the neighborhood crowds so Janet and Lydell could make it to the door. Later, discussing Janet's brief visit with *New Movie Magazine*, Ralph rubbed his stubbly cheek and said, "Why, I haven't shaved this spot on my cheek yet, where she kissed me. I don't want to shave it off."

Frank never received credit for Janet's career and in fact, never even bragged about being Janet's father to anyone:

> Even a great many of Frank Gainer's acquaintances and some of
> his closest friends did not know he was the father of the star. And
> many people in the Frankford section of Philadelphia have known

the Gaineirs for years without even knowing there was any relationship between the Gainers and the Gaynor of the films.[157]

Frank had never asked for or received a piece of Janet's wealth, and was offended when others suggested perhaps she should share with her old man: "Me? Me take money from Lolly? Not on your life...I won't take money from anybody as long as I can go out and earn $10 a day." So when Janet met with her father that night, she was visiting the one person who had not profited from her career, had not groomed her for stardom, and had not been anything to her except Dad. Janet was reclaiming some shreds of normalcy when she saw Frank again and introduced him to her new husband. Frank pronounced Lydell a "fine, upstanding fellow," and Janet danced with everyone in the little house. Sadly, this was the last time Janet saw Frank. He died three years later when he was struck by a streetcar as he was walking home.

Janet was searching for answers when she visited her childhood during that critical point in her life. She was trapped in a disastrous marriage, no matter how normal it seemed to outsiders. She had left her career behind and there was no guarantee she was getting it back. Public opinion was turning against Janet, too, as the Depression deepened. The people who came to see her movies were concerned with feeding their families and holding down any available jobs. Janet was no Greta Garbo, aloof and foreign, who could command an astronomical salary and keep people coming to the theatres. She was an American girl from blue-collar roots who made good but then renounced the American Dream. Walking away from $2,000 a week when a loaf of bread cost eight cents was sacrilegious to most Americans and made Janet seem like a spoiled brat.

The press was turning against Janet, too. In a rant that was typical of Janet's press, Hollywood jour-

Newspaper photo of Frank Gainer, 1930.

nalist Mollie Merrick observed, "The way public interest is wavering nowadays between darlings of the screen and favorites of the stage makes this proceeding an exceedingly dangerous one." Using words like "huff," "tantrum," and "the grand gesture" to describe Janet's strike, Merrick's tone was both condescending and cautionary. Merrick noted that Fox was already grooming several starlets to take Janet's place, including a "charming Irish lassie" named Maureen O'Sullivan. According to one newspaper clipping of the time: "The little O'Sullivan has the kind of eyes which create a poignant wistfulness in the heart of the beholder…and meanwhile a little lady whose brimming eyes captured the heart of a whole world some three years ago is sitting waiting for the phone to ring…That's the way Hollywood goes." [158]

Meanwhile, Fox took the Gaynor/O'Sullivan switcheroo one step further, casting Maureen with Charles Farrell in *The Princess and the Plumber*, directed by Alexander Korda. In the film, Maureen played Louise, the princess of the imaginary kingdom Daritzia, who is being pressured by her bankrupt father (H.B. Warner) to marry a wealthy Count (Lucien Prival). Her father is also planning to rent their castle out to a wealthy American, so he hires a plumber (Charles Farrell) to install radiators in all the rooms. Naturally, the Princess and the plumber fall in love, and all of the royal family's monetary needs are answered when it is revealed that Charlie owns his own plumbing company and is a wealthy man.

Alexander Korda was fired after *The Princess and the Plumber* was complete, supposedly because Sol Wurtzel's eleven-year-old son had seen the film and decreed, "It stinks."[159] Despite the young master Wurtzel's disdain, *The Princess and the Plumber* garnered great reviews, particularly for O'Sullivan and Farrell. O'Sullivan began receiving the kind of praise usually handed out to Gaynor by the press. Louella Parsons' review was characteristic: "You will love Maureen; she is so naïve in her role of Princess Louise…Lucky girl to have Charles Farrell as her plumber. Charlie has a boyishness that is captivating to this reviewer who can never decide how much is acting and how much is real." *Film Daily* added, "Maureen O'Sullivan steps it up another notch with her captivating performance as a sheltered princess, while Charles Farrell is right in his element as the plumber." Whitney Williams, writing for the *Los Angeles Times*, added, "The picture belongs to the actress, who it is to be hoped, will be teamed with Farrell again."

By August 15, Janet had talked to Fox and was reinstated on payroll. She had been off-salary for twenty-one weeks and four days, and had lost over $40,000 (the equivalent of half a million dollars in 2007). Although

Charles Farrell and Maureen O' Sullivan, *The Princess and the Plumber*, Fox, 1930.

Janet was prepared to leave it all behind at the beginning of the year, something had changed her mind by the summer. She certainly realized that she was not irreplaceable and that Fox had the upper hand. She understood that she would lose millions of dollars by leaving her Hollywood career—and this during the Depression. Maybe her visit home and her time alone made her appreciate that she really was quite a lucky woman. Of her demands, she had only won the right to an eight-hour day, and perhaps a certain amount of story approval. Sheehan won her over by admitting, "Janet, we can't get you the three best properties of the year. There's just so much to go around all of the studios, but I guarantee you one, and we'll do the best we can with the other two."[160] Remarking on her return in the 1950s, Janet remembered Win Sheehan taking her aside to say, "You know, Janet, you can do the greatest artistic picture in the world, but if no one sees it, it's not going to do you or anyone else any good."[161] That October, Janet began filming *The Man Who Came Back* with Charlie.

The Man Who Came Back was originally published by John Fleming Wilson in 1912, and had been filmed by Fox in 1924 starring George O'Brien and Dorothy Mackaill. In June 1930, after sending the Digest of Demands to Lydell Peck, Fox began adapting the book for a new film.

This may have been the film that enticed Janet to return to Fox, for *The Man Who Came Back* was a tough, hard-hitting drama. In the original book, Henry Potter is a wealthy playboy whose drunken exploits continually embarrass his father. He is sent out to one of his father's branch offices, to swim or sink on his own. Slowly he descends into alcoholism, moving further and further away from New York and his family, until he winds up in an opium den in Shanghai. He hocks his fraternity ring for rotgut gin and befriends an opium addict named Marcelle. With Marcelle's help, he begins his journey home to New York. As he sets off on his journey, Marcelle overdoses, and it is in her memory that he renews his life. His odyssey retraces every mile of his descent: he repays all the money he lost, rights all the wrongs he committed, and marries the girl he should have wed in the first place, Miss Sadie Price.

In the film adaptation, Henry Potter becomes Stephen Randolph (Charles Farrell), and Marcelle's character is morphed with Sadie's, becoming Angie Randolph (Janet Gaynor). Stephen's descent into drunkenness is shortened and hastened along by his father's business associates, who 'shanghai' him to Shanghai to set him straight. Implausibly, Angie

Janet and Charlie in *The Man Who Came Back*, Fox, 1930.
With Mary Forbes and William Worthington.

follows him to Shanghai, and they somehow meet in the opium den where she is a hopeless addict. They resolve to get clean and to support each other every step of the way on their odyssey to New York. They only make it so far as Hawaii before Stephen's father interferes.

From there the film slides down into a muddle of misunderstandings, deliberate trickery, and "testing"; for example, Angie pretends to be under the influence when Stephen's aunt comes to take him away, as a test to see if Stephen will stay with her or go home. He chooses Angie, and once she is assured of his loyalty, she sends him to New York to patch things up with his father. His father has Angie followed by a henchman, Captain Trevelyan (Kenneth MacKenna), who places all manner of temptations before her to trip her up. When Angie and Stephen are reunited by his father in New York, everyone has passed every test and temptation, and everything is hunky-dory.

Janet referred to *The Man Who Came Back* as her worst film, second only to *High Society Blues*, and often said it was the studio's way of showing her she was not the great artist she thought she was. But the problem with *The Man Who Came Back* is not Janet's performance, nor Charlie's, but a script that managed to be both sensational and dull at the same time, and an unexpectedly wooden direction from Raoul Walsh. Walsh's films need action, movement, punch; *TMWCB* is introspective and overly talky. The script, written by Broadway import Edwin J. Burke, cuts out much of what made the book a fascinating exploration of addiction and redemption. Because we do not see their struggles, Stephen and Angie have an alarmingly quick plunge and a ridiculously fast cure. Most of their troubles come not from their cravings, but from Stephen's meddling old man. In the pre-Alcoholics Anonymous era, not to mention the pre-Code era, *TMWCB* should have been a compelling study of salvation instead of just a Gaynor/Farrell vehicle co-starring liquor and opium. They were first-rate actors. They could have handled strong subject matter just fine without the addition of a June-Moon-Spoon romance.

The one redeeming scene in the film occurs in the opium den, as Stephen and Angie are reunited. Set designer Joseph Urban created a seedy, depressingly authentic dive, with rickety bunks and filthy pillows on which strung-out frails recline. Cinematographer Arthur Edeson, who had filmed the fantastic *Thief of Bagdad* (1924) and the poetically realistic *All Quiet on the Western Front* (1930), filmed the scene through drifting clouds of smoke. Into this moody, desperate place Stephen Randolph stumbles, having hocked his fraternity ring (and symbolically, his last vestiges of honor, faith, and courage) for a quart of stinking gin. He is unshaven, his eyes are dulled, and his clothes are rumpled. He sits on a broken chair and singsongs, "Anyone care to join me for a drink? Anyone gonna keep a white man from drinkin' with a…?" A woman's legs, bared below the knee, swing out from one of the bunks. A slow, drugged voice drawls, "I'll join ya'…"

It is Angie. As Stephen gazes at her haggard face and emaciated body covered in a sleazy kimono, he slowly comes to his senses. Charlie's face registers horror, disbelief, and finally a slow-burning anger at what she, and by extension he, has become. He drops the liquor, and begins choking her, hissing, "You're going clean, do you hear? *Clean!*" until Angie faints. It is an eerie callback to the final scene in *Street Angel*, where Gino chokes Angela until he sees her portrait over the altar. Stephen then carries her out of this hellhole, up the stairs and into the light—just as Gino carried Angela out of the church and into the mist. The most memorable scene in the film is an homage, or outright cribbing, from Borzage.

Popular reception of *The Man Who Came Back* was tremendously favorable; the public was hungry to see Janet and Charlie together again and the film did exceedingly well at the box office. Critics knew something was off about the picture, but could not determine exactly what the weak link was. *Film Daily* laid it on the actors and director: "Janet Gaynor is miscast and Farrell moves through many dramatic scenes in a rather mechanical manner. Maybe they picked the wrong director, for this team of all others requires delicate handling."[162] The *Los Angeles Record* chalked it up to pacing:

> Perhaps the sudden changes of mood, tempo, and locale, not to mention the complications, have something to do with the undeniable fact that the picture fails to be convincing. All of the complications, by the way, are of that type which could be cleared up in a minute by a word which the characters are never allowed to speak. Miss Gaynor and [Mr.] Farrell have never had so many troubles to overcome as they have in this picture. They both strive nobly, and at times successfully, to bring a degree of reality to the picture.[163]

In November, after *The Man Who Came Back* wrapped filming, Charlie was rushed into *Body and Soul* (aka *Squadrons*), starring Elissa Landi, Myrna Loy, and Humphrey Bogart. Landi was an aristocratic beauty and an intellectual who had already, by the time she landed in Holly-

Charlie takes a break during the filming of *Body and Soul,* with an unidentified friend.

wood, written two novels. *Body and Soul* was her first American picture. Loy had already toiled for years in silent films, usually as a villainess or vamp, but had not made her mark as "The Perfect Wife" of the 1930s. Bogart was a recent Broadway transplant who had made a couple of films for Fox but was not faring very well in his film career at this point. Starting with *The Princess and the Plumber* and continuing with *Body and Soul,* Charlie's star power carried a film while he served as a foil to a young starlet on the rise.

This was a practice that should have put Charlie on notice; for his studio was becoming less concerned with finding suitable material for him, than with using his fame to promote fresh young talent. Therefore, the plotline of *Body and Soul* is pretty silly: Charlie and Bogart are officers in a flying squadron during WWI. When Bogart is killed, Charlie sets off to find both Bogart's widow and the other woman he loved; one is a German spy, the other is a fine, upstanding female. Which one is which? "From this point on," one reviewer wrote, "the story is moviefied and will lose some of its interest for the adult audience…It is Farrell's best work to date in the talkies…Miss Landi is a stimulating new personality."[164]

As for Janet, she returned to Hawaii as soon as *The Man Who Came Back* wrapped, leaving Lydell Peck behind. On November 12, George and Ira Gershwin signed a contract with Fox to write the songs for the next Farrell-Gaynor picture, *Delicious*. This was further proof that Fox had no intention of caving to Janet's demands. On the other hand, if Janet had to do a musical picture, at least she was performing in one that showcased the Gershwins' glorious music. On December 18, Janet was rushed to the hospital in Honolulu with an attack of appendicitis. Lydell Peck was not with her, but was scheduled to join her on Christmas Day. Janet's recovery was slow; she was in a delicate state of health after her prolonged fight with the studio. She spent the holidays in her hospital bed and was not released until after the New Year, when Lydell finally joined her.

Further tragedy struck over the Christmas holidays. Estelle Farrell, who had been suffering from recurring migraines and dizziness, died of a sinus infection on Christmas Eve. In the days before antibiotics, sinus infections could spread to the brain and cause an entire host of infections, such as meningitis, encephalitis, or brain abscesses. Estelle's death was swift and painful, and none of her son's money, fame, or connections could prevent it. Estelle had been the peacemaker and the nurturer and she had always believed in Charlie's talent. Even when she felt he made poor decisions, she had never shunned him as David had. One fan magazine said that her death "hit him pretty hard." In truth, Charlie was absolutely devastated.

Once again, Charlie suffered through a Christmas funeral. He laid his mother to rest on December 27, 1930. The service was held at the Wee Kirk O' the Heather Chapel and she was buried at Forest Lawn, Glendale. After the funeral was over and Janet had been released from the hospital, Charlie sent a wire informing her of Estelle's death.[165] Janet sent her condolences, but there was precious little she could do. She empathized with Charlie but could not see him; she was still on bed rest in Honolulu and any special response from her would have provoked a jealous confrontation from Lydell.

Bereft of the peaceful bulwark that was Estelle Carew Farrell, and denied access to Janet's wise and warm presence, Charlie was drifting without an anchor; but, there was another woman who had also always been there for Charlie. She had been his Hollywood dream girl; she had been the reason for his breakup with Janet Gaynor; and she had remained in the background, a serene and sophisticated presence among all the women he dated for the past five years.

Mr. and Mrs. Charles Farrell on the *S.S. Augustus.*

Charlie asleep on the deck of the *S.S. Augustus*.

On February 2, 1931, Charlie was granted a ten-week leave of absence from Fox, and on February 14, he eloped with Virginia Valli to Yonkers, NY. The bride wore a blue suit with a corsage of gardenias pinned to her shoulder. The groom wore a dark blue suit and a slightly forced, wan smile. The newlyweds then left on the *S.S. Augustus* for a three-month tour of Europe, a trip that Charlie called, with dazzling yet characteristic understatement, "a well-deserved holiday."[166]

Chapter Eight

Heartbreak

"I'll just keep on waiting, Waiting 'til I see/ Somebody from some-where, For nobody but me."

— "Somebody from Somewhere"
by George and Ira Gershwin

"How can I say whether or not six months from today I will still be living with Lydell?" Janet admitted to *Photoplay* magazine, shortly before her December vacation in Hawaii. "I don't know. I can't even be sure that six months from today I will be with Fox. I live for today." Then, backpedaling furiously, she added, "Now that, no doubt, sounds as if I am considering a divorce, but I promise you I am not."[167] In reality, Janet had been considering a divorce from Lydell since the earliest days of their marriage. Her declaration, which ran in the most popular fan magazine of the age, was read by thousands of people around the world. Surely her husband read it. Though she immediately recanted her confession, the handwriting was on the wall.

Their marriage was breaking down in a very public way. During a huge party at the home of a studio executive, Janet and Lydell quarreled openly. Lydell went home in a fury, but Janet remained at the party. Their argument was so spectacular, so overt, that it made all the fan magazines and gossip columns. During another fight, this one at their beach home in Playa Del Rey, Janet walked out and was gone for so long that Lydell called the police, fearing Janet had committed suicide. Their marriage was collapsing in private as well. Lydell had developed a nasty habit of sneaking up to Janet's bungalow on the Fox lot. He would suddenly kick the door open, attempting to "catch her in the act" of cheating. He also enjoyed

137

perusing her fan mail, picking out any unfavorable or spiteful letters, and reading them aloud to Janet. To someone as sensitive as Janet, Lydell's behavior was a torment, disrupting her ability to concentrate on her work. Ever fearful of Lydell's jealous rampages and jeers, Janet began to retreat further and further within herself.

Lydell's behavior made him increasingly unsympathetic. Fans of Janet Gaynor hated him passionately and Fox was deluged with letters scolding her for choosing Lydell over Charlie. Typical of the fan response, a Tijuana Bible (a pornographic comic book popular in the era) was devoted to Janet and Charlie rekindling their sexual relationship after her marriage to Lydell. "Now I'm sorry I didn't marry you, my husband can't do any of these tricks!" Janet says to Charlie by page 5, and the message was clear: everyone, even pornographers, thought she married the wrong man.

Lydell may have earned the wrath of the general public because he was not Charles Farrell, but that was not the only factor contributing to his misery. For any man to be Mr. Janet Gaynor at this time, he would

What Janet Never Knew (and oh boy did she like it): A Tijuana Bible from the 1930s.

have needed deep reserves of confidence and character. Janet was earning an enormous salary, much more than Lydell ever made as an attorney. Although Lydell was listed as the head of household in the 1930 census, Janet was the breadwinner. She was one of the most famous women in the world and was the number one box-office attraction across the country. Her job also required her to spend long hours on a movie set, often kissing and embracing other men—especially her cinematic soul mate. Moreover, the press blamed him for Janet's walkout. *Photoplay* went so far as to call Janet a "pawn between Lydell Peck and the Fox Studio," completely ignoring any role Janet may have played in her own strike. Other publications were content with saying Lydell just advised Janet badly. By doing so, the press placed Janet on an unwarranted pedestal; but placing the blame squarely on Lydell may have been the only way the press could justify Janet's behavior.

Lydell also realized that the woman he married was not the woman he dreamed of when he saw *7th Heaven*. Rita Hayworth once said, "Every man I have ever known has fallen in love with Gilda and awakened with me," and this is absolutely true of the Gaynor-Peck marriage. Lydell Peck fell in love with Diane and awakened with Janet Gaynor. She was not a waif needing rescue, nor could she be controlled. In marrying Janet, Lydell Peck also, in a sense, married Laura Gaynor. Laura was a constant presence in their married lives. When they traveled to Europe, Laura traveled with them. When Janet fled to Hawaii, Laura was with her. Janet was Laura's greatest accomplishment and she guarded her investment closely. Lydell was an interloper in their relationship, for a husband had the power to take Janet away. Paul Gregory commented on this years later, when discussing his own marriage to Janet:

> Laura liked her martinis, and we'd sit in the kitchen and have a martini. Janet would go out of the room and Laura would say, "You bastard! You've taken my daughter away from me!" and Janet would come back in and she [Laura] would say "Paul, Paul, dear, how are you?" But she was a funny gal and I loved her.[169]

If Laura was behaving that way when the daughter in question was well into her fifties and had a son in college, one can only imagine what choice words Laura had for Lydell Peck. Given all these dynamics, it is no wonder that Janet and Lydell Peck's marriage was on the rocks. The wonder was, since Janet had known "she blew it" three days into their honeymoon, that it lasted as long as it did.

While Charlie was still in Europe on his honeymoon, Janet began work on her first solo effort since her return to the studio. *Daddy Long Legs* began as a best-selling novel by Jean Webster in 1912, and later became a play and the basis of Mary Pickford's 1919 film. In the 1931

Janet in *Daddy Long Legs*, Fox, 1930.

remake, Janet played Judy Abbott, an orphan who beguiles a wealthy older man named Jarvis Pendleton (Warner Baxter). He arranges to anonymously sponsor her education. The only way Judy can identify her benefactor is from his lengthened shadow as he leaves the orphanage, so she nicknames him "Daddy Long Legs." Judy writes to Daddy Long Legs to inform him of her progress over the years; when they finally meet, they fall in love and marry. Of her performance, the *New York Times* curtly noted, "Miss Gaynor reveals a great improvement in her diction," and gave the laurels to Una Merkel as Judy's college buddy, Sally McBride: "This young actress never misses an opportunity to score, and her lines are a source of considerable fun."[168] Janet's lackluster performance could be blamed on her personal troubles; also, being cast once again as a waif probably added to her despair. In fact, the one bright spot of the entire film was the costume design: Fox borrowed the illustrious Adrian from MGM to complete Judy's transformation from drudge to chic young woman. If Janet was going to play yet another urchin, she might as well do it in the finest wardrobe in Hollywood.

Charlie returned from his honeymoon on April 10 and reported for work on April 20. His vacation lasted ten days longer than originally scheduled, but Sol Wurtzel had granted the extension via telegram several weeks earlier. Upon his return, Charlie and Janet began work on *Merely Mary Ann*, an adaptation of the play by Israel Zangwill. Charlie played John Lonsdale, a penniless composer who lives in a cheap London boarding house, and Janet played Mary Ann, an orphaned slavey who earns fifteen shillings a month cleaning up after the residents of the boarding house. Mary Ann is devoted to music and idolizes Lonsdale, who tries to better her by making her wear gloves, as his mother and sister always wore them. Eventually, after going through many difficulties, Lonsdale composes a successful operetta and Mary Ann inherits $1,000,000, and the two are reunited in Lonsdale's cottage by the sea.

Merely Mary Ann had been filmed by Fox twice before, in 1916 and 1920. Beginning with *The Man Who Came Back* (1912), continuing with *Daddy Long Legs* (1912), and *Merely Mary Ann* (1904), Fox was mining the Edwardian era for material for its brightest Art Deco stars. Before talkies, Charlie and Janet had parts custom written just for their interpretations; now they were fast becoming the remake king and queen of the lot. Moreover, these stories were not in keeping with the current cinematic vogue. The same day that Mordaunt Hall reviewed *Merely*

Wistful still of Janet from *Merely Mary Ann*, Fox, 1930.

Mary Ann, he reviewed *My Sin* starring Tallulah Bankhead and Frederic March, *Caught Plastered* starring the comic team of Wheeler and Woolsey, and *I like Your Nerve* starring Douglas Fairbanks, Jr. and Loretta Young. In reviewing *Merely Mary Ann*, Hall said:

> It is a vehicle which creaks a little in its joints, but its generous supply of sentiment and gentle humor evidently appealed to an

audience yesterday afternoon... It is a simple, appealing little affair and Miss Gaynor does remarkably well by her scenes. There are some charming scenes in this film, and throughout there is a laudable note of restraint.[170]

As filming wrapped on *Merely Mary Ann* towards the end of May, Janet attended the premiere of *Daddy Long Legs* on Lydell Peck's arm. Janet was "dainty in a white chiffon frock, tight-fitting, trimmed with silver...Everyone turned to catch a glimpse of Janet Gaynor and her husband, Lydell Peck, as they passed through the crowd." Also in attendance were Mr. and Mrs. Charles Farrell: "Of great interest was the appearance of Virginia Valli, a recent bride, beautifully gowned in black and white wrap, escorted by her husband." All eyes were on Charlie and Janet, and the press tried to surmise if the pair would ever work together again after Charlie's marriage. Columnist Eileen Percy announced, "another screen romance has hit the rocks and the most famous lovers of motion pictures will come to a parting of the ways." Percy added that James Dunn, who had just been paired with Sally Eilers in Frank Borzage's *Bad Girl*, would be Janet's new screen partner. Louella Parsons took it a step further, stating, "Undoubtedly the Janet Gaynor and Charlie Farrell team will not continue. Janet and Charlie are going their separate ways and Sally Eilers and James Dunn will take their place on the Fox program."

Despite these rumors, Fox had always planned to star Janet and Charlie in *Delicious*, the musical the Gershwins had been signed for in December 1930. Before filming began on *Delicious* in August, however, Charlie was rushed into *Heartbreak*. The film, which was serialized in the newspapers just before its release, was another WWI love story, with Charlie as an American aviator in love with a Viennese countess (Madge Evans). When war breaks out and the two are parted, Charlie accidentally kills her twin brother (Hardie Albright) in a dogfight. He deserts and crosses enemy lines to tell the Countess about the accident in person; when he returns to his unit, he is ostracized and imprisoned. Charlie's performance was singled out as "splendid" and "dashing as ever," his pairing with Evans declared "fine," but with an unknown supporting cast and an unremarkable director (Alfred Werker) at the helm, *Heartbreak* had the markings of a B-picture. Charlie's charisma and star power were being used more and more to carry sub-par films or provide a foil to an actress on the rise.

This marked change in Charlie's status extended even to an all-star A-picture like *Delicious*. The Gershwins collaborated on their first full movie score for the film; David Butler directed and Ernest Palmer worked his cinematographic magic. The story, adapted from Guy Bolton's *Skyline*, concerned a Scottish immigrant named Heather Gordon (Gaynor) who is denied entry upon her arrival in the US because her parsimonious uncle has refused to support her. Larry Beaumont (Farrell), fabulously wealthy polo player, met Heather on the voyage and was enchanted with her. When Heather is set to be deported, she stows away in Beaumont's horse's stall, and spends the rest of the film fleeing the clutches of Detective O'Flynn. She stays with a kind Russian immigrant family she met on the boat. The Russians are also musicians, which provide the setup for the Gershwin score. Their son, Sascha (Raoul Roulien) falls in love with her and wants to marry her. To his dismay, Heather wants Larry Beaumont, and after he is injured in a polo match, she defies everything to be by his side. Beaumont's spiteful girlfriend (Virginia Cherrill) turns her in to the authorities and Heather is once again on the run—until, exhausted from the chase, she turns herself in. Larry comes to consciousness (and his senses) in time to make her boat back to Scotland, and naturally they will be married by the ship's captain as soon as possible.

While the film was ostensibly another Gaynor-Farrell partnership, in reality it was a Janet Gaynor picture. Her character's struggles take center stage and Charlie is relegated to looking handsome in evening clothes. Anyone could have played Larry Beaumont, for there is nothing for Charlie to bring to the part. In fact, one could argue that Charlie probably took the part only because his character was a polo player, a sport he had taken up with great enthusiasm some years earlier. Beaumont was merely a rich, bland object of desire for Heather Gordon, nothing more. *Delicious* also shows that Janet won part of her battle with the studio. She only sings one verse of one song, the wistful "Somebody from Somewhere," and does very little dancing. Although Janet gave a sincere performance, her Scottish accent is quite awful. While she is the star of the film, the Brazilian actor Raoul Roulien runs away with the picture. His singing is lovely, his characterization by turns sweet, jokey, earnest, and tender.

Naturally, the Gershwins' music soars above the commonplace storyline and "scarcely inspired" (according to Mordaunt Hall) dialogue. The imaginative musical sequences were directed with flair by David Butler, especially Heather's dream sequence about her arrival at Ellis Island (the "Melt-

Together again—Charlie and Janet in *Delicious*, Fox, 1931.
Photograph by Hal Phyfe. Courtesy of Gina LoBiondo.

ing Pot" number) where she is greeted by reporters, photographers, and about fifty Uncle Sams before being showered with money by Lady Liberty. George Gershwin's "New York Rhapsody" (originally called "Rhapsody in Rivets") underscores Heather's desperate journey through the unfriendly city, effectively echoing the careless noise and bustle. As with so many Gershwin compositions, the "New York Rhapsody" has a plaintive strain that is a counterpoint to the syncopated energy of the score; in the film this theme echoes the few bright flashes of humanity Heather finds in the anonymous city. George then expanded the "New York Rhapsody" into his "Second Rhapsody," which was premiered by the Boston Symphony Orchestra (with Gershwin on piano) January 9, 1932.

Delicious was released December 26, 1931, opening to throngs of eager theater patrons. *Film Daily* called it "topnotch entertainment for all classes—dandy heart-interest romance and swell musical numbers." Very few reviews singled out the performances of Gaynor or Farrell, calling attention to the music and the direction instead, and one reviewer breezily mentioned, "If you're a Gaynor-Farrell combination fan, you'll like this latest offering, bringing them together in another love story." *Delicious* may have been their latest film partnership, but it was not a Gaynor-Farrell film. It was a Gershwin musical directed by David Butler, and any other romantic team could have played their roles.

The story of *Delicious* does not end with its premiere, however. In 1932, a woman named Corrine Mannix Swenson sued Fox Films for over a million dollars, claiming that *Delicious* infringed upon her own story, "Lucky Molly Bawn," which she had submitted to the Fox scenario department several years before. Swenson included Guy Bolton, Sonya Levien (who adapted Bolton's story), David Butler, and the Gershwins in her suit. Alfred Wright, Fox's legal counsel, carefully examined the two stories and found them to be completely disparate. He settled with Swenson by buying out the rights to her story for $3,000, a princely sum but far less than Swenson had originally planned. When researching Swenson's grievances, Wright contacted the scenario department and was told that Swenson was a considered a "crank." The secretary noted that they received several calls a month from Swenson, who declared that Janet Gaynor was sabotaging Charlie Farrell's career. Swenson averred that Farrell needed a few good storylines to set his career back on track—without Gaynor— and that she could provide said scenarios.[171] Perhaps Swenson was a crank, but there was a vague ring of truth about her assertions. Although Janet was not deliberately harming Charlie, their onscreen partnership was beginning to take its toll on his career.

The week after filming wrapped on *Delicious*, Lydell and Janet sailed to Europe on a three-month holiday that was a last-ditch effort to save their marriage. (Unsurprisingly, Laura Gaynor tagged along on this second honeymoon.) By going on holiday, Janet forfeited a chance to make *After Tomorrow* with Charlie and Frank Borzage. Her part went to Marian

Last-ditch effort: Janet and Lydell Peck leave for a three-month holiday.

Nixon, one of the handful of starlets Win Sheehan had groomed as a Janet Gaynor replacement during Janet's strike.

After Tomorrow is worth examining for a moment because it is the last Farrell-Borzage collaboration and the next-to-last film Borzage did for Fox, before moving on to greener pastures. It is the story of Sidney Taylor (Nixon) and Peter Piper (Farrell), two hard-working kids who have been engaged for years. As they save their pennies for a "marriage fund," their hopes for happiness are thwarted at nearly every turn by their selfish parents. Sidney's mother (Minna Gombell) is having an affair with their young boarder; Peter's mother (Josephine Hull) relies on his salary for support and refuses to move in with the young couple so they can be married. The

Last film with Borzage: Charlie and Marian Nixon in *After Tomorrow*, Fox, 1932.

film is a cycle of hopelessness and despair: every time they get ahead, they are slapped back by fate. When they finally have enough money to be married, Sidney's mother runs off with the boarder, which gives Sidney's father a heart attack, which means all their extra cash must be used to pay for his doctor bills. Borzage wanted the film to have a tragic ending but was overruled by Sheehan. The requisite happy ending has a tacked-on quality: they finally marry because Peter's investment in a new type of chewing gum pays off. The first three-quarters of the film lack that Hollywood polish; James Wong Howe's cinematography gives it a gritty, almost documentary quality. When Sidney complains of roaches in the kitchen, the audience can almost feel them underfoot.

Any trace of sentiment is rubbed out from Sidney and Peter's romance. His pet name for her is "funny face," and she often calls him "a big lug." When they are first thwarted in their plans to marry, Sidney breaks down sobbing. "After all those tears, we'll have to go on a honeymoon to Niagara Falls," Pete jokes, and Sid tearfully replies, "Sure, it's probably the closest we'll get to Niagara Falls, ya' big lug." "Thata baby, always comes up wisecracking," laughs Pete, holding her close. Unlike earlier Farrell-Borzage heroes, Peter is not immune to temptation. When Sidney catches him ogling the office floozy, she makes a frank offer that is still, decades later, a little shocking to the audience, "Well, I thought—listen Pete, why can't we have a holiday together? Well, why can't we go away somewhere together? We could come back...and nobody would have to know. Well, wouldn'tcha?" Pete is a little shocked himself, and replies, "You poor little kid, somebody's been telling you a lot about the differences between women and men...self-control. Maybe it's true, and maybe again it's just a lot of applesauce. Anyway, as far as I'm concerned, and this is on the level, it's got nothing to do with sex. It's just on the level, that's all. Get me?" Such an open discussion of premarital sex would disappear from the silver screen once the Production Code came into effect two years later.

After Tomorrow received decidedly mixed reviews when it was released the following March. Mordaunt Hall of the *New York Times* hated the film, calling it a "humdrum tale [which] possesses none of the dramatic value or poetic charm of [*7th Heaven*]." Hall continued damning with faint praise, calling Charlie's performance merely "fairly good."[172] *After Tomorrow* fared better with small-town critics, who perhaps could relate to the story and its characters better than Hall. One such reviewer called it a "tensely human drama of the present day American home, [which] makes for one of the most beautiful romances of the present season."[173] Another reviewer praised the film as "stripped of all sentimentality and clothed only in stark realism," adding, "Charles Farrell, in the leading role, gives a performance that exceeds anything he has done in many a day and ranks with his memorable "Chico" in *Seventh Heaven*."[174] Nowadays, *After Tomorrow* is considered a minor Borzage film and a minor Charles Farrell film, made at a time when both had a foot out the door at Fox. But what *After Tomorrow* offers us is a glimpse of what could have been, had their collaborations continued well into the 1930s. How would they have developed the Charles Farrell hero, once the lyricism of the silent screen gave way to the realism of the talking picture? In that respect, *After Tomorrow* is a distinctly melancholy picture, marking the end of a partnership that should have continued for years.

While Charlie's career was still going strong, his wife had retired from films altogether. Virginia's career was on the wane as early as 1928, when her option was not renewed with Fox. After a few films for Columbia, she was making B-pictures with Poverty Row studios like First National and Tiffany. Her marriage was the perfect excuse for retirement, and she devoted her energies to being Mrs. Charles Farrell. But less than

Charlie gets a boost from the 1932 German women's track and field team
on a visit to Fox Movietone City.

a year into matrimony, Charlie and Virginia were on shaky ground. Frank Bogert felt that Virginia was more of a mother figure than lover to Charlie, noting that they had separate bedrooms from the earliest days of their marriage. Charlie spent much of the summer of 1932 attending the Olympic Games, which were staged in Los Angeles. He was photographed at several events without his wife. Some columnists noted that he was rooming with Johnny Weissmuller, a former Olympic athlete recently signed to MGM, which indicates that he and Virginia were living apart.

When Janet returned from Europe, her marriage to Peck was effectively over. She and Charlie began seeing each other again, and arranged clandestine meetings at Marion Davies' house parties at San Simeon. The isolated castle provided a prefect cover: a private train carried the Hearst guests from Glendale to San Luis Obispo; from there, a convoy of limousines carried the Hearst party guests up to the Castle. No personal servants were allowed. Davies and Hearst, who were themselves carrying on a decades-long extramarital affair, were discreet hosts. According to frequent guest Louise Brooks, "As long as [Hearst] had Marion's drinking under control and nobody was busting up his objects d'art, he didn't give a damn about their sexual activities."[175]

Actor Joel McCrea, also a San Simeon regular, observed the renewal of Janet and Charlie's relationship. He frequently stayed in the same guest villa with Virginia and Charlie because "Farrell was never there, he was still in and out with Janet Gaynor; not lovers, but very *close* friends. After *7th Heaven*, who wouldn't be?"[176] Whether or not Janet and Charlie actually became lovers again is open to question, at least according to McCrea; on the other hand, whether their relationship was physical or not, it was an *affaire de l'esprit*. Virginia must have noticed her husband's absence, which

Charlie and Janet in *The First Year*, Fox, 1932.

begs the question: did they in fact have an open marriage? It's possible. Her first marriage to Demerest Lamson was anything but ordinary. Virginia may have realized that there was no way she could prevent Charlie from seeing other women, particularly Janet. So she simply shut her eyes to his transgressions and made the best of her situation.

The first Farrell-Gaynor film for 1932 was *The First Year,* an adaptation of Frank Craven's stage play, directed by William K. Howard. Fox had already filmed it before in 1926, making another remake for the team. Originally, Janet had turned down the role of Grace Livingston but changed her mind when she learned Marian Nixon would get the part. *The First Year* takes up where other Farrell-Gaynor films fade out, beginning with their wedding.

The First Year takes as its motto "the first year of marriage is the hardest," and follows the trials and tribulations of Grace and Tommy Livingston as they adjust to married life. Their marriage nearly ends after a disastrous dinner party which nearly costs Tommy a huge real estate deal, but in the end, everything works out all right and they are restored to matrimonial bliss. *The First Year* was more of a balance for the Farrell-Gaynor partnership and it received good reviews across the board. The *New York Times* called it "highly gratifying... Not since their days of silent pictures have Miss Gaynor or Mr. Farrell appeared to such advantage on the screen as they do in this current study."[178] The *Los Angeles Times* offered a most astute critique of the Farrell-Gaynor partnership, noting "one grades their vehicles in the light of their other vehicles— good Gaynor-Farrell, fair Gaynor-Farrell, excellent Gaynor-Farrell, etc... *The First Year* is good Gaynor-Farrell."[179]

Janet thwarted the next Gaynor-Farrell picture by refusing to remake *Rebecca of Sunnybrook Farm*; the film was made with Marian Nixon and Ralph Bellamy instead. She also passed on the role of Salomy Jane in an adaptation of Bret Harte's *Salomy Jane's Kiss* (retitled *Wild Girl.*) The part went to Joan Bennett, and Charlie was cast opposite her as Billy, the Stranger.

Director Raoul Walsh moved the cast and crew out to the wilderness of Sequoia National Park for the last part of the summer. While on location, Charlie received word that he would be loaned out to Warner Bros. for a film called *Central Park*. For the first time in his career, Charlie said no. Filming on *Wild Girl* was running long anyway—*Central Park* was starting on August 15, and *Wild Girl* was not completed until the 22nd.

The cast of *Wild Girl.* Seated are Charlie, director Raoul Walsh, and Joan Bennett. Standing: Morgan Wallace, Irving Pichel, Ralph Bellamy, Eugene Pallette, and Minna Gombell.

Charlie's refusal could be excused as a scheduling conflict; on the other hand, Charlie definitely stated he "did not wish to play the part." *Wild Girl* was another forgettable feature in which Charlie supported another actress on the rise, but what makes it memorable is Charlie's first step at controlling his own destiny. *Central Park* was made with veteran character actor Wallace Ford in Charlie's place.

In August, Fox acquired all the interests of the Mary Pickford Corporation, and with these interests, the rights to the next planned Farrell-Gaynor picture: *Tess of the Storm Country.* Louella Parsons noted, "The Mary Pickford fans are especially interested in [this remake], as it is the one picture Mary thought well enough of to bring to the screen twice"—in 1914 and 1922. Pickford must have been especially fond of *Tess,* for she played hardball with Fox's lawyers and "drove a hard bargain—we were forced to surrender to a very objectionable clause, to wit, that the contract be held in escrow by the Chase National Bank until all payments are made."[180] Essentially Pickford allowed Fox to proceed with the making of the film, but if they missed one payment as stipulated in the contract, all bets were off and they forfeited all the money already paid and any rights to the film. Pickford was nobody's fool. Fox president Harley Clarke had just been replaced by Sidney Kent, formerly of Paramount Pictures, but the studio was on financially shaky ground. Pickford was protecting herself in the event that Fox finally declared bankruptcy, which seemed imminent.

Tess of the Storm Country was the story of Tess (Gaynor), her seafaring father, and their struggle to keep their home on the Maine coast, after being unfairly evicted by the wealthy landowner, Frederick Garfield. Tess saves Garfield's son (Farrell) from drowning, and later, when her father is accused of a murder he didn't commit, young Garfield comes to the rescue. Somewhere along the way, Tess also accepts responsibility for Teola Garfield's (June Clyde) baby out of wedlock. Originally, Charlie passed on the role of Frederick Garfield, Jr. The story clearly belonged to Tess and gave his character very little to do other than be a rich object of desire, along the lines of Jack Cromwell in *Sunny Side Up*. At first Lew Ayres was approached but he turned down the role, Joel McCrea was also offered the part but passed. Charlie finally took the role as a favor to Janet.

Tess was also yet another old-fashioned story for the Farrell-Gaynor team. *Film Daily* noted: "Old time meller [melodrama]...Where it misses is in not providing any really fine love or romantic scenes between the great young sweetheart team that distinguished so much of their former work. It has gobs of the old hoke [hokum]."[181] The *New York Times* agreed: "Janet Gaynor is enduring the torments of all misunderstood and rather aggressively virtuous little heroines of the pre-war era in a pleasant resurrection of *Tess of the Storm Country*...If the sorrows of Tess seem more appropriate in their infinite number and variety to the nineteenth century, that is something for which the book must be praised or blamed."[182]

Upon completing *Tess*, Charlie was offered the part of Joe Buck in *The Face in the Sky*. The story concerned the adventures of a sign painter who travels through the countryside painting ads on barns, and the young woman (Marian Nixon) who loves him. After reading the script, Charlie refused the part. He had already completed four films for the year and of those four, he had only done really good work in *After Tomorrow*. In fact, Charlie had been completing three to four pictures a year for Fox since Janet's walkout from the studio. Upon her return, Janet had only averaged about two pictures a year, each picture an A-level production. In

Janet and Charlie in *Tess of the Storm Country*, Fox, 1932. Photograph by Hal Phyfe.

refusing the part, Charlie was making an attempt to salvage his career, which was in serious danger of being run into the ground by the studio executives. He also desperately needed a break.

Charlie's refusal to do *The Face in the Sky* touched off a series of memos between Fox comptroller George Bagnall and Fox legal counsel Alfred Wright. It is interesting to note that Bagnall first consulted with an attorney before appealing to a studio executive. Bagnall asked Wright for his opinion on what options Fox had: Wright replied that they could either take Charlie off payroll until he came to his senses, or they could simply terminate his contract. Wright enclosed two letters to that effect in his reply, needing only Win

Sheehan's signature. Bagnall then forwarded Wright's reply to Sheehan in New York. Sheehan offered none of the "wait and see" pragmatism he had applied to Janet Gaynor; Charlie was removed from payroll immediately, effective November 2, 1932, less than forty-eight hours after refusing the part. Either Sheehan had learned his lesson with Gaynor and had no more patience for strikes, or he simply treated Janet more gently because he had a personal interest in her career. Whatever the reason, Sheehan treated Charlie's walk out with cold-blooded efficiency. By November 3, the *Los Angeles Record* noted that "Spencer Tracy replaces Charles Farrell in the Fox picture, *The Face in the Sky*. Studio advanced no reasons why the switch." Fox attorney George Wasson then sent a separate memo to Win Sheehan, reminding him that Fox had to make a reasonable effort to find work for Farrell and put him back on payroll.

Charlie took refuge in his home at 906 N. Beverly and appointed his manager, Harry Edington, to deal with Fox. For the next ten days, Charlie was, according to Edington, under the care of a doctor and could not return to the studio. On November 12, Edington sent a telegram to the studio, informing them that Charlie would be well enough to report for work on the 14th. The studio replied with a curt telegram:

> As an employee of Fox Film Corp., you will be expected to and required to discuss matters pertaining to your employment with officers of the corporation and not through agents or representatives…
> The suspension of your services will continue. We will advise you just as soon as we are able to find a part in which you may be cast.[183]

Privately, Alfred Wright told George Bagnall, "If Farrell wants to employ an attorney, then the attorney can deal with me."[184] He did not consider Edington Charles Farrell's representative and refused to talk to him. Unlike Janet, Charlie had no list of demands and regretted his strike. Charlie was willing to come back to work without demanding anything and had reconsidered taking the part of Joe. He did not need counsel. He changed his mind.

His employer did not. By November 23, Charlie's contract with Fox was terminated, effective November 14—the date he had intended to return to the studio.

Chapter Nine
Change of Heart

"I didn't quit pictures. They quit me."

– Charles Farrell

After William Fox lost control of his own company in 1930, Fox Film Corporation had undergone a metamorphosis. Fox was no longer the most artistic studio in Hollywood and had chased off its two star directors, Murnau and Borzage, by meddling in their projects. When Sheehan and Fox's creditors took control, their focus shifted to family-friendly and homespun films, palliatives for Depression-weary audiences. Indeed, when the Production Code[185] went into effect in 1934, it hardly mattered to Fox, as one Hollywood columnist noted:

> MGM, for instance, may have to bring about the cinematic regeneration of most of its stars. Will Norma Shearer, Joan Crawford, Jean Harlow, Myrna Loy, Greta Garbo, Constance Bennett, and others be given a purification of character? Fox, on the other hand, just happens to have, at the moment, more stars with a clean bill of health than any other studio. Not one of them has a flaming reputation![186]

To further augment its "clean bill of health," and its emphasis on homespun humor, Fox signed Will Rogers, the American humorist whose dry wit and straightforward observations on American life and politics made him a beloved star of newspaper columns and radio shows. Rogers signed with Fox in 1929 and for his first few years his film career was not as enormously successful as in other media, but that was about to change.

When Sheehan essentially fired Charlie over one role, he lost Fox's most popular and hard-working male star. In 1932, Charlie ranked #4 at the box office, and was the #1 male box-office draw in the country. He received more fan mail than anyone on the lot, except for Janet. His films, even when they weren't very good, made money. His films with Janet Gaynor made huge box office; in fact, *The First Year* was breaking records, especially in small towns, where it was held over for weeks. All of this begs the question: *What was Sheehan thinking?* Fox was deluged with angry letters from fans around the world, who furiously demanded that Charlie be given his job back and featured with Janet in another film without delay. "How can you play characters that have no character?" Charlie complained bitterly when he left Fox, and it's true that his roles had changed over the years. No longer an equal counterpart in the Farrell-Gaynor team, he had become Janet's romantic foil. For the time being, he accepted his termination from Fox with some grace, then spent the next few months on a quail hunt in Mexico.

Newspaper columnists made the split sound like an amicable parting of the ways, with both parties satisfied at the outcome. For his part, once the initial shock wore off, Charlie may have actually felt relieved. He was now a free agent. He could choose the number of films he made per year. His career was no longer directly tied to Janet's. Explaining his departure to a reporter years later, Charlie said, "I played so many sweet boy lover parts that I actually discovered myself becoming more juvenile, naïve, and downright dumb every day. I stopped thinking for myself, battling for myself. Life just ambled along serenely. I was a perfect vegetable."[187]   Charlie's departure from Fox forced him to think about his career, to make active decisions, something he had left up to the studio bosses since 1926.

Charlie's explanation also points out the troubling change that had come over his career once talking pictures transformed the film industry. In the silent era, especially under Frank Borzage's direction, Charlie had perfected a unique brand of hero, capable of warmth and naiveté while, at the same time, maintaining a masculine virility. Something happened, though, that eliminated this kind of hero from the screen after 1930. The new hero was brash, hard-hitting, and tough as nails: think James Cagney or Clark Gable. It could be argued that the onset of the Depression contributed to this change: people were better able to deal with the chaos in their lives by enforcing inflexible gender roles. Black and white concepts of "man" and "woman" offered a sense of normalcy in a topsy-turvy world. Any hero with traditionally "feminine" traits, such as the ability to nurture, or who was capable of great tenderness, was rendered obsolete. Whatever the reason, the Charles Farrell brand of hero became suddenly unfashionable and disappeared from the screen until he was resurrected, in some ways, by actors like James Dean and Montgomery Clift in the 1950s. If this seems far-fetched, try imagining Clark Gable as Timothy Osborne. Now, imagine James Dean in the role. One can easily imagine Dean washing Mary Tucker's hair, or gently wrapping her up in his old Army jacket. It is impossible to imagine Gable doing the same—not without a wisecrack and a threat to the lady's jaw.

Over the years, Charlie's explanation changed and he blamed his departure directly on his voice. "Winnie was a *New Yohker*. He'd arrive on the set and start complaining right away, making little jokes about Bostoners having to '*pahk theah cahs*,'" Charlie told the *Los Angeles Times* in 1976. "A lot of silent people ran into trouble, you know. I think with the Kennedys, it's all right to talk like a Bostoner now."[188] He reiterated this Boston accent theory in another interview: "Good voices sounded lousy in those days. I saw myself in quite a few pictures, late pictures and my voice was awfully good – when I first started they didn't like my voice. Well, the studio didn't like my Boston accent you know, and then of course Kennedy came in and made it famous."[189] There's just one problem with this theory: there is no evidence in any of the Fox legal or employment files that back it up. There are no memos from Sheehan regarding Farrell's voice; there is nothing to indicate the studio was worried about his accent or that they were taking steps to correct it. Charlie's popularity had not lessened with the takeover of talking pictures; even though his roles changed dramatically, he was more popular with audiences than ever.

So why did Charlie perpetuate the myth that his voice was responsible for his downfall? For one thing, it was an easy, shorthand explanation. Most people believe that a huge number of silent film stars lost their jobs to the microphone; movies like *Singin' in the Rain* reinforce that theory. This generalization falls apart under scrutiny; more often studio politics could be blamed for a star's downfall.[190] Even though this assumption has been proved wrong again and again by film historians, it is still widely accepted by the general public. Moreover, this myth blames outside forces (coming of sound, Win Sheehan's prejudice), taking the heat off Charlie himself. In blaming those outside forces, Charlie did not have to share his own reluctance to stand up for himself, his own culpability in accepting inferior roles. Perhaps, over time, Charlie began to believe it himself.

There is also some question as to what role Janet played in Charlie's departure. In the 1950s, she said, "It was dramatic when Charlie left the studio. He left the studio quite a long time before I did. I don't know whether it was wise for him to do it or not, but he felt that perhaps it would be better if we went our separate ways."[191] Twenty years later, she reversed her position and took credit for their breakup, saying, "He became so nervous that I finally said, 'Charlie, get out of the studio and get away from *me*. I am ruining your career!'"[192] Charlie's family offered a more direct theory: that Charlie left Fox because of his relationship with Janet Gaynor. "They were meeting all the time," Charlie's cousin Belle Lundstedt explained, noting that their affair was hurting Virginia Valli.[193] Whether Charlie left because Janet was hurting his career or hurting his marriage (or both) is open to some question, but she clearly played a part in his final decision. Their careers had been inseparably intertwined since *7th Heaven*, and "they gave us a lot to live up to—and it was really up to us. Janet would walk into the front office and insist upon having the parts that were right for her...I just took what they gave me. But we began as stars together, and that's the kind of stories I wanted."[194]

Janet lost her onscreen cinematic partner just as her marriage to Lydell Peck finally ended in divorce. In November 1932, Janet moved out of their home in Playa Del Rey and took refuge with Laura. A month later, Janet's personal attorney Lloyd Wright issued a formal statement to the press, which the *Los Angeles Times* said was "not a surprise to the cinema colony, [but] it came with startling suddenness yesterday after attempts to keep the news quiet appeared futile." In his statement, Wright blamed the separation on "clashes of temperament and the requirements of their profession upon their time and abilities."[195] In March, Peck issued a decree to Fox, informing them that anything Janet had earned since September 11, 1929 was community property and not to make any disposition of Janet's assets until he, Lydell Peck, gave them the go-ahead. In the days before prenuptial agreements became common in celebrity marriages, Peck was doing the lawyerly thing (if not exactly the gentlemanly thing) in protecting his interests. Even though he declared himself the head of their household, he was determined to have a piece of the fabulous Gaynor gold mine. Janet was earning $2,500 per week during their last year of marriage; half of that alone would have set Lydell up for life.

In April 1933, Janet's divorce was finally granted after an embarrassing and painful public trial. She described Lydell's abuse to Superior Judge Shinn, calling Lydell her "severest critic," and admitted she had been unhappy most of her married life. Laura Gaynor corroborated her daughter's testimony but added she had only recently become aware of how unhappy the marriage really was (a highly unlikely story). Newspaper photos captured Janet looking pale and exhausted, wearing an unflattering black hat and white coat that emphasized her haggard appearance. The newspapers did not disclose the final "satisfactory" property settlement, but apparently it was good enough that

Newspaper photo of Janet on the witness stand during her divorce trial.

Peck left Janet in peace for the rest of his life.[196] Two weeks after the final decree, Janet was spotted at the Club New Yorker, celebrating with Charlie and Virginia.

During her separation from Peck, Janet made *State Fair*, an adaptation of the novel by Iowa newspaperman Phil Stong.[197] The film was Win Sheehan's pet project, one perfectly in keeping with the studio's new emphasis on straightforward Americana. Although Janet was officially starred as Margy Frake, the young woman who longs to get away from farm life and "raise hell," the film really belonged to its other stars, Will Rogers as Abel Frake and Dike of Rosedale as Blue Boy the prizewinning hog. In August 1932, the crew journeyed to the real Iowa State Fair to film the midway and racing scenes, to give the film a more authentic quality. Among those who journeyed to Iowa in the dead heat of summer were Janet Gaynor, Will Rogers, and if local newspaper accounts can be believed, Charles Farrell. If Charlie was originally chosen as reporter Pat Gilbert, he was quickly dropped. Fox had an extremely difficult time finding a replacement: James Dunn and Joel

Lew Ayres and Janet in *State Fair*, Fox, 1933.

McCrea were tested, and the role finally went to Lew Ayres (who had gone fishing rather than except the part in *Tess* that Charlie eventually took on as a favor to Janet).

Indeed, the producers had more luck in casting the animals than Janet's love interest: Dike of Rosedale actually won the Iowa State Fair and was imported to play Blue Boy for the film. Although Mordaunt Hall praised Janet's performance as her "best performance in talking pictures,"[198] *State Fair* was tailor-made for Rogers' gentle, rambling humor, and it officially launched his career at Fox. By 1933 he replaced Charlie as the top male box-office draw in the nation and held that position until his death in 1935.

For Janet's next picture, *Adorable*, French actor Henry Garat was imported by Fox. "For Janet is now to have a new leading man; *a man of her own choosing*, a man so different from Charlie Farrell and so directly opposite in temperament to Janet's husband, Lydell Peck, from whom she recently separated, that one can scarcely credit the credibility of the new Gaynor-Garat romantic screen team," purred Virginia Maxwell in *Photoplay*.

Garat was given tremendous buildup by Fox in the press and *Adorable*, while ostensibly a Janet Gaynor vehicle, was tailored to launch his American career. In *Adorable*, Janet played the princess of a mythical country who slums as a manicurist; Garat played the dashing lieutenant who falls in love with her. *Adorable* was a charming musical remake of the German film *Ihre Hoheit Befiehlt*, one that took "All sorts of cinematic liberties...the Princess's slippers dance after she goes to bed, and her bed also begins to sway to the music."[199] Janet only hummed one verse of one song, the rest of the singing and dancing given to Garat and the supporting members of the cast. The critical reception of the film was lukewarm, with the *New York Times* declaring that "Miss Gaynor does fairly well by her role...Garat is ingratiating."[200] Apparently, Garat did not generate enough heat to keep him in America; he immediately returned to his homeland, where he enjoyed a long and prosperous career.

While Janet made *State Fair* and *Adorable*, Charlie returned from Mexico and embarked on his freelance career. He began with *Aggie Appleby, Maker of Men*, for RKO, which co-starred the wisecracking blonde Wynne Gibson. Charlie played Adoniram Schlump, a pampered mama's boy and nerd, who is made over by Aggie (Gibson) as a two-fisted he-man named Red Branahan. The real Red Branahan (William Gargan) happens to be Aggie's common-law husband who is in jail for beating up cops; when he escapes and finds Aggie and Adoniram living together, the usual complications (and fistfights) occur. "In its rather crude fashion, this offering affords a good deal of amusement," the *New York Times* noted, adding, "Charles Farrell gives but a surface conception of Adoniram Schlump."[201] However, it must be noted that all of the characters in the film were somewhat caricatured, and later in the review, Hall called out director Mark Sandrich for being "too eager at times for the characters to be mere puppets."

In August 1933, Charlie signed with his former studio, Warner Bros., to make *The Big Shakedown* with Bette Davis and Ricardo Cortez. For his services, Charlie was given $17,500, or $5,833.33 per week for two months' work, nearly twice what he and Janet were making at Fox. The story was a typical Warner Bros. Pre-Code exposé of some seedy underbelly of modern life: in this instance, the imitation drug racket. Charlie played a pharmacist who is pressured by gangster Cortez into manufacturing useless imitations of drugs; in doing so, Charlie inadvertently causes the death of his unborn baby son. The *New York Times* called the film "specific and believable" in its depiction of the racket but added scathingly, "Thus it maintains a moderate sum of interest and excitement in the face of a routine assortment of gang-film impedimenta, including Charles Farrell and a howling dénouement in which the racketeer expiates his sins in a vat of acid."[202] Indeed, *The Big Shakedown* is considered such a minor Bette Davis B-picture that it is ignored in most of her biographies. Obviously, in making *The Big Shakedown*, Charlie didn't make high art, but he did make a lot of money.

When Charlie was not making films, he devoted his energies to his other passions: tennis and polo. He began spending a lot of time at his desert home in Palm Springs, where he and fellow actor Ralph Bellamy would spend hours playing tennis tournaments against each other. The courts they used belonged to the El Mirador hotel. According to legend, one particular tennis tournament was interrupted by Marlene Dietrich, who complained to hotel staff that others should be allowed to use the courts, too. Charlie and Ralph were chased off the courts by Warren

Charlie with his string of polo ponies.

Pinney, the hotel manager. They were furious until they remembered they owned 53 acres of desert sand, perfect for creating their own private courts. They built two courts and a shelter house. However, they never got a chance to play, because all their friends began using the courts too. Next, Ralph and Charlie decided to charge everyone 50 cents each to use the courts, but "when our friends came up grinning and said, "Here's your 50 cents, fella!' we couldn't stand it. So we decided to have a club—a racquet club. Then it would be all right to have dues and there'd be none of this 50-cent business."[203] And thus, out of spite to a hotel manager, the Palm Springs Racquet Club was born.

Charlie and Frank Bogert in the 1930s.

Charlie avidly pursued his interest in polo, becoming a charter member of the Palm Springs Polo Club. It was here that he met another charter member, Frank Bogert, a cowboy actor and stuntman who had migrated to California from Colorado in 1927. Bogert and Charlie became good friends and remained close for the next several decades. Both men had a hand in taking Palm Springs from a dusty village to a world-class resort destination.

While Charlie continued freelancing and building his desert empire, Janet made two more films: *Paddy, the Next Best Thing* and *Carolina*. *Paddy* was a remake of a 1923 film of the same title, about a younger sister (Gaynor) who rescues her older sister (Margaret Lindsay) from an unwanted marriage to one man (Warner Baxter) by marrying him herself. The film was a sparkling romantic comedy that went over well with audiences and critics alike; the *New York Times* said "Miss Gaynor puts her heart into her work and she laughs and pouts prettily... It is a simple little Irish romance in which the comedy is gentle and natural. All the incidents are set forth in an effortless fashion and the Hollywood conception of scenes of the Emerald Isle are extraordinarily good." *Paddy* also introduced Janet to Margaret Lindsay, who played her sister Eileen in the film; the pair became instant best friends. Lindsay, who was born in Dubuque, Iowa, had received stage training in New York and London before making it out to Hollywood. The slight British accent she could affect after her time in London got her a job in the "all-British" production of *Cavalcade* (1933). She continued to use her sham British glamour to land other parts until she was finally signed to—and "Americanized" by—Warner Bros. in 1934. The "absolutely authentic" Gaynor found Lindsay's artifice amusing and Lindsay began boarding with Janet and Laura, staying with them and often vacationing with them for the next several years.

Their friendship has been scrutinized by writer David Ehrenstein, and he concluded that Lindsay and Gaynor carried on a long-term affair. However, Paul Gregory denied this claim:

And the nasty-mouthed people tried to make it say that they were lesbians and then this woman, I guess, happened to turn out to be a lesbian later on in life. She married or she lived with fellow John Boles or someone like that for a while and then later became that and Janet was tagged with that and I can tell

Margaret Lindsay and Janet in *Paddy, the Next Best Thing*, Fox, 1933.

you that uh, she [Gaynor] and I often sometimes our conversation would come around to it...It didn't hurt her because she was annoyed by it, not hurt by it. She just thought, how dumb people are, and you can investigate it to the moon and you won't be able to find anybody that can say they were in bed with her.[204]

At the time, Janet's other girlfriends were busy. Irene Selznick was preoccupied with babies and helping David build his film empire. Fay Wray was married to playwright John Monk Saunders and was raising their daughter, Susan. Janet, liberated from her miserable marriage, found in Lindsay a friend with whom she could raise hell. Lindsay had the gift of making Janet laugh, and their hi-jinks on the set of *Paddy* nearly shut down production on several occasions. They had perfected a duet of "Edie Was a Lady" that dissolved cast and crew in hysterics. In this respect, Lindsay's gift of laughter could be considered more valuable than all the possible romantic entanglements in the world. For the first time in years, Janet was happy.

Around this time, a bizarre rumor surfaced that Janet had secretly borne a son by Lydell Peck and kept him in hiding for three years. At first Janet refused to make a statement in the hopes the rumor would simply die down. After months passed and the rumors continued to grow, the studio finally issued a statement from Janet that, "it is not true, but it would be nice if it were true." The rumor dated the pregnancy to Janet's appendix operation in 1930 and there is the vague possibility that Janet had been pregnant, and had a miscarriage or abortion (and an appendix operation to cover it up). This could explain, in part, Lydell's reluctance to join Janet in Hawaii and his hasty departure when she was released from the hospital. It may also explain another strange piece of the puzzle— a picture of Margaret Lindsay and Janet in Palm Springs ran in all the newspapers that summer, captioned:

> CELEBRATING DIVORCES both on grounds of incompat-
> ibility, Margaret Lindsay (left) and Janet Gaynor of the films stroll
> in the sun at Palm Springs, Cal. Miss Lindsay recently divorced
> her husband, and Miss Gaynor was parted from her appendix.

There are a couple of things that make this caption strange: first, Margaret Lindsay was never married. Second, Janet's appendix operation had been performed three years before her divorce from Lydell Peck, and hence, three years before the caption was written. There's something fishy about that news item—it could be a simple mistake, or perhaps the writer was saying that Lydell was as expendable as an appendix. Or perhaps there was something more to Janet's surgery in 1930, something that contributed to the rumors that summer.

After *Paddy*, Janet made *Carolina*, based on Paul Green's play, *The House of Connelly*. In this post-Civil War epic, Janet played Joanna Tate, a Northerner with Southern relatives, who befriends the proud Connelly family. After much persuasion, she convinces the Connellys to grow tobacco rather than cotton, and the family's former glory is restored. As her reward, Joanna weds Will Connelly (Robert Young).[205] The film had a stellar cast: in addition to Gaynor and Young, it featured Lionel Barrymore as the head of the Connelly clan and Shirley Temple as little sister Joan Connelly, in her first Fox film role. Although Janet had shared onscreen romances with Lew Ayres, Warner Baxter, and Robert Young since Charlie's departure, none of these pairings had the same chemistry or elicited the

Sheet music from *Girl without a Room*, Paramount, 1934.

same audience response as her work with Charlie. For her next two scheduled films, Janet asked for and got Charlie Farrell, which indicates two things: first, that whatever Janet's initial role in his departure had been, she now recognized Charlie's worth; and second, that Charlie was, whatever he felt upon leaving Fox, ready to work with Janet again.

Charlie had just completed *Girl without a Room* for Paramount, the studio that originally had tried to buy him out from Fox in 1926. The film was a "lively piece of nonsense,"[206] in which he played Tom Duncan, a wannabe artist from Tennessee, who goes to Paris on a scholarship. While he is living the artist's life in a bohemian garret, he falls in love with Kay Loring (Marguerite Churchill). Their love inspires him to paint "The Wheel of Life," a futuristic masterpiece that becomes a sensation, but Tom is forever disillusioned when the painting is displayed upside-down. When filming wrapped on *Girl without a Room*, Charlie signed a two-picture deal with Fox. For his services in *Manhattan Love Song* and *One More Spring*, Charlie was given $70,000, or $35,000 per picture. Both films were to feature Charlie and Janet, and Charlie's name would be featured in the credits and all advertisements in "equal size and prominence" to Janet's.

Filming on *Manhattan Love Song* (later renamed *Change of Heart*) began February, 1934. The film concerned four recent college graduates, Catherine (Gaynor), Chris (Farrell), Madge (Ginger Rogers), and Mac (James Dunn) who move to New York City to follow their ambitions. Catherine wants to be a writer but winds up working in a salvage shop, Chris gets a place in a law firm, Madge becomes an actress (but only by marrying a wealthy patron), and Mac gets a job as a "crooner" on the radio. Chris loves Madge and is devastated when she marries her sugar

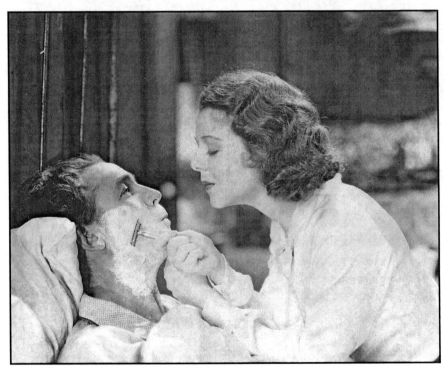

Janet and Charlie share a warm moment in *Change of Heart*, Fox, 1934.

daddy; he sinks into despair, losing his job and developing a serious illness. Catherine, who loves Chris, comes to his rescue and nurses him back to health. When Chris recovers, he and Catherine are married; but, just as they find happiness, a newly divorced Madge comes along to try and break them up. In the end, nothing can break apart Chris and Catherine, and Madge and Mac find happiness together.

Change of Heart differs from other Farrell-Gaynor romances in that they share a great deal of their screen time with the other couple in the picture, Rogers and Dunn. It has little of the quiet intimacy that marked their best onscreen partnerships, except in the scene where Catherine nurses Chris from delirium back to health. When Chris is well enough to sit up, Catherine gives him a shave. Charlie can hardly speak through the lather covering most of his face; Janet scrunches her mouth up and around as she concentrates on her work. He flirts with her, scolds her for nicking him, and finally, asks her to marry him. "Shut up," is her response to all the attention, until finally and happily accepting while wiping his face clean with a towel. This scene is a little jewel in the Farrell-Gaynor *oeuvre*, showcasing how naturally and easily they played off each other. There was always a warmth, a glow between them, a chemistry that neither shared with any other co-star. Whenever Farrell looked at Gaynor onscreen, his features always softened, as though he melted a little with every glance at her.

Change of Heart was released in May, 1934, to mixed reviews. The *New York Times* called it an "innocuous little romance which steadfastly refrains from indulging in any suggestion of subtlety,"[207] but the film fared better with small-town reviewers, who were pleased to see Janet and Charlie together again, especially in a modern, realistic storyline. One such review ran:

> Dealing in very human fashion with the joys and sorrows of four young people who after leaving college, struggle against the trials and vicissitudes of a great city, the theme, and its trenchant handling of common problems, make the picture a unique one in the Gaynor-Farrell annals, and one that promises to become an outstanding screen hit of the year.[208]

Despite the few golden threads it contained, *Change of Heart* is a distinctly anticlimactic film, because it marked the close of the Farrell-Gaynor partnership. Their partnership ended not with a bang, but with a whimper, even though Charlie had agreed to make *One More Spring* with Janet the following September. In May, around the time *Change of Heart* was released, Charlie and Virginia Valli had a terrible fight. According to Frank Bogert, Virginia had caught Charlie with an unnamed "other woman" and ordered him out of their home. Charlie immediately departed for London, where he stayed alone for nearly six months, effectively walking out on his wife—and Fox. In September, Fox agreed to buy Charlie out of the remainder of his contract, giving him half the $35,000 fee he commanded. The fee was wired directly to the Dorchester Hotel, where Charlie had taken up residence. The newspapers caught wind of the buyout, reporting it as: "one of those 'agree to disagree' arrangements. But Virginia Valli, or Mrs. Farrell, if you please, is in New York. She will spend some time there and then come to Hollywood to attend to some of Charlie's business for him. An emphatic denial of any pending divorce is made by both Charlie and Virginia."[209]

Though they denied it to the press, their marriage almost ended. Frank Bogert did not know the "other woman" in the case, but given Charlie's womanizing ways, it could have been anyone. Of course, it is possible that Virginia discovered the extent of Charlie's relationship with Janet. They had rekindled their friendship earlier during house parties at San Simeon; perhaps, spending time together on the set and playing those comfortable romantic roles, they became lovers once again. The fact that Charlie left for London and settled for a buyout of his Fox contract reinforces this theory; after all, his next scheduled picture was another Farrell-Gaynor partnership. Had he just been caught with an anonymous starlet, and summarily kicked out by Virginia, Charlie could have roomed with any of a dozen friends, just as he had roomed with Weissmuller during the Summer Olympics. He could have made the film with Janet and moved on, but that's not what happened. Moreover, Charlie and Janet stopped speaking to each other, which indicates that something happened between them—something beyond a professional disagreement. Whatever happened, and whoever was involved, it was bad enough that Charlie felt the need to put most of a continent and an ocean between him and Virginia for nearly half a year. He also stopped speaking to one of his closest friends for another four years.

While Charlie was in London, production on *One More Spring* was stalled to see if he would return. In the meantime, Janet made *Servants' Entrance*, a light comedy in which she played the daughter of a Swedish

Charlie and Janet aboard the *Flying Cloud*, 1934.

financier who has fallen on hard times. In preparation for a life of work, Hedda Nilsson (Gaynor) and her fiancé (G.P. Huntley, Jr.) decide to take on jobs as servants. Once employed, Hedda falls in love with Karl, the chauffeur (Lew Ayres), and the usual romantic complications arise. The film was praised for its light comic touch and fine cast (Walter Connolly, Louise Dresser, and the incomparable Ned Sparks shared the honors), and an imaginative animated dream sequence, directed by none other than Walt Disney. *Motion Picture* called the film "a novel background for the Gaynor charm and whimsy,"[210] and the *New York Times* added, "The problems solved during the films course are not of the gravest import... [but it] is an agreeable romantic comedy."[211]

Once filming on *Servants' Entrance* wrapped and it was clear that Charlie would not return from London, production began on *One More Spring*. The film was based on Robert Nathan's 1933 novel[212], about a group of outcasts displaced by the Great Depression, who begin living in an abandoned tool shed in Central Park. The film, directed by Henry King, discarded most of the satire of Nathan's novel, instead focusing on the humanity of its three main characters: Mr. Otkar (Warner Baxter), a former antiques dealer; Mr. Rosenberg (Walter King), a has-been violin virtuoso; and Elizabeth, "who, out of deference to the Legion of Decency and Miss Janet Gaynor's following, has abandoned the scarlet vocation which the author designed for her and has now become an unemployed actress."[213] The three misfits help each other, and several other displaced souls, through a barren Depression winter. The film was well-received by critics and audiences alike, with the *New York Times* leading the praise:

> Doubtless your enjoyment of this fantastic and rollicking fable will be greater if you have not encountered the joys of bedding down on Winter evenings in Central Park or allowing your stomach to go on three-day vacations. But "One More Spring" in any case is a credit to Hollywood and a genuine treat for the filmgoer.[214]

This is the film that should have wrapped up the Farrell-Gaynor partnership. It would have been the perfect bookend to their careers together, beginning with the outcast sewer worker and street waif dwelling in a Parisian garret in *7th Heaven,* ending with those same outcasts, different careers, in a Central Park tool shed. But Charlie remained in London, and made a quickie film, *Falling in Love,* with the "British Jean Harlow," Margot Grahame. Charlie played a matinee idol who falls in love not with his co-star (Grahame), but with a little country miss named Ann Brent (Mary Lawson). The film was directed by former Mack Sennett comedian Monty Banks for Vogue Pictures, as one of three pictures Vogue ever made. It is safe to assume that the film was never meant to be more than a lark for those involved; it barely caused a ripple when released in the United States.

Detail from press release of *Falling in Love*, Vogue Pictures, 1935.

Charlie returned home in October. "With the age-old defense of, 'we're deeply in love,' Charles Farrell and his actress-wife, Virginia Valli, today scouted rumors of a pending divorce," ran the story in the local papers. "Returning home from Europe, the first person who greeted Farrell was his wife. 'Rumors of a separation are bunk,' they echoed. 'We're as deeply in love as ever.'"[215] Charlie did not set foot on the Fox lot, nor did he attempt to see Janet upon his return. Instead, he made a film for the newly formed Poverty Row film company, Republic Pictures. The film, *Forbidden Heaven*, bore a striking similarity to *One More Spring*. Charlie played Nibs, a Cockney working man, who is part of a "quartet of derelicts" living under a bridge in Hyde Park; included in the quartet is Ann (Charlotte Henry) a young café dancer who attempts suicide. Mr. Nibs rescues her, and works to better not only her life but uplift his entire class. As a B-picture, *Forbidden Heaven* was ignored by major critics, but was welcomed in the small towns with high praise. Typical of the response, a small-town reviewer called the film "a simple tale, but one which will hold the members of every audience enthralled...Charles Farrell's performance is one that will never be equaled, while the portrayals of all of the players are positively inspired."[216]

If 1934 marked the end of an era with the final Farrell-Gaynor partnership, it also ended the era with an abrupt shakeup at Fox. After several attempts at staving off bankruptcy, in 1933, Fox's West Coast Theatre chain went into receivership, which effectively bankrupted the entire company. Sidney Kent, Fox's president, began casting around for solutions when he found the answer: a merger with 20th Century Pictures. 20th Century was a production company founded by producer Joseph Schenck and former Warner Bros. employee Darryl Zanuck, which released films through United Artists (owned, in part, by Mary Pickford). 20th Century was looking for a way to produce and release its own films, without sharing the profits with another company; Fox was looking for a way out of bankruptcy. The merger, completed in May 1935, installed Schenck as Board Chairman, retained Kent as President, and installed Zanuck as Vice-President in charge of production. In doing so, Zanuck replaced Win Sheehan entirely; Sheehan was forced out of the company he had helped create—the company he had taken over from William Fox. The industry catch-all term "amicable settlement" was used to describe Sheehan's departure, and *Time* noted, "last week's settlement might really have been amicable was indicated by the terms revealed. Producer

Sheehan kept his fat block of Fox stock, got something like $360,000 for his contract which had 14 months to run."[217] Sheehan left on a European vacation and within months married Maria Jeritza, prima donna with the Metropolitan Opera Company. With Sheehan's departure, Janet lost her biggest champion and protector at Fox. With Charlie's departure, she had lost her cinematic soul mate. She was very much on her own at Fox, and her next year at Fox was a decided turning point.

Chapter Ten

A Star Is Born

"Hollywood isn't cruel, except to those who want things that Holly-wood won't give them."

— Janet Gaynor, 1958

The contract Janet signed with Fox back in 1933 was different from the others she had signed before. No longer given a set weekly salary and the nebulous promise of work, the new contract paid Janet per picture. Each year, in April and in November, Janet had to report to Fox offices in either New York or Los Angeles to select her material for the coming year. Under the contract, she was paid $100,000 for her first film, $112, 500 for her second and third films, and $115,000 for her fourth through sixth films, split into weekly payments of well over $6,000. This contract was a far cry from the very first she signed with Fox, which had estimated her worth at $500 per week by May 1930.

On March 28, 1935, Janet appeared at Fox after her mandatory month-long vacation following *One More Spring* (another stipulation of the 1933 contract). She agreed to three pictures for that year: *The Farmer Takes a Wife*; *Way Down East* (a remake of D.W. Griffith's 1920 master-piece); and *Red Night*. Less than a month later, however, with the dust settling from the merger between 20th Century and Fox, Janet's 1933 contract was cancelled. A new contract, effective January 1, 1936, was drawn up, stipulating that Janet would make one picture (option A) be-tween January 1 and February 3. Another picture (option B) would be made June 1, 1936. Thus, Janet had the studio's guarantee that she would make only two pictures a year, and she knew exactly when she would be expected to report for duty. Even more than money, Janet valued her time off, as she later explained:

> I found that I really did nothing but work and go home and go
> to bed and sleep and try to get rested to get up the next morn-
> ing. When I finished a picture, I would try to leave town, be-
> cause if you stayed there would be publicity pictures or inter-
> views or you'd have to talk about your next picture, or some-
> thing like that...Often I would say, "I don't want more money,
> but I want..." For instance, I wanted shorter hours, because I
> worked terribly hard and I wasn't awfully strong.[218]

In the meantime, it was business as usual for Janet. Even though Fox officially merged with 20th Century two weeks later, she began work on *The Farmer Takes a Wife*. The film began as a novel, *Rome Haul*, by Walter Edmonds, a somewhat bawdy tale of American life during the birth of the Erie Canal. The book was then adapted into a play by Marc Connelly and Frank Elser, and a struggling actor named Henry Fonda played the shy farm boy, Dan Harrow, on Broadway. Fonda was imported by Fox to play Dan to Janet's Molly Larkin, marking Fonda's film debut.

Margaret Hamilton, Henry Fonda, and Janet in *The Farmer Takes a Wife*,
Fox, 1935.

Of her young co-star, Janet recalled:

Cameras and camera angles enthralled him. He studied them and everything else on the set. Big red-headed Charlie Bickford was cast as the heavy. He and I would gossip and play practical jokes, but Henry would have none of it.[219]

The Farmer Takes a Wife was a critical success, and most of the honors went to Fonda. The *New York Times* remarked, "Mr. Fonda is the bright particular star of the occasion," but felt Janet was miscast: "Miss Gaynor is really too nice a person to be playing bad girls like Molly Larkin."[220] *The Farmer Takes a Wife* launched Fonda's legendary film career, and he shared enough chemistry with Janet that Fox cast him as the lead in *Way Down East*, Janet's second film for 1935.

Way Down East had been filmed in 1920 by master director D.W. Griffith, and starred Lillian Gish and Richard Barthlemess. It was the story of an innocent girl who is deceived into a sham marriage by a smooth Lothario, and has a baby by him. The baby dies and the girl finds refuge as a servant for a family in Maine, until they find out the truth about her past. In 1920 the film's depiction of unwed motherhood was shocking; in 1935 the dialogue was described as "spotless" so it could be "slipped past the vigilantes of the Hays Office." Both *Way Down East* and *The Farmer Takes a Wife* were the kind of sanitized slices of Americana that Win Sheehan favored and promoted at Fox since his 1930 takeover.

Filming on *Way Down East* began June 1, but abruptly halted in mid-July when Janet suffered an accident on the set. During one scene, Janet and Henry Fonda collided, bumping their heads, and Janet fell to the ground, stunned. She was given the rest of the day off to recuperate and reported for work the next day, but immediately collapsed. Dr. S. M. Alter diagnosed a brain concussion and Janet was taken off the film. (It was completed with Fox actress Rochelle Hudson in her place.) Janet departed for her vacation home in Hawaii aboard the *SS Lurline*, with Laura and Margaret Lindsay in tow. Also aboard was Hilary Gordon, neé Helen Gaynor, who had flown from New York to care for her sister. According to the 1930 census, Hilary was living in the Bronx as a lodger with John J. "Jack" Gordon. She was listed as a writer; he was a packer in a meat-processing plant. A year later they married, and suddenly Jack got a job with Fox Movietone as a newsreel producer. Hilary's inclusion in the Hawaiian vacation shows that, to some extent, she had cleaned up her act after her embarrassing Oscar night performance and she was welcomed by her family. Sadly typical of Hilary's neglect by the press, however, her presence on the *Lurline* was either ignored or she was mistaken as "a nurse." Only one newspaper got the story right and gave Hilary proper credit as Janet's sister. Hilary divorced Jack Gordon in 1939; a few months later, Walter Winchell reported that "she will next blend with a San Fran biz man." That is exactly how Paul Gregory characterized her later years: "well, she married one man after another and went in and out of houses that, where they try to make you well, you know," but she never conquered her alcoholism.[221]

Janet and her family stayed the rest of the summer in Hawaii, but Margaret Lindsay only stayed about a week before reporting back to Warner Bros. to star with James Cagney in *Frisco Kid*. During their Hawaiian vacation, Janet recovered as her home studio went through the biggest upheaval since William Fox lost control five years' earlier. She was gone when Win Sheehan left. He had produced all of her films, from her earliest role in *The Johnstown Flood* to the halted *Way Down East*. He had groomed her for stardom, protected her, advised her, and argued with her through her tempestuous tenure at Fox. Where other producers would have thrown up their hands in vain and fired her, Sheehan worked with Janet. When he was gone, it was the end of an era. Never would any one producer put so much effort into Janet Gaynor's career again. When she returned to Fox (now 20th Century-Fox) in September, she was given her choice of supervisors to replace Sheehan: Sol Wurtzel, whom Janet had fought so bitterly in 1930; Buddy DeSylva, of the songwriting team of DeSylva, Brown and Henderson; former silent film comedian Raymond Griffith; former drama critic Kenneth MacGowan; or scriptwriter-cum-producer Nunnally Johnson. Of the supervisors she was offered, Janet probably would have worked best with MacGowan, who had run the Provincetown Players Theater with Eugene O'Neill and later became chair of the Department of Theatre Arts at UCLA. MacGowan had the artist's touch that Janet needed. She could have gotten along with Johnson, too, who was a former journalist and critic who went on to win an Oscar for Best Screenplay for *The Grapes of Wrath* (1940). Either of these men was qualified to take over where Sheehan left off—at least, as far as Janet's career before the camera was concerned.

It is doubtful, though, that any of these men would have given her the personal care and attention she received from Sheehan, who made sure fresh flowers were delivered to Janet's bungalow every day. "Not a morning on the set without a personal visit from Sheehan to see if everything was all right...On her own lot she was a pet, coddled, pampered and catered to— a queen bee: Miss Movie Star in person."[222] In fact, after Janet left for Hawaii to recover from her head injury, her bungalow was loaned out to visiting actors. The studio manager, Jack Gain, assured Janet via telegram that this move was merely "because of the number of important players being used on the lot now between our own company and 20th Century."[223] Whether it was done as a cost-cutting measure by the studio, or merely as a convenience, it was a very personal affront to Janet, and made her realize her status as queen bee was in jeopardy. Janet made a special request: that Darryl Zanuck himself would supervise her films. In a way, this was an obvious choice: Sheehan had been her producer as well as Head of Production over the entire studio; since Zanuck had taken his place, why not have him take over her career, as well? Moreover, with Zanuck as her producer, she could bolster her position as the number-one actress on the lot. She sent her wish to Zanuck, who responded that he was "most happy" to serve as her producer.[224]

When 20th Century merged with Fox, Darryl Zanuck emerged as the studio's new dominant personality. Born in Wahoo, Nebraska in 1902, Zanuck received little formal education. When he was fourteen, he lied to an Army recruiter about his age and joined the Nebraska National Guard, with whom he served in France during World War I. Returning to the U.S. after his stint in France, Zanuck began selling scenarios to various producers, including Irving Thalberg. In 1924, he was officially hired as a scriptwriter for Warner Bros., where he began a series of films that made Rin-Tin-Tin an international star. Using Gregory Rogers as a pen name*, he also wrote the screenplay for one of Charlie's earliest films, *The Love Hour* (1925). In 1929, Zanuck was promoted to management; two years later, he was Head of Production. Despite these promotions, Zanuck realized he would never be anything but an employee to the tight-knit, clannish Warner Bros., so he left to form 20th Century with Joseph Schenck and William Goetz in 1933.

Whatever Zanuck lacked in terms of formal education, he possessed in an innate understanding of not only the motion picture industry, but

---

*Some sources credit Bess Meredyth with the scenario for *The Love Hour*, but according to records in the Warner Brothers Archives at the University of Southern California, Gregory Rogers wrote the scenario for the film.

Janet as Kay Brannan in *Small Town Girl*, MGM, 1936.

the art of film. Zanuck was a micromanager; overseeing every aspect of production. He was famous for spending hours in the cutting room, editing or re-editing films. Zanuck was preoccupied with reshaping the studio in his own image; when Janet returned to the studio, Zanuck was not exactly sure what to do with her. Plans for Janet's third film under her old contract, *Red Night*, were scrapped when she was injured, so no projects were on her immediate horizon. In November, a month after agreeing to supervise all Janet Gaynor films, Zanuck began negotiations to loan Janet out to MGM. The project was *Small Town Girl*, co-starring the dashing Robert Taylor. 20ᵗʰ Century-Fox was to receive $11,500 in compensation for the loan, and filming would keep Janet occupied for ten weeks. Under Option A of her new contract, Janet was supposed to make a film during the first two months of 1936; however, production of *Small Town Girl* began December 20, 1935, just a few weeks early.

Small Town Girl was a light romantic comedy-drama based on Ben Ames Williams' novel and directed by William Wellman. It focuses on a young woman named Kay (Gaynor) who lives in Carvel, a waypoint between Harvard and Yale. During the big annual football game, Kay is picked up by handsome, wealthy young doctor Robert Dakin (Taylor), and after a night of drunken partying, they end up married. They agree to stay married for six months, and then have a quiet divorce, but Kay spends the time falling in love with Bob and trying to get him to reciprocate. She also encourages him to give up his wastrel habits and devote himself to his brilliant surgical career. Janet does her best work in the film when Kay fairly seethes with impatient rage to shake the dust of Carvel off her feet and see the world; she shoots murderous glances at her family "in a rebellious mood, distracted by the monotony of grocery store keeping, Saturday rice puddings, and supper conversations."[225] Her performance is a potshot at the homespun, downtrodden roles she had tired of playing at Fox. Gaynor's role was originally intended for Jean Harlow, and a constellation of MGM talent rounded out the cast, including James Stewart as Kay's hometown sweetheart Elmer, and Binnie Barnes as Bob's original fiancée Priscilla. Despite the talent involved, critical reception to the film was cool, and the *New York Times* acerbically commented, "It takes Miss Gaynor, we regret to say, almost the full period to show Mr. Taylor the error of his ways and rescue him for science. Miss Harlow, we are quite sure, could have done the job over the weekend."[226]

Filming on *Small Town Girl* wrapped on February 28, 1936, and Janet was given four weeks' vacation, as was agreed, and returned to the studio in April to discuss her next project, under Option B of her contract. The film was *Ladies in Love*, an ensemble "woman's picture" based on a play by Ladislaus Bus-Fekete. The story, which took place in Budapest, was about four young women who find and lose their chances at love. Along with Janet, who agreed to play Martha, three other heavyweight female stars were assigned to the picture: Loretta Young (Susie), Constance Bennett (Yoli), and Simone Simon (Marie). Although Janet had made several films with large casts, such as *Sunny*

Side Up, and heavyweight talent, such as Lionel Barrymore in *Carolina*, and had shared billing with another star, Charles Farrell, in several pictures, *Ladies in Love* was the first film in which Janet was required to share equal billing with other actresses in the cast. Just like sharing her bungalow, this was a warning that Janet was slipping from her top post at the studio. On the other hand, Janet was granted an extension on her vacation and did not have to report for filming until July 6, even though she was technically on payroll as of May 20, which shows that Zanuck was not entirely heartless.

Ladies in Love was not a remarkable picture, but Janet did good work in it, and the *New York Times* said of her performance, "Miss Gaynor, too, has played her scenes with charm and humor, and, although I hate to drop an apple of discord into Hollywood's Olympus, she impressed me more favorably than the Misses Young, Bennett, and Simon."[227] What makes *Ladies in Love* memorable is not so much the picture itself, but what happened behind the scenes. While Janet was scrambling to keep her stature at the studio, Loretta Young was struggling to heighten hers. When Young later refused a part for which Zanuck had cast her, Zanuck wrote a letter to attorney Neil McCarthy, in which he discussed Young's part in *Ladies in Love*:

Don Ameche and Janet in *Ladies in Love*, 20th Century-Fox, 1936.

I have already told you earlier in this letter how much Miss Young wanted to play the part, once we assigned her to portray the role. Several times during the production of *Ladies in Love* Miss Young came to see me about production matters, asking that certain favors be done for her, such as adding certain scenes or incidents which she thought might improve her role. I went out of my way to accommodate Miss Young and personally saw to it that these scenes were included...if Miss Young will tell you the truth and the facts, you will know how careful I have been to personally protect her interests for which, at the time, she profusely thanked me.[228]

Studio politics aside, the film is also memorable because Janet actually fell in love in *Ladies in Love*: with her handsome co-star, Tyrone Power. Power, scion of an acting dynasty that included his father, Tyrone Power Sr.,[229] was just beginning his film career when he was assigned to *Ladies in Love*. Power had seen *7th Heaven* when he was only thirteen years old and fell head over heels in love with Diane; working with Janet Gaynor he was "a fan meeting a star, and so was speechless."[230] The day after they met on the set, he anonymously sent three dozen roses to her dressing room; he then upped the ante by sending three dozen roses to Gaynor three times a week, from different florists so the orders could not be tracked. Power continued his affair with ice-skater turned movie star Sonia Henie, but remained a secret suitor of Janet's until the following spring, when he finally asked her to lunch at the Brown Derby. In the meantime, until Power asked her out, Janet was seen with Al Scott, Gene Raymond, and most often, Robert Taylor. She also dated a New York dentist by the name of Dr. Veblen.

When filming on *Ladies in Love* wrapped September 5, Janet's obligation to 20th Century-Fox was complete; but even so, there was no reason to anticipate any major change in Janet's connection with the studio. On September 25, however, the studio issued a statement to the press, which read:

Complete change of policy in the future casting of Janet Gaynor's future screen roles has been decided upon by 20th Century-Fox as a result of an exhibitor tabulation made by John Clark, general sales manager of the company.

> When Miss Gaynor is used in future 20th Century-Fox pictures she will be co-starred in important productions like her present picture, *Ladies in Love*, in which she shares billing with Loretta Young, Constance Bennett, and Simone Simon, according to the new plan.
>
> The contemplated plan of producing a series of pictures in which Miss Gaynor would be individually starred has been abandoned.[231]

The effect of that announcement was electrifying and columnists everywhere began sharpening their knives. In releasing that statement to the press, the studio had essentially called Janet, their top star, a has-been who would only be called on in future to lend support to other, bigger stars. Such a statement, publicly made by a studio, had the power to completely wreck a career. If John Clark had indeed made a study of Janet's box-office power, there is no report of it and there is a suspicious absence of any memos regarding it in any of Janet's legal or personnel files.

Immediately, Janet replied with her own statement to the press, which appeared in *Variety* under the headline GAYNOR-ZANUCK WAR:

> My contract with 20th Century-Fox ended with the completion of LADIES IN LOVE. I was asked to make a new contract with that company but several days ago, and before the announcement appeared in the trade papers, I notified Mr. Zanuck that I would not make a new term contract.
>
> It seems regrettable that any producer, and particularly one with whom an artist had been associated for several years, would go so far and make a statement which has no basis in fact for the very apparent and only purpose of injuring the artist who has refused an offer of a new term contract. I am asking my attorneys to study the matter with a view to a possible suit against 20th Century-Fox for its wholly unwarranted statement.[232]

If anyone could take on an entire studio and win, it was Janet Gaynor. One could almost pity Darryl Zanuck. Did he have any idea what he was getting into? Janet Gaynor was a notoriously litigious actress. What happened between September 5 and September 25, to cause such a public and acrimonious parting of the ways?

According to Paul Gregory, Darryl Zanuck had tried a little personal inducement when negotiating Janet's new contract:

> Well, he was a nasty old man. He locked her in the office and exposed himself and tried to tie her into a relationship that she didn't want. And that's what the problem was, nothing else. He thought that that's his, like a dog that stakes out his territory. She wasn't going to be it.[233]

Janet had never submitted to the casting couch in her entire career; protected first by Laura Gaynor, and later by her own good sense and self-respect, she had climbed the ladder of success based on her own talent as an actress, and nothing else. She was certainly not going to yield to an affair with Zanuck simply to keep her rightful place on the lot.

The day after Janet's rebuttal appeared in *Variety*, 20th Century-Fox issued a confused retraction to the press:

> The recent statement concerning our future policy with respect to producing all star pictures was the expression of a decision based upon a tabulation which shows the public preference for casts with multiple starring names.
>
> The company for some time has been successfully casting its more important productions in accordance with this preference, as in the case of LADIES IN LOVE wherein Miss Janet Gaynor shares co-star billing with artists of similar magnitude.
>
> The reference to Miss Gaynor in said statement was merely an example of the application of said policy and was in no way intended to injure Miss Gaynor or to detract from her artistic achievements, which we anticipate will redound to our benefit in the future as well as in the past.[234]

Of course, this was studio lawyerspeak trying to cover 20th Century-Fox for a statement that was, in fact, pointedly aimed at injuring Janet's career. The original box-office tabulation, as implied, had shown not a preference for multiple starring names, but a decline in Janet's drawing power. In the original statement, only plans for Janet Gaynor vehicles had been abandoned. Of course, the "multiple starring roles" plan was bunk; after all, the studio's biggest star for the next several years was

The Racquet Club, Palm Springs, California.

Shirley Temple, who obviously shared billing with no one. Whether the studio's retraction quelled Janet's anger or whether she simply decided to cut her losses and go, her meteoric but turbulent career at Fox ended in 1936. For the first time in a decade, Janet was free.

While Janet was battling with the studio, Charlie spent 1935-1936 engaged in expanding the Racquet Club. From the original two courts they began with, Charlie and Ralph added another four courts and a swimming pool. Then they added a bar, which was enlarged to a dining room. As Ralph recalled, "The thing seemed to grow of itself. It wasn't at all what we planned."[235] To offset the cost of expansion, and to limit the number of people using the courts, Charlie and Ralph did away with their 50-cent court usage fee. Instead, they sent out over 170 letters to friends and acquaintances, offering single memberships for $75 and family memberships for $100 for a limited time. After that, the rates would increase exponentially. By the time their first deadline passed, they had thirty members;

every time they increased the cost of membership, more people joined. The Club had its grand opening on Christmas Day of 1934; by the end of 1936, they had so many members they had to close the membership list. At that time, Racquet Club covered five acres of their twelve acre plot of land. It boasted six tennis courts, a swimming pool, a clubhouse, two locker and shower rooms, a bar and a dining room. When Charlie wasn't at the Club,

Charlie at the helm of *Flying Cloud.*

he was sailing his yacht, *Flying Cloud*, often taking her out for week-long trips. Sometimes Virginia accompanied him on these excursions, but more often Charlie went alone, or with a pretty companion.

Adding to his personal troubles, Charlie suffered the destruction of his $20,000 Malibu beach home in a devastating wildfire in October, 1935. The fire destroyed hundreds of homes and consumed 30,000 acres of land, the destruction estimated at eight million dollars. No one was injured in the blaze that consumed his home, but the property was a total loss.

Charlie's only film for 1935 was *Fighting Youth* for Universal, in which he played a college football hero, Larry Davis, who is seduced by Carol Arlington (Ann Sheridan) into becoming a Communist. The Communist agents plan to take over State College, beginning with their take-over of Larry Davis. The film was a B-picture, panned by critics, who said "*Fighting Youth* is neither impressive in its stand for Americanism nor as an exposé of the extra-curricular activities of Left Wing students."[236] *Fighting Youth* was one of Ann Sheridan's first billed roles, and Charlie tried to help her out, as he recalled:

> I liked her, I gave her lots of—lots of lectures because I knew she had a hell of future and I introduced her to some very big writers. And she said "What am I gonna do with those guys?" I said "Just go around with them, go around with them." One writer, they became great friends and neither one remembered that I had introduced them. One night when it was raining and I was taking her home and it had been raining and it was at one of those little hamburger stands. Myles Connolly. A fat writer by the name of Connolly. And I said "Come over here I want you to meet this girl. She'd be great company for you." And later on he said "Oh, Annie Sheridan I know her very well." I said "Yeah, I introduced you to her one rainy night."[237]

The film also featured football players from the All-American team, who were at first cautious not to make the football scenes too realistic, as Charlie remembered:

> Yeah, funny you know they were trying to be careful of me so they wouldn't kill me. I invited them to come out and see a big polo game one Sunday; I was playing in a big polo game. It

was a hell of a big match about 5,000 people there. So I came back the next day and they said "We don't have to be careful of him, he rides Roman[238]." You know when you're riding somebody off; you hop on somebody else's horse. Jesus boy I'm telling you they tore me apart.[239]

In January, 1936, Charlie signed on to make a film about the Flying Medical Association of Australia, written and directed by multitalented actor Miles Mander. To add authenticity, *The Flying Doctor* was going to be completed in Australia with a primarily Australian cast; indeed, Charlie (as "sundowner" Sandy Nelson) was the lone American in the cast. Charlie

The girl Charlie wanted: Mary Maguire.

left for Australia late January, unaccompanied by Virginia Valli. He stayed on location for nearly six months. When he returned to California that summer, he came home to ask Virginia for a divorce before leaving again for England. The gossip columnists picked up on the seemingly final rift between the two, and reported:

> The long anticipated separation of Charles Farrell and Virginia Valli has finally reached the stage of an understanding. This was confirmed when Mr. Farrell returned to Hollywood after a lengthy absence in Australia where he starred in a film and immediately left California for England to head the cast in a Gaumont-British vehicle...As a result of the Farrells' separation, gossipers will not be able to resist the opportunity of fabricating a new romance for Miss Gaynor and Mr. Farrell, but the latter is said to be interested in an Australian screen actress.[240]

Charlie and Janet were not on speaking terms, and he made no attempt to see her during his brief return to the States. The "Australian screen actress" alluded to by the press was also the reason behind his demand for a divorce—his seventeen-year-old *Flying Doctor* co-star, Mary Maguire. Maguire was described as "five foot tall, weighs 104 pounds, and has very nice architecture...She most resembles Janet Gaynor."[241] Maguire had started her career as a child actress in her native Australia; her father Michael was an ex-prizefighter turned hotelier and her mother Peggy stayed home to groom Mary for stardom.

On his way back to England, Charlie stopped to visit his sister Ruth and her family in Onset Bay, where they had returned following Estelle Farrell's death. Charlie told Ruth that he wanted out of his marriage, but that Virginia declined to grant him a divorce.[242] Why Virginia refused is a mystery, as are many of Virginia's actions: as a biographical subject, she remains cold and aloof. Very few of her contemporaries wrote about her in their memoirs; visitors to the Racquet Club and Charlie's own extended family only recall Virginia as very nice and very quiet. Virginia had to know as early as 1931 that Charlie was not fulfilled in their marriage; he constantly sought companionship with other women. Did she love Charlie so much, that despite his flaws she was willing to remain with him no matter the cost? Virginia was raised as a Catholic—did she suddenly become devoutly religious? Whatever the reason, the outcome was the same:

Together but apart: The Farrells in the late 1930s.

Charlie left for England, and his affair with Mary Maguire ended abruptly—possibly called off by ex-pugilist Michael Maguire, when he found out Charlie could not marry his daughter. Maguire came to America and enjoyed a brief tenure with 20th Century-Fox; but her career never really took off and by the early 1940s she disappeared from the screen.

Upon his arrival in London, Charlie made *Moonlight Sonata*, directed by Lothar Mendes, a fairy-taleish fable about two plane crash survivors, one of whom is Ignace Jan Paderewski, the famous Polish pianist. When the survivors find haven in a Swiss castle, Paderewski changes its inhabitants' lives through his music, especially his interpretation of Beethoven's "Moonlight Sonata." *Moonlight Sonata* is infused with a romantic, dreamlike quality; of Charlie's talking pictures, this comes closest to recapturing the magic of his silent films. Emphasizing the economical use of dialogue and the importance of music to the story, Mendes opens with a half-hour long concert given by Paderewski, featuring his "Minuet in G." This was Paderewski's first film and he was nervous and unsure of himself, but he and Charlie became close friends. Paderewski spent most of his off-screen time in Charlie's dressing room, playing bridge and discussing polo, which may have led to his famous quip: "You are a dear soul who plays polo; I am a poor Pole who plays solo."

Charlie and Binkie Stuart in *Moonlight Sonata*, Pall Mall Productions, 1937.

Charlie's second film during his English sojourn was *Midnight Menace* (aka *Bombs over London*), directed by Sinclair Hill for Grosvenor Films. Judging by the handful of films Grosvenor made, it is safe to assume it was the British equivalent of a Poverty Row company. In the film, Charlie played Briant Gaunt, a newspaper cartoonist, who stumbles upon a Balkan plot to bomb London via remote control planes. The film was hardly noticed in America, but critic Sandra Brennan of the *All Movie Guide* called it a "chilling war movie that successfully predicted the type of bombs Hitler later used."

While Charlie finished 1936 in London, Janet began negotiations for her next film. Even if Zanuck went out of his way to make Janet sound like a washed-up has-been, producer and close friend David O. Selznick had faith in her. He called Janet just after her bitter fight with 20th Century-Fox and said, "Janet, would you like to listen to a story that Billy Wellman and Bob Carson would like to come over and tell you?"

As Janet later recalled:

> So over they came, and they sat in my living-room and just outlined the story of *A Star Is Born*. They did not have that title then. It was a story of a small town girl who comes to Hollywood, and her success. I said immediately I would do it. Up until that time I had always played very young little girls. In this, I had the chance to begin as a little girl and then to become a woman of the world. I thought that would be fascinating. Also I wanted to make a picture with David because I had such confidence in him that I somehow felt it would be a good one.[243]

On October 5, 1936, Janet signed with Selznick International Pictures to make *A Star Is Born*. Originally, Janet's salary was set at $125,000 but she requested instead a salary of $100,000 and ten percent of the profits. (As usual, this was an astute business move on Janet's part. Her initial share of the profits totaled $45,454.55. By 1940, three years after the film's release, Janet's share of the profits still averaged $400 a month.) On October 8, Marlene Dietrich's dressing room was cleared out to make way for Janet's arrival. Once again, Janet Gaynor was queen of the lot, and David Selznick lavished her with the attention she deserved. Daniel

Janet as Vicki Lester, *A Star Is Born*, Selznick International Pictures, 1937.

Selznick, son of David and Irene, enthused, "What a brilliant choice my father made in casting her in *A Star Is Born*. What an actress!"[244] The top-notch cast included Frederic March as Norman Maine, Adolphe Menjou as agent Oliver Niles, and May Robson as Grandmother Nettie. Irene Mayer Selznick called the film "the movie David promised me," remembering it as "one movie I got to know in advance, scene by scene, because

David used me as a sounding board. Contrary to myths and credits, the story was largely his."[245]

A Star is Born has been remade twice, in 1954 with Judy Garland and James Mason, and in 1976 with Barbra Streisand and Kris Kristofferson, so the storyline is familiar—almost cliché— to modern audiences. In 1936, however, stories about Hollywood and the underside of fame were taboo, so the film's "overtones of truth, because they didn't try to make everything sweetness and light"[246] were still considered bold. Janet brought to Vicki Lester everything she had learned about fame and Hollywood since her days as an extra, going the rounds of the casting offices only to be disappointed in her search for work. In the party scene, where Esther is employed as a waitress, she mimics famous actresses to try to enchant the oblivious producers; we see Lolly in the mirror, imitating Norma Talmadge. In the Academy Awards scene, where Vicki accepts her Oscar only to be humiliated by Norman, we see Janet's pain at Hilary's drunken behavior on her Oscar night (adding to the scene's authenticity, Janet carried her own Oscar). Vicki's marital problems due to her blossoming fame echoed Janet's own problems with Lydell Peck. In fact, it is safe to say that Janet *lived* Vicki Lester. Her performance was the finest solo effort in her career; as Hedda Hopper said, she should have gotten another Oscar for *A Star Is Born*.

As a special thank you for Janet's brilliant work, David made a gift to her that Christmas of several costumes she had worn in the film. Stopping just shy of the $1,000 ermine coat Janet favored in one scene, Selznick gave Janet the silver dress she wore under the coat, two pairs of crepe pajamas, and the black velvet dress Janet wore in the Academy Awards scene. The costumes and all their accessories were wrapped up especially for Janet, with a handwritten note from David.

In March, 1937, when production had wrapped and retakes were finished, David hosted a private screening of the film. In a telegram to Janet, who was vacationing in New York, he wrote:

Dear Janet: Ran the picture last night for about thirty people all of whom went off their heads about it many being so extravagant in their praise as to call it the best picture in a year STOP Douglas Fairbanks says he has never been so delighted or moved in his memory STOP Walter Wanger thinks it will be one of the greatest successes ever made STOP Everyone exceedingly enthusiastic about your appearance and performance and feel it is the best thing you have ever done Affectionately, David[247]

If there was ever any doubt in Hollywood about Janet's stature as an actress or her ability to draw in the crowds, it would all change when *A Star Is Born* was released that spring.

Chapter Eleven

Retirement

"I just wanted to know about other things that I couldn't find time to know about. Some people seem capable of living more lives. I had to live one at a time."

— Janet Gaynor, 1958

The April 20, 1937 gala premiere of *A Star Is Born* was a shining example of life imitating art imitating life. It was held at Grauman's Chinese Theater, a pivotal location in the film's final scene as Vicki spies Norman's footprints in the forecourt and nearly collapses. Of course, in real life, Janet had placed her own footprints there in 1929; the day after the premiere, Frederic March (Norman Maine) immortalized his footprints in cement. The Mutual radio network hosted a nationwide broadcast of the premiere, with George "Hollywood Whispers" Fisher describing each celebrity's arrival, just as in the movie, when Vicki Lester introduced herself to her fans with the film's famous last line: "Hello, everybody. This is Mrs. Norman Maine." Critical and popular reception of *A Star Is Born* was, as Selznick predicted, a smash.

Columnists fixated on the new Janet Gaynor, both in her rebirth as a star, and her transformation from little girl roles to "her spirit, up-to-date 'it,' yes—and sex-appeal." Janet, who had only ever appeared in black and white films until *A Star Is Born*, was now considered the "best color subject discovered"[248] and her beauty received much praise:

> But most of all, Janet's alluring beauty was revealed for the first time; her soft coppery hair with its golden lights, the deep brown of her eyes, the white luster of her throat, and even the fascinating freckles that sprinkle her pert little nose and make her so

warmly human—all these took on a subtle new quality that made audiences glamour conscious.[249]

One fan magazine laughed: "It's darn [sic] funny that Hollywood, of ALL places, has taken ten years to discover Janet Gaynor has a BODY!"[250] Janet was flattered and embarrassed by the attention given her looks; but, the notion of being a "star re-born" annoyed her. The phrase, coined by head of advertising at Loew's Theatres, caused a flurry of memos from David O. Selznick. He asked Daniel O'Shea, vice-president of production, to contact both Janet and her attorney, Loyd Wright, adding, "Janet has no idea that she has changed…and I would like her to know what others think…but diplomatically!"[251] However tactfully Mr. O'Shea shared the news, it still exasperated Janet. "What do you mean, comeback?" she snapped at one columnist. "I was always on top."

There was no doubt that, even if a few people thought Janet had temporarily slipped from the top rung of fame, *A Star Is Born* put her back in the limelight. "Right now, Janet Gaynor is causing more excitement in Hollywood producing circles than you'd think possible for a lady her size," avowed columnist Kent Bailey. "The question isn't 'Is she worth a starring picture?' It's 'Can we get her to star in our picture?'" Bailey added, "The bids are high and very handsome. They're in the Garbo and Dietrich class, if money talks to you."[252] Janet was deluged with offers from other producers; in fact, B. P. Schulberg wired her constantly when she was on vacation in Europe, trying to get her for *Flower of France*, written by William Saroyan. Janet chose to stay with Selznick. After much debate about salary, working hours, and days off, she signed a two-picture deal in July 1937 at $137,500 per picture.

While Janet's career was in orbit, her romantic life was also on the upswing. Following her divorce from Lydell Peck, Janet had grown too absorbed with Laura again, mentioning in an interview, "[Laura's] the life of the party…we go to football games and are the noisiest rooters in our section. We attend symphony concerts, plays and pictures, love to travel and are never bored when we are together."[253] Obviously, it was time for Mrs. Gaynor's daughter to get a social life—and she did. Gossip columnist Walter Winchell ran an item in his column that Janet was "long-distancing a Hollywood producer but he has wife trouble,"[254] and columnist Jimmie Fiedler mused, "How can Janet Gaynor leave a path strewn with broken hearts but still maintain that sweet girl stare?"[255]

After *A Star Is Born* was released, Tyrone Power finally gathered his courage and asked Janet out. At the time he was still dating Sonia Henie, but soon he and Janet became inseparable. In fact, it was on a Hawaiian holiday with Power that Janet finally signed her contract with Selznick.

Janet genuinely loved Tyrone Power; of all her Hollywood romances, she only ever spoke to her son Robin of two men: Power and Charles Farrell. At the time, though, it appeared that Tyrone was completely smitten with Janet while she was proceeding with more caution. In November, Power tried to modify the "no marriage" clause in his contract so that he and Janet could wed, while Janet kept denying any rumors that she would be married. By January 1938, their engagement announcement was supposedly imminent, but suddenly Power began issuing denials: "I'm at the formative period of my career and I'm going through enough readjustment without that one. It wouldn't be fair to either party."[256] By June, their romance had definitely ended. Neither said what caused their breakup, but as Annabella, Tyrone's first wife, said, "Tyrone was the nicest man in the world. The only thing was, he was a little weak." Annabella recalled that, on their honeymoon, Power allowed a studio publicity man to follow them everywhere until she protested; they ditched the publicity man by leaving their hotel at 4 a.m. "That was the fault of Tyrone, but he had no others that I know. He was too, too sweet."[257] Given that Power was under contract to 20th Century-Fox, and his "no marriage" clause was a part of that contract, Power's sudden switch to focusing on his career may have been encouraged (or pushed) by Zanuck. Janet observed this weakness and knew what it meant for married life. Scarred by her marriage to Lydell Peck, Janet was eager to find someone self-fulfilled and strong. She loved Tyrone, but he was not the man for her.

While Janet's career and love-life blossomed, Charlie was stuck in limbo. He returned to the United States in March 1937 after making *Midnight Menace*. He loved making films in England, "where you do your work like a banker and then come home and mingle with a delightful, cosmopolitan crowd." He took a flat in Mayfair, which he said reminded him "very much of the attic in *7th Heaven*. It had dormer windows looking out on a penthouse roof,"[258] and he signed a ten-year lease so he could return at any moment. Upon his return, Charlie was given a hero's welcome by his own Uplifters Polo Club.[259] The team played a special match in his honor, during which he served as umpire.

Virginia, Charlie, and Guinn "Big Boy" Williams at a Santa Monica polo match.

Only a few months after his arrival, Charlie was on the move again, this time to Skowhegan, Maine. He had been invited by director Melville Burke, whom he had met at Fox in 1930, to do summer stock at the oldest summer theatre in the country, the Lakewood Theatre. "Accordingly he sent Burke a wire, jumped into his car and drove to Lakewood where he will spend several weeks," the local newspaper reported. "As a result of this decision he is acting this week in Owen Davis's farce, 'Two-Time Mary' and will have an important role next week in 'Reno.'"[260] Charlie also appeared as Senator Keane in the Lakewood's production of *First Lady*, and Sir John Romany in *God Save the King*. Charlie's stint at the Lakewood put another few months and a few thousand miles between himself and Virginia. The gossips at the Lakewood reported his "nightly long-distance phones after the performance," but whom was he calling? Virginia?—or Mary Maguire? Always one to duck a confrontation, Charlie found that constant traveling was the only way he could deal with his unhappy marriage.

When he came home to Palm Springs that fall, Charlie devoted himself to the Racquet Club, which had been run—almost into the ground—by Ralph Bellamy during Charlie's prolonged absence. Bellamy was also no businessman and despite the Club's unprecedented popularity, profits were rapidly draining. Bellamy wired Charlie in London for help and hired a private investigator, who found out that a bartender and waiters were running a scam that sapped their profits. Charlie rectified the situation by installing Frank Bogert as General Manager. Ralph wanted out of the Club so he could devote more time to his stage career, so Charlie bought out his shares and Ralph returned to New York.

Charlie always described the birth of the Racquet Club with characteristic modesty, saying, "The Racquet Club started in a haphazard way and grew in the same crazy, mixed-up fashion. Nothing was ever really planned. We just built, added on, or changed as we saw the need."[261] He neglected to mention that the bar they installed, the Bamboo Room, was designed by famed director Mitchell Leisen and was reportedly the first bar ever built from bamboo. Virginia oversaw the interior decoration of the rest of the rooms, bringing a refined elegance to the formerly indiscriminate Club. As an expert short-order chef, Charlie took a special interest in the cuisine, which was considered particularly fine. Celebrities flocked to the Racquet Club to play tennis, relax by the pool, and party; Tex Greggson, the new

Charlie teases John Barrymore at the Racquet Club, circa 1938.

Where it all began: the Racquet Club tennis courts.

bartender, created the Bloody Mary (originally called Farrell's Flip) to cure Charlie's monumental hangovers. The roster of members reads like a Who's Who of Classic Hollywood: Clark Gable, Carole Lombard, William Powell, Rudy Vallee, Douglas Fairbanks, Jr., Mary Pickford, Buddy Rogers, Bing Crosby, Bob Hope, Robert Taylor, Busby Berkeley, Errol Flynn, and Frank Capra—to name just a handful in the early days of the Club. Charlie was the Club's consummate host, its emcee, its ringmaster; his laid-back charm set the Club's tone and made it a welcome haven for Hollywood, a "celebrity refuge from columnists, photographers, and autograph hounds."[262] In some ways, Charlie was reliving his carefree fraternity days, but this Club was even more exclusive. In another way, Charlie was recreating his role as Liliom, the carousel barker who knew everyone but was close to no one. The Club was "something tangible to play with, and I forgot about pictures," Charlie explained.[263]

Enter Janet Gaynor. She went to New York in 1938 with Laura to visit Hilary, and Charlie happened to be in the city at the same time. Hilary ran into Charlie when she was out running errands, and insisted on bringing him back to the hotel to see Janet. After four years of silence, the ice was broken. Janet was still seeing Tyrone Power at the time, so she was not looking for romance; Charlie may have been carrying a torch for Janet but accepted her friendship as better than nothing. Janet inaugurated their renewed camaraderie by bossing Charlie around, inquiring, "Farrell, what are you going to do?" Charlie replied that the Club was fun and was making money. "But not for the rest of your life. You can't go on being a playboy," she admonished him, "Get yourself back to Hollywood, back to work. Stay in town more, be seen about."[264] When Charlie returned to Hollywood, he made the sci-fi thriller *Flight to Fame* for Columbia Pictures. "Terror Rides the Air Lanes!" screamed the advertisements for the film, which featured Charlie as ace aviator Robert Lawrence. In the film, a newly invented "death ray" falls into the hands of a madman, forcing Charlie to save the entire Air Force from destruction. *7th Heaven* it wasn't, but it did bring Charlie to director Irving Cummings' attention. Cummings felt Charlie would be ideal to play Shirley Temple's father in *Just around the Corner*. With that, Charlie signed a two-picture deal with 20th Century-Fox on April 16, 1938, at a salary of $1,000 per week.

Shooting on *Just around the Corner* began a week later; in the meantime, Janet helped Charlie get prepared. They rehearsed scenes together, just as they had in the old days, with Janet coaching and encouraging him

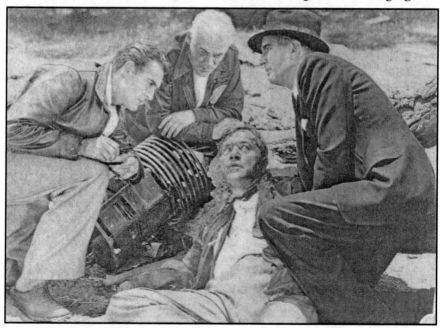

Detail from lobby card advertising *Flight to Fame*, Columbia, 1938.

so that when he met Shirley "One-Take" Temple, he could save face. According to the shooting schedule, Temple was in almost every scene; Charlie was in about 75% of them, so it was imperative that he stay on his toes. In the film, Charlie played an idealistic architect, Jeff Hale, who goes broke building large apartment buildings during the Depression. Temple plays his daughter, Penny, who manages to win the heart of a curmudgeonly old millionaire (Claude Gillingwater) who gives Jeff a career-resurrecting commission. Incidentally, this commission also ends the Depression. The film was a charming Temple vehicle, featuring catchy songs and a great supporting cast that included Bert Lahr, Bill "Bojangles" Robinson, and Joan Davis. Charlie was billed third in the picture, which was a comedown even from his days supporting Rin-Tin-Tin, but it was a job and it put him back in the movies.

While Charlie worked on *Just around the Corner,* Janet made her first film under her new Selznick contract, *Young in Heart.* Based on a short story, *The Gay Banditti,* by I. A. R. Wylie, it was a mellow screwball comedy about a family of confidence tricksters, who make their living mooching off the rich. The cast was splendid, including Roland Young as Colonel

Richard Carlson, Douglas Fairbanks Jr., and Janet in *The Young in Heart,* Selznick International Pictures, 1938.

Robert Montgomery and Janet in *Three Loves Has Nancy*, MGM, 1938.

Anthony "Sahib" Carleton, Billie Burke as the matriarch, Mamy Carleton, Douglas Fairbanks, Jr. as wastrel brother Richard, and Janet as gold-digger George-Ann. The family takes up with rich old dowager Miss Fortune (Minnie Dupree) in hopes of inheriting her wealth when she dies; however, under her good influence the entire family reforms. Richard Carleton makes the supreme sacrifice of getting a job selling cars ("The Flying Wombat," which cost Selznick $12,000 to build) and earns the love of Leslie Saunders (Paulette Goddard). Janet sets her sights on Scottish millionaire Duncan Macrae (Richard Carlson) and winds up finding true love. The *Los Angeles Times* called the film a "pleasing, if slightly slow-paced contribution to the more illuminated fall season of the films," but singled out Janet's performance as "warm and sympathetic."[265]

Charlie's last film under his Fox contract was *Tail Spin*, an Alice Faye vehicle in which Miss Faye plays an aviatrix who enters a cross-country derby against her wealthy rival Gerry Lester (Constance Bennett). Of the film, the *New York Times* dryly noted: "Though history may not consider his contribution equal to that of Orville Wright, Mr. Darryl Zanuck may ultimately be remembered as the man who brought sex to aviation." Naturally, as Alice Faye's love interest, Bud, Charlie had very little to do. "The male portion of *Tail Spin* isn't important," the *Times* concluded, "but here's how it is: Charles Farrell gets Alice, Kane Richmond gets Constance, and Nancy and Edward Norris (already married) are reunited in death."[266] In both films under his new 20th Century-Fox contract, Charlie had played supporting roles, and in neither film did he have an opportunity to shine. When his options came up on November 9, Zanuck chose not to renew his contract.

As Charlie worked on his final film for Zanuck, Janet began her last film, a loan-out to MGM. Janet agreed to do the film after reading the script in June, perhaps spurred on by Daniel O'Shea's comment that "Katie Hepburn is most anxious to play it, and while MGM would rather have you, they will find Hepburn tomorrow if you don't want it."[267] On June 20, she went to MGM to make *Three Loves Has Nancy*; in exchange, Selznick got James Stewart for *Made for Each Other* with Carole Lombard. *Three Loves* was a mild romantic comedy, about a small-town girl (Janet) who goes to New York to search for her missing fiancé (Grady Sutton). Once in New York, she is pursued by novelist Mal Niles (Robert Montgomery) and publisher Bob Hanson (Franchot Tone); but, eager to avoid another bad romantic experience, she sets up housekeeping with both men in a chaste ménage-a-trois to see which man is most worthy of her affection. "The dialogue is liberally sprinkled with *bon mots* (some are bon, and some are *comme ci comme ca*)" the *Los Angeles Times* critiqued. "The performances are sprightly. Miss Gaynor's Nancy comes close to being a genuinely fresh creation…the film should please the majority."[268] If the film was not a memorable romantic comedy, it was memorable for the real-life romance it sparked between Janet and the film's costume designer, Adrian.

In 1917, French critic Colette had lamented the cinema's lack of original fashion sense and called for a couturier to "dress the screen." "He will be required to have the talents of a painter, a sculptor; he will have to play with a master hand over the keyboard of tonal values," Colette proclaimed.[269] Eight years later, Colette got her wish. Adrian was Hollywood's fashion auteur, a master designer whose works exploited the fantasy of the silver screen. He was born Adrian Adolphe Greenburg in Nagatuck, Connecticut in March, 1903. His family was devoted to fashion and the arts: his father Gilbert was a furrier; his mother Helena was a milliner; and his uncle Max was a scenic designer for the stage. From childhood, Adrian was a compulsive artist: one teacher remembered keeping him behind after school to write lines as punishment, only to find Adrian had perfected an entire mural on the chalkboard instead. In the 1920s, Adrian's older sister Beatrice went to New York to study dance with Vernon and Irene Castle; Adrian went with her and began studying at Parsons School of Fine and Applied Art. Adrian's first job as a designer came during one season at the Gloucester Playhouse. His most memorable accomplishment during that period was choosing a new professional name, encouraged by director Florence Cunningham. She convinced him to change to simply "Adrian" to emulate his heroes, artists Bakst and Erte. When Adrian did so, his father was hurt and angry, so Adrian adopted his father's first name, Gilbert, as his own. For the rest of his life, Adrian was known as Gilbert Adrian, legally, and Adrian professionally.[270] Much later, when the Greenburgs retired, they moved to Los Angeles to be near Adrian; showing the rift had healed, his father changed his name from Greenburg to Adrian, too.

In 1922, Adrian transferred to Parsons' branch in Paris for more challenges and enlightenment. It was in Paris, at the Bal du Grand Prix, that Adrian met Irving Berlin, who hired him on the spot for the *Music Box Revue* he was staging in New York. Although most of his designs were ditched by the *Revue's* official designer, Charles LeMaire, the gig gave Adrian his start. He began working as a costume designer for the *Greenwich Village Follies* and the *George White Scandals*. In 1925, he came to Natacha Rambova's attention, and she hired him to do the costumes for *Cobra*, starring her husband, Rudolph Valentino. This marked Adrian's first foray into films; afterward he worked for Cecil B. DeMille. However, Adrian's film career was officially launched in May 1927, when he signed a contract with MGM. His costumes for Greta Garbo's *A Woman of Affairs* caused a furor; from then on, Adrian was responsible for dressing Miss Garbo and MGM's two other queen bees: Norma Shearer and Joan Crawford. He worked with the actresses' personalities and created a signature look wholly individual to each one: for Crawford, the padded-shoulder look for which she became famous; for Shearer, her elegant soignée style; and Garbo wore his most theatrical costumes with ease.

Daniel Selznick recalled that Louis B. Mayer had complete trust in Adrian, but added, "The demands for his time at MGM swamped everything else, clearly."[271] A dedicated workaholic, Adrian led a quiet, austere existence outside of the studio. He ran an antique store and painted, and when possible, would retreat to his Palm Springs ranch, which did not have running water or electricity. He was responsible for most of MGM's important and lavish films, often designing for several at the same time;

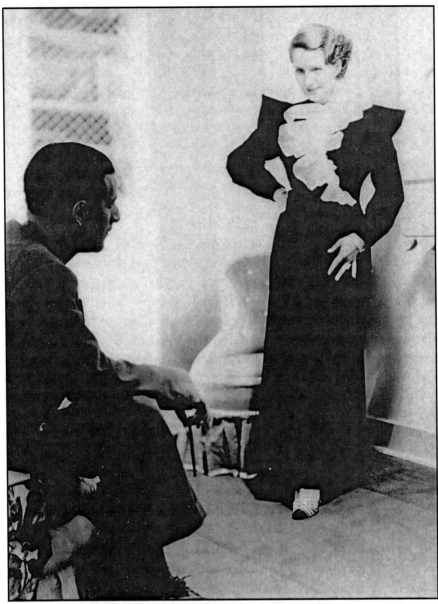

Adrian looks over his handiwork—Norma Shearer is the model.

in later years, Janet told their son, Robin, that upon Adrian's retirement, they had to hire five designers to replace him. "He was aided by an eye and mind which could immediately discard the nonessentials. With this convenient grace, he produced paintings, costumes, rooms, and dinners of opulent simplicity," biographer Robert Riley affirmed.[272]

Janet had known Adrian professionally for several years, at least since Irene Mayer had her wedding gown and those of her bridesmaids designed by him for her wedding to David Selznick. Janet had requested Adrian for her film *Daddy Long Legs*; though they worked together well, Robin recalled, "It was not love at first sight. I think they were cordial to each other and my understanding is that that all went fine," but there was no personal spark between them. When Janet worked at MGM for *Small Town Girl*, the film was not considered important enough for Adrian's talents, so Dolly Tree handled all of Janet's costumes. At the time Janet made *Three Loves Has Nancy*, she had broken up with Tyrone Power and was dating her *Young in Heart* co-star, Richard Carlson. Adrian was a loner and Janet was still searching for a self-fulfilled man; their courtship was hesitant and unsure.

When Janet completed *Three Loves*, she had also completed her Selznick contract. Janet made a conscious decision to only make films if she felt like it—and those films never appeared. Selznick scrambled around, trying to hold her interest. He offered to broker a loan-out to Columbia, so Janet could appear in *Holiday* (the role went to Katharine Hepburn) and *You Can't Take It with You* (the role went to Jean Arthur), but Janet refused.[273] Selznick then all but handed Janet the role of Melanie Wilkes in the most important film of his career, *Gone With the Wind.* "I have a sneaking hunch that Janet Gaynor might be persuaded to play Melanie after all and that she might further be persuaded to take a substantial cut to play it," Selznick wrote to O'Shea in October, 1938, "in view of her apparently sincere indifference to money and her anxiety to do more pictures only if and when great roles come along."[274] Despite Selznick's gut instinct, Janet refused, and the role went to Olivia de Havilland. Indeed, as late as 1942, Selznick was still offering plum roles to Janet, including a sequel to *A Star Is Born,* with Vicki Lester mentoring a child star. On each occasion, Janet gracefully declined. As a parting gesture, she sold the rights to *Forever,*[275] a story she had purchased, to MGM as a vehicle for Norma Shearer.

Janet chose to retire, because, as she said:

> I stopped because I really wanted to have another kind of life. I wasn't disgruntled. I'd really had such a good time and such a great success—but I also had no other life, and I just wanted to know about other things that I couldn't find time to know about.

I think it's a matter of energy. I just didn't have the energy to do other things. My time between pictures was spent just resting to get ready to go back to work.[276]

Janet chose an auspicious time to call it quits; if she had retired after her fight with Zanuck, she would have been forever branded as a has-been and her retirement would have been cast up to her lack of box-office appeal. Janet left after proving Zanuck wrong, and she went out on top. She had surpassed all of Laura and Jonesy's expectations of her; she made enough money that her family was comfortably taken care of in perpetuity. She was more than ready to leave the career she never wanted, to seek the life she always had.

Charlie also renounced films, despite Janet's advice. He found happiness in managing the Club; indeed, he managed the Club better than he ever had his own career. As David and Estelle's son, he knew how to successfully run a small business; as Charles Farrell the movie star, he avoided confrontations and decisions, which ultimately led to his downfall. Charlie did not so much choose retirement as he chose to give up the fight.

In April, 1939, Janet attended the Big Top Ball at the Racquet Club, one of the glittering social events of the Palm Springs season. She came in costume as Pierrot, only to find that her host, Charlie, was there in an identical costume. Both insisted that this was a mere coincidence, but what a coincidence! Even if it were accidental, the incident shows how alike and in synch they were and had always been. Frank Bogert photographed them dancing together later that evening. Charlie held Janet and faced the camera, with an expression of resignation and sneaky adoration in his eyes, the "Charles Farrell Hero" (self-mocking and hesitant) smile on his face. Janet, elusive as ever, laughed and turned away from the camera's glare. Four months later, Janet eloped with Adrian to Yuma, Arizona. Her chauffeur, Clifford, acted as their witness.

Janet's romance with Adrian surprised Irene Selznick, who became Janet's confidante. "I thought they were both crazy...they had nothing in common," she wrote in her memoirs. But later she admitted she was wrong:

With consummate ease Janet became a fashion plate and hostess, the kind of transformation one usually witnesses only on the screen. As she grew, essentially she remained the same, because she had absolute authenticity. She and Adrian never looked

Janet and Charlie in identical costumes at the Big Top Ball.
Photograph by Frank Bogert.

back...or sideways. Until his death twenty years later, the marriage was one of the best, if not the best, I've ever encountered.[277]

Robin analyzed his parents' initial attraction:

I think that they both had a love of adventure and I think that was part of the connection. They were both interested in other things and they weren't egotistical which in that business, par-

Janet and Adrian together, circa 1939.

ticularly with actresses—I'm sure because my father knew so many of the Metro actresses and so many of them were just into their own careers and their own egos and my mother was not that kind of a person. I think that they just found each other interesting and that was part of the attraction. I'm sure there was a physical attraction because both of them were attractive looking people. But they connected on another level.

That "other level" was the desire to have a life outside the studio, something Janet had never kept secret. In an interview published five years before her retirement, she said, "Of course I hope to marry again, some day. *I hope I have a baby.* No woman should go through all of life without that supreme experience."[278] Soon after their marriage, Janet got her wish: she became pregnant with Robin. In high delight, Adrian designed a maternity smock for her that became a sensation when she was photographed in it for *Vogue* magazine. On July 7, 1940, Janet delivered Robin Gaynor Adrian by caesarian section at Good Samaritan Hospital in Los Angeles. Adrian celebrated his son's birth by constructing a circus top canopy to fit over his crib. Careful not to exploit their son, and eager to protect their privacy, the Adrians did not allow any pictures of Robin to be published until nearly a year after his birth.

Shortly after Robin was born, Adrian began experiencing difficulties at MGM. His lavish designs were his trademark, and they were as magnificent in reality as they appeared on the silver screen; for example, a single embroidered panel on one gown for *Queen Christina* cost $1,800 to make. MGM was feeling a budget crunch due to a decline at the box office, and so they began slashing unnecessary expenses, beginning with wardrobe. Moreover, the studio began a makeover campaign on Greta Garbo for her next film, *Two-Faced Woman.* Adrian was asked to supply costumes that made the aloof, dramatic Garbo seem like the girl-next-door—a mighty task, indeed. As the pre-production process stagnated, Adrian grew increasingly frustrated: no one would approve his sketches. One night, after a particularly bad day at MGM, Adrian confided to Janet that the handwriting was on the wall: his days at MGM were numbered.

Adrian had already been visited by luxury retailing magnate, Herbert Marcus of Neiman-Marcus, earlier that year; and Marcus had urged him to go into retail. Looking around Adrian's workroom, Marcus had seized a simple black-beaded party dress, and said, "I can sell at least fifty of these in each store!"[279] Marcus's visit stuck with Adrian, and that night as he discussed *Two-Faced Woman* with Janet, he asked her about retiring from MGM to start his own *prêt-a-porter* line. Janet was ecstatic, and offered to bankroll the entire operation with her own life savings. The next day, Adrian handed in his resignation. His contract officially terminated on July 16, 1941, but he stayed on until September 5 to assist in the transition to a new designer. When Greta Garbo—who had been Adrian's biggest clotheshorse and was indirectly responsible for his departure—heard of his retirement, she told him, "I am very sorry you are leaving, but you know, I never really liked most of the clothes you made me wear."[280]

Adrian began Adrian, Ltd. with Janet and former employees Woody Fuert and Hannah Lindfors. Discussing Janet's role in the venture, Robin recalled that "Of the two she was the more practical. He was more of a dreamer, he was the one with ideas and I think he wanted whatever it was done at any cost,"[281] so her main job was to bring Adrian down to earth. Adrian's first showing was in January 1942 in their home on Toluca Lake in Hollywood. Several retailers, including Neiman-Marcus, signed up for the retail line at $10,000 per collection. The following show, in June 1942, was an absolute triumph: it took all day to write up the orders for stores like Bonwit Teller and Marshall Fields. He followed that show with one just for customers in August, and most of his former clients attended, including Joan Crawford, Norma Shearer, Greer Garson, and Bugsy Siegel's girl-friend, Virginia Hill. With that show, Adrian's retail success was assured. With the onset of World War II, Adrian became the leading advocate of American fashion, and his designs were endlessly copied by others.

Throughout the war, Janet stayed busy between assisting in Adrian's thriving business and raising Robin. She appeared in a few plays but never seriously considered a comeback. Her only real Hollywood connection at this time was her participation in the "Stars over America" War Bond Tour. Along with a constellation of fellow actors (including Bette Davis, James Cagney, Henry Fonda, Norma Shearer, Gene Tierney, Robert Young, and Dorothy Lamour), Janet trouped across the country to raise war bond sales to the billion-dollar mark. Her life, though, was devoted to Adrian, because, as she said, "He took me into another whole world, the world of fashion…I found it fascinating. I wanted to know the world of art. I wanted to travel. I wanted to do all these things, and I have done them. I'm very, very grateful."[282] In Adrian, Janet found her self-fulfilled man, the man who gave her everything she had missed when she was working in Hollywood.

While Janet found happiness in marriage, Charlie was still deeply unsatisfied with his marriage to Virginia. He was seen publicly with other women, including former leading lady Alice Faye. Their fling was reported matter-of-factly by the press: "At Ciro's, Alice Faye, radiant in a black crepe dinner suit, danced with her latest beau, Charles Farrell."[283] He devoted himself to sports, which had the added benefit of taking him away from home for long periods of time. He played countless charity polo matches. He went on a national celebrity tennis tour with actors Errol Flynn, Paul Lukas, Gilbert Roland and tennis champion Bobby Riggs to raise money

Candid snapshot of Janet, circa 1940s.

for the British War Relief Association. He went on week-long trail rides with the Vaqueros del Desierto. When Charlie came home, he devoted his efforts to making Palm Springs and the Racquet Club a world-class destination, causing one Hollywood columnist to remark:

> Whenever a movie actor gets the sniffles, or [is] sore at the boss, or figures he's got to get away from it all, he comes to Palm Springs, 110 miles due east of Hollywood. Here he sees other actors; spends his evenings in cocktaileries like those at home, and pays $30 a

day for a room overlooking an endless expanse of sagebrush and sand. Charles Farrell seems to be one of the leading citizens. He runs the racquet club, plays polo on Sundays, and functions as associate editor of one of the three weekly newspapers. He has a regular column in this paper, which he signs "Charles Libelous Farrell"— and which seems to be no exaggeration.[284]

As a lark, Charlie made one last film, *The Deadly Game* (1941), for Monogram Pictures. Charlie played Barry Scott, an FBI agent working against Nazi spies and counterspies. "It's a hectic story of espionage and sabotage that moves at a mile a minute pace, and which finds all the naughty Nazi boys and girls headed for jail while Mr. Farrell acquires the somewhat delectable June Lang,"[285] ran one review. If *The Deadly Game* was an anticlimactic epitaph for Charlie's topsy-turvy film career, it may have been responsible for the next phase of his life. As Henry Fonda declared, "I don't want to be in a fake war in a studio," so Charlie joined Fonda, Clark Gable, James Stewart, Tyrone Power, and Douglas Fairbanks, Jr. as just a handful of the many Hollywood actors who actively fought in WWII. At 42, Charlie was nearing the draft age limit, but thanks to all his athletic endeavors, he was in fine physical condition.

In June 1942, the first notices of Charlie's enlistment appeared in the papers; by October he had received his first commission in the United States Navy. He attended officers' training school at Quonset Point, Rhode Island that winter, but made time in New York for one last flirtation that was captured by columnist Louella Parsons: "Charles Farrell, who is reported as being the handsomest man in New York wearing a uniform, created a lot of interest when he danced with Eva Gabor at the El Morocco."[286] That was Charlie's last appearance in the gossip columns for the next few years. Charlie's stint in the Navy gave him the structure he needed; away from the Racquet Club and stripped of his playboy lifestyle, Charlie became the remarkable fellow Janet always knew he could be.[287]

Chapter Twelve

Comeback

"If it's possible to have another life besides pictures, then I think that it isn't sad at all."

– Janet Gaynor

When Charlie left the School of Indoctrination at NAS Quonset Point, he had little chance to make an impression on his superiors. His course grades were unexceptional and he was designated as "average" by the officer in charge. Since Charlie was in training at the time, Lt. Commander Zitzewitz noted, "It was impracticable to observe his capabilities sufficiently for proper marking."[288] Lieut. Farrell was then transferred to NAS Bunker Hill, Indiana (now known as Grissom AF Reserve Base), which was a training base for naval pilots. Charlie's background in the Racquet Club decided his first post; as Aide to the Commanding Officer, M. T. Seligmann, he was responsible for the morale, recreation, and welfare of the men on base. He was only at NAS Bunker Hill for a few months, from March 1, 1943 to July 28, 1943, but he made an outstanding impression on Lt. Commander Seligmann. He gave Charlie excellent marks in all sections of his Report on the Fitness of Officers, giving Charlie especially high ratings in initiative, cooperation, loyalty, and military bearing and neatness of dress. Seligmann added, "This officer has performed all his duties in a highly satisfactory manner. His personal and military character is excellent. He is a good shipmate. I take pleasure in recommending him for promotion when due."[289]

With that, Charlie moved to NAS Alameda, on the San Francisco Bay, which was his home for the next ten months. NAS Alameda was one of the newest and most advanced naval air stations of WWII. In April

1942, the *USS Hornet* (CV-8) had departed from Alameda under the command of General Doolittle, to perform the famous Doolittle Raid on Honshu, Japan. By the time Charlie reached Alameda, the base employed over 200 workers skilled in 271 trades, capable of repairing and manufacturing any part of any aircraft. In this exhilarating atmosphere, Charlie was made Assistant Domestic Transportation Officer and supervised the Commissioned Officers' Mess. He fairly itched to get into combat, as noted by his commanding officer, Lt. Commander F. R. McCrary, who added, "This officer has a very good personal and military character. His industry and perseverance in the performance of his assigned duties has set an excellent example for others."[290]

In April 1944, a fighting squadron called the Fighting 17 (VF-17) was formed at Alameda under the command of Lt. Commander Marshall U. Beebe. [291] The group flew the newly designed, 2,000 hp Grumman Hellcat. The Fighting 17 was assigned to the aircraft carrier *USS Hornet* (CV-12). (The *USS Hornet* that had launched the Doolittle Raid had been sunk in the Battle of the Santa Cruz Islands in October 1942; CV-

Charlie in uniform, with unidentified friend, during WWII.

Charlie on the deck of the *USS Hornet*. He is standing by the Hellcats
that were flown by the men of the Fighting 17.

12 was originally called the *USS Kearsarge*, but was renamed the *Hornet*
in her honor.) The newly christened *Hornet* had a hasty history: it was
commissioned only 15 months after the keel was laid in Newport News,
RI. The "shakedown cruise," in which the ship's performance was tested,
lasted only 14 days instead of the usual four to five weeks. On April 19,
Charlie got his wish: he was assigned to Fighting Squadron 17 as Administrative and Personnel Officer under Lt. Commander Beebe.

As his ten-month training period got under way, Charlie's wrist-watch, along with several other officers' watches, was stolen by a seaman. The sailor, Albert David, was caught by Oakland police when he tried to pawn the watches and was sent to Leavenworth for committing burglary on U.S. property. That was the mildest incident in Charlie's life for the next year or so. At the close of his training period, during which Charlie had spent the final month in combat, Commander Beebe gave Charlie superior marks in all areas. Beebe was compelled to add, "Lieut. Farrell has a most pleasing personality and has been a big help in the squadron in maintaining a high standard of morale."[292]

Once aboard the *Hornet,* Charlie acted as Beebe's right-hand man, serving as administrative and personnel officer. Another lieutenant, ace pilot Ned Langdon, served as head aviator and executive officer. Charlie was in charge of all the administrative and personnel duties for the Fighting 17, which included 54 men, only 24 of whom were enlisted crew; the rest were officers. The last month of Charlie's first reporting period under Beebe was spent as the VF-17 participated in air strikes against Chichi Jima and Iwo Jima, in preparation for the invasion of Iwo Jima. Once the area was secure for the Marine invasion, the *Hornet* turned her attention to Tokyo, annihilating its airfields. Then, on March 18, *Hornet* began a forty-day preparation for the invasion of Okinawa, launching strikes continuously on 32 of the 40 days. The pilots flew over 4,000 combat sorties during that period. On April 1, Marines hit the beaches of Okinawa, with the air groups from *Hornet* riding shotgun overhead. In retaliation, the Japanese sent their most powerful battleship, *Yamato,* on a kamikaze mission. The air groups from *Hornet* were the first to strike *Yamato,* hitting her with four torpedoes and three bombs, which crippled her and caused her to sink.

Amazingly, during these months of heavy combat, the *Hornet* was never hit by bombs, torpedoes, or kamikazes. Indeed, it took a force of nature to stop her: a massive typhoon struck the entire Task Force 58 on June 5. The *Hornet,* facing 120 knot winds and 60 foot waves, lost 24 feet of her forward flight deck. Grant MacDonald, an AP reporter aboard another carrier, witnessed the planes "flipped around like bean bags" on deck. The next day, the *Hornet* backed down at a speed of 18.5 knots while her aircraft were launched over the stern end, in order to reassemble the Task Group. This, it seems, was a characteristic act of daring and "can-do" of the men of the *USS Hornet;* during her eighteen months

Charlie and an unidentified crewmember of the *USS Hornet*.

at sea, the ship's guns shot down over 660 Japanese planes, sunk 73 Japanese ships, and damaged another 413. Her air groups flew over 18,500 sorties, and 10 of those pilots achieved "Ace in a Day" status for scoring five or more aerial victories. Ten days after being hit by the typhoon, the *Hornet* returned to NAS Alameda to repair the crippled flight deck, while her officers and crew enjoyed a well-deserved 30 days' leave.[293]

In his last Officer's Fitness Report for Charlie, Beebe ranked him within the top 10% of all the officers in his class in the areas of initiative, understanding and skill, and leadership. In the report, Beebe noted: "He is willing, cooperative, and carries out instruction in an excellent manner." Beebe also gave Charlie a commendation for outstanding performance of duty.[294] After five months of intense battle, Charlie stepped off the *Hornet* that July a changed man; his hair had even turned grey. On August 6, Charlie was given additional leave to attend to matters at the Racquet Club, but within a few weeks, the war had officially ended. In November, 1945 Charlie received an honorable discharge, with the rank of Lt. Commander. In July, 1946, Task Force 58, including the men of

Charlie and Pops Farrell before the war. Photograph by Frank Bogert.

the *USS Hornet*, was given the Presidential Unit Citation by President Harry Truman for extraordinary heroism.

Overall, the war had a grounding effect on Charlie, who returned to the Racquet Club full of purpose and ambition—not for a film career, or polo, or tennis, but for his beloved Palm Springs. Virginia had successfully managed the Racquet Club by herself during Charlie's three-year absence; under her care even the Club's tiny sports shop, no bigger than a closet, netted $30,000 a year. When Charlie returned, the Club was a common interest that bonded them; Charlie once again became the Club's ringmaster while Virginia retired to the front office. David Farrell, known to everyone as 'Pop' Farrell, was imported to help run things; he ruled the food and liquor storerooms with an iron fist and kept careful track of everything taken by the bartenders and chefs. (Pushing eighty, David had also married a very young woman of whom no one approved.) Charlie diversified his interests by establishing another resort on Catalina Island, called the Toyon Bay Resort. Toyon Bay, which cost $450,000 to build (Charlie had originally estimated the cost at $90,000) was called "Noel Coward Swank" by the columnists, but it was not as lucrative as the Racquet Club. Charlie sold Toyon Bay in 1950 to Julian King, who turned it into a dude ranch, called the Catalina Island Guest Ranch.

Charlie branched out from resort life into politics, something he had shown an interest in as early as 1940. Before the war, Charlie began petitioning the Palm Springs City Council for different reasons. The most popular and amusing was the poem he wrote to the City Council, calling for an ordinance banning bare-chested men from public places:

> We like our girls to wear their shorts,
> For walks in town or active sports.
> We like our men to wear them, too.
> But please in town respect the view.
> A man's torso on a public street,
> Is seldom handsome, never neat.
> We shouldn't like to spoil your fun,
> While basking in our desert sun.
> Palm Springs *is* yours so keep it clean,
> Keep your chests where they can't be seen.

When Charlie returned from the war, he ran unopposed for District 6 of the City Council. He served only two years of his four-year term before being elected by his fellow city council members as Mayor of Palm Springs. Charlie was the fifth mayor of the desert community, and the only one so far to serve a six-year term. Although some dismissed the post as largely ceremonial, Charlie took an active interest in improving life for residents. He petitioned the Civil Aeronautics Board in Washington, D.C. for better airline feeder service during the winter months. He had palm trees planted down Palm Canyon Drive. As a joke, he made Bob Hope the honorary mayor of Palm Springs during the Desert Circus events of 1948 (for which Charlie also decreed a city-wide holiday). Hope repaid the favor by calling Palm Springs "the vacation spot in the heart of the California money belt...of course, ever since Charles Farrell became mayor, it's no longer called Palm Springs...it's known as the sun-soaked Seventh Heaven."[295]

Did Charlie miss acting?

"Good heavens, no," he told a reporter in 1951. "I do a few radio and television shows to work out whatever ham is left in me."[296] Charlie was referring to a few radio shows Jack Benny had broadcast from the Racquet Club, and on which he had appeared as a guest. Just a few months

Charlie with Jane Russell and Bob Hope during the Desert Circus.

Together again: Charlie and Janet during the *Lux Radio Theatre* broadcast of *7th Heaven*.

later, Charlie reunited with Janet on *Lux Radio Theatre*, in a presentation of *7th Heaven* in honor of the Academy Awards. It was a moment that captured the imagination of an entire generation of fans, who had always wanted Farrell and Gaynor to reunite. Even though Charlie had not been nominated for the Academy Award, he gracefully took up the role of Chico and even joked about his former fame with reporters: "When I was on a ship in the war, the boys heard I was in pictures, but asked, 'Who is he?' Some weeks later, after they had written home about me, their mothers and grandmothers told them who I was."[297]

Charlie and Janet had seen each other socially ever since Charlie returned from the war; in fact, his first appearance in the gossip columns came in September, 1946, when he was spotted talking to Janet at a party. Janet scotched any rumors of a romantic reunion, telling a reporter, "We are both happily married now. Charlie, as you know, operates the Racquet Club in Palm Springs with his wife, the former Virginia Valli. It's a wonderful place and they're wonderful people, and Adrian and I love to visit them. We're all good friends, and Charlie is still terribly handsome."[298] Their first professional reunion in 17 years was a lucky charm for Charlie; it was the catalyst that jump-started his comeback in show business.

In a rare moment of mistaken judgment, Janet and Charlie's former boss, Darryl Zanuck, had said that television "won't be able to hold any market it captures after the first six months. People will soon get tired of staring at a plywood box every night." He was wrong, of course, and by the end of the 1950s, television had eclipsed film as the most popular entertainment medium in the country. *I Love Lucy* was the most beloved sitcom running at that time, and when it went off the air for a summer break in 1952, Charlie was approached by Hal Roach, Jr. to star in its replacement, *My Little Margie*. The sitcom centered on perky Margie Albright and her handsome widowed father, Vern; most of the plots dealt

Charlie and Gale Storm in a publicity photo for *My Little Margie*.

with Margie's schemes to keep gold-digging women away from Vern. Movie star Gale Storm signed on to play Margie as soon as she heard Charlie had been cast, remembering him as a "great-looking person, a distinguished gentleman who was perfect for the part as my silver-haired and slightly helpless father. He had such a childlike quality that I actually felt older than he." Since summer replacement shows rarely succeeded, CBS only ordered nine episodes rather than the usual thirteen. Filming began April 1952, and the first shows aired that June.

To everyone's surprise, *Margie* became a hit. In fact, the show did so well that it was purchased by NBC and moved to their Saturday evening lineup, then moved back to CBS in January of 1953, where it stayed for the next two years. Initially panned by critics as "silly," the show was, according to Gale Storm, "successful because it was fast and funny and had characters an audience could love."[299] Much of the quick tempo of the show was due to director Hal Yates, who would not permit any pauses or hesitations from the actors. This was a problem for Charlie, as Gale Storm recalled:

> He was a bit of an absent-minded professor and very nervous about returning to acting. He always had his script with him, and he was always reading it and trying to memorize his lines between takes. He'd be studying the next scene while we were shooting one and forget his lines for the one we were shooting. We had to hit our marks, and he'd miss them…And Hal would holler at Charlie until we all felt sorry for him.[300]

Gale enjoyed working with Charlie, despite his absent-minded ways:

> Charlie was the single most considerate man I have ever known in my life. I bled internally for him, but he took the ill treatment in stride. He had no vanity at all. He just loved *Margie*— he never complained to Hal or about Hal and he was happy to be back in the spotlight. [301]

To capitalize on *Margie's* popularity, the producers approached both Charlie and Gale about doing a radio version while the television show was still running. The radio programs would feature completely different plots from the television shows, which the producers reckoned would draw in even more audiences. Hal Roach, Jr. offered to give them each a day off from filming (they were working six days a week as it was) to record the radio broadcasts, and sweetened the deal by offering them each a ten percent ownership in both the radio and television versions of the show. Though, as Gale recalled, it meant "more madness," they relented. "I don't know why [Charlie] gave in, but I am sure it was hard on him,"[302] she said. Indeed, Charlie was working so hard that he regretfully resigned as mayor of Palm Springs. He did, however, make time in June 1955 to accept an honorary degree from his alma mater, Boston University. Approximately ten years later, after his retirement from show business, Charlie gave a huge bequest (some estimates speculated the donation was in the tens of thousands of dollars) in grateful homage to the University.

When *Margie* concluded its run in 1956, Charlie was approached by Hal Roach, Jr. to do another show, this one based on life at the Racquet Club. "It looks like I am back in business," Charlie told a reporter. "You'll just have to put me down as a ham that's been smoked out of its resting place." Originally aired as a summer replacement for *I Love Lucy*, and intended as a "pleasant and lucrative way to spend the off-season away from Palm Springs,"[303] *The Charles Farrell Show* became another hit. It ran for two years on CBS. Charlie's co-stars were Charles Winninger, as 'Dad Farrell,' Leon Askin as 'Pierre the Racquet Club chef,' and Kathryn Card as 'Mrs. Papernow.' Exteriors were filmed at the Racquet Club to add some authenticity, and several Racquet Club habitués, including Bob Hope, made guest appearances on the show.

In 1959, Charlie abruptly sold his beloved Racquet Club to two California businessmen, at a profit of more than a million dollars. Exactly why he sold the Club is a mystery, but he had spent very little time there once his television career took off. He was retained as the managing director and figurehead, which meant that the business details were handled by other people. He was still the Club's "face." With the stressful details handled by someone else, Virginia retired as Charlie still played at the Club.

While Charlie spent this era as a television star, Janet was a wife and business partner to Adrian and a mother to Robin. Adrian, Ltd. continued to grow during the war years; Robin remembered, as a child, being taken to Adrian's office for lunch as a treat. "It was always a big deal to get to see what was going on and watch him do some of his designs. He worked very quickly. He might do a design while I was sitting there," he recalled.

Charlie and Virginia together at the Racquet Club, before the war.
Photograph by Frank Bogert.

He might be sitting there doing a design and then somebody would come in and do a fitting and I do remember seeing – he had a really large office. It was more like this giant room because on the floor were bolts of material and the room also served as storage for all that so he could sit there and be looking at that while he had his ideas. Beyond that I didn't really see the process of the dress makers sewing them and doing that. I probably had a tour of the whole thing when I was five or six years old.[304]

After the war ended, Janet and Adrian began traveling again, taking a safari to Africa in 1948. While on safari, they visited the Masai tribe and drank the ceremonial cup of cow's blood mixed in milk. Adrian spent the entire trip with brushes in hand, painting everything he saw. When they returned, his works were exhibited in the Knoedler Galleries in New York City, where each one commanded about $1,000.

Adrian branched into stage and film design again, creating costumes for the national company of *State of the Union* and the MGM film *Lovely to Look At*. The pressures of working for a studio proved too much for Adrian's workaholic nature; he suffered a heart attack shortly after completing the costumes for *Lovely to Look At*. Janet immediately took over

Janet and Adrian together during the 1940s.

as his watchdog and protector as he recovered; she also filled in for Adrian during the showing of his fall 1952 collection. This shows how much faith Adrian had in Janet, for he was a perfectionist and it was a daunting task for anyone to try to step into his shoes. The fall 1952 collection was the last for Adrian, Ltd; under doctor's orders, the Adrians closed it at the end of the year.

Suddenly free of all business responsibilities, and encouraged to relax, the Adrians began traveling and enjoying life. Janet dabbled in television, appearing in *Medallion Theatre*'s presentation of "Dear Cynthia" and the *Lux Video Theatre*'s presentation of *Two Dozen Roses*. She also presented the Best Actor Oscar to Gary Cooper (for *High Noon*) at the 25th Annual Academy Awards (John Wayne accepted on Cooper's behalf, as Cooper was on location and unable to attend). On a lark they accepted an invitation to the 1954 Brazilian International Film Festival in Rio de Janeiro. They were accompanied by a junket of celebrities, including Irene Dunne, Joan Fontaine, Robert Cummings, and Fred MacMurray. With their characteristic sense of curiosity, Adrian and Janet decided to accompany an acquaintance to the interior of Brazil: "So we arranged to fly in on an old DC-3 with crates of parrots and heaven-knows-what. We went up to the state of Goias and were absolutely smitten. So we bought a ranch," Janet recalled.[305]

The 200-acre fazenda became their idyllic retreat from civilization. Adrian designed their house and local workers built it from scratch, which Robin recalled as "kind of a nightmare." None of them were fluent in Portuguese, so Janet's Academy Award-winning acting abilities were called into play more than once, as she acted out Adrian's instructions for the building crew. Their home was a kind of jungle Eden; it had no electricity and only a wood stove for cooking; they did, however, relent to one modern convenience and installed indoor plumbing. They were unfazed by local wildlife, coexisting with snakes, armadillos, and an ocelot that wandered into the kitchen and scared their cook. This was a far cry from their Bel Air mansion on Bellagio Road, but it was the kind of adventurous life Janet enjoyed. Janet and Adrian spent much of their time painting, a hobby Janet had tried back in the 1930s, but took up again with renewed fervor. She was inspired by the hues of Brazilian nature: "The colors are magnificent down there. Every day we get a downpour of an hour or so and everything looks clean and washed. And the skies are gorgeous. The most beautiful blues you've ever seen."[306]

The Adrians' love for Brazil extended to their friends, who often braved the jungle wilds to enjoy their rustic hospitality. When Broadway star Mary Martin finished her year-long stint as Peter Pan, she and husband Richard Halliday came to see Janet and Adrian and fell in love with Brazil, too. Richard was particularly impressed with the land across the valley from the Adrians' home, on a hill. "If that's ever for sale, let me know," he informed Adrian. A year later, when Martin was appearing on Broadway in *The Skin of Our Teeth*, the property did come up for sale and the Hallidays bought it sight unseen.

Unfortunately, the Hallidays purchased the land from a woman who swindled them out of their money. When *Skin of Our Teeth* closed and they were free to visit their new acreage, they were obliged to stay with the Adrians for nearly six weeks while the legal entanglements were worked out. In the end, the Hallidays had to purchase a different farm, two miles away and accessible mostly by horseback. The Hallidays came to Brazil once a year, when Martin was between television shows or stage engagements. Robin became close friends with the Hallidays' daughter, Heller, who was about his age.

Janet had been friends with Richard Halliday before he married Mary Martin in 1940. Halliday was a story editor and later head of West Coast production for Paramount in the late 1930s when Janet was freelancing; she consulted him about a few roles before she went into retirement. Later, when Janet married Adrian and Halliday married Mary, they would visit the Adrians' home in Bel-Air. When Mary's film career did not take off, the Adrians advised the Hallidays to try Broadway, advice for which Mary Martin was forever grateful. Over the years, Janet and Mary became good friends, but their friendship, just like Janet's friendship with Margaret Lindsay, has come under close scrutiny. Stacy Wolf, in her book *A Problem Like Maria*, offers a typical examination:

> There is no "proof" that Gaynor and Martin were lovers. Nevertheless, the intimacy and interdependence of what was always referred to as their "uniquely close relationship" were extraordinary and are necessary to an account of Martin's married life.[307]

Wolf then describes her discovery, in one of Mary Martin's personal scrapbooks now in the Museum of the City of New York, a note from Bea Traub.[308] The note read, "Dear Mr. Halliday, Here are the black satin bras you ordered. I hope Janet likes them." This piece of paper is, to Wolf, "an object that accrues lesbian overtones,"[309] even though it is addressed to Richard Halliday—which would indicate, if anything, that Janet might have had a relationship with him. However, the truth is much simpler, much less sensational, and even a little poignant. In 1955, Janet underwent a mastectomy in Brazil, an operation that left her very ill for quite a few months. Robin thought, "It may have been an overreaction because she was a celebrity and they saw this – I can tell you today they would have done a lumpectomy, it would have been done and nobody would have thought again about it."[310] At the time, especially in rural Brazil, mastectomy bras were extremely difficult to come by. Richard Halliday handled all of Mary Martin's theatrical costume needs; of anyone, he would know a how to find a prosthetic bra for Janet. While Mary was appearing on Broadway in *Skin of Our Teeth*, Halliday found the bras and brought them to Brazil after the show closed. In the meantime, Adrian stayed with Janet, helping her recover.

Paul Gregory resolved the "was she or wasn't she" question in an interview with the author: "And then [Mary] became a big Broadway star and they stayed friendly and to try to tie them together is like trying to tie Holy Mary with Greta Garbo." In the A&E documentary about Janet's life, Paul further elaborated, "The Mary Martin rumor is absolutely ridiculous. I just know. I know my gal. I can tell you this much, if it had been true with Janet, she would not have hidden behind anything. She would have said, 'That's the way it is, old boy, take it or leave it.'" Given what we know about Janet's personality, that is an absolutely spot-on assessment.[311]

Breast cancer was not the only illness the Adrians' faced in Brazil. In 1956, Adrian developed a low-grade fever that would not abate. Paul Gregory insists that Adrian was bitten by an insect, and because of his weakened immune system and physical condition, was never really able to shake it off. Despite these illnesses, they loved Brazil and their lives followed a happy, tranquil pace: long stretches at the fazenda, followed by brief visits to Los Angeles to put Robin in school, or follow an interesting project.

One such project was *Bernadine*, a teen musical comedy that was Pat Boone's film debut, produced by her old studio, 20th Century-Fox. The studio was undergoing another period of change: Darryl Zanuck had just moved away to concentrate on production in Europe. So when Jennifer Jones, an actress and David O. Selznick's second wife, begged Janet to take the part as a personal favor, Janet relented. She played Mrs. Ruth Wilson, mother of Sanford Wilson (played by Dick Sargent, of *Bewitched* fame). It was her first film appearance in 19 years; but at 51, Janet looked even more beautiful than she had in *The Young at Heart*. Naturally, she was dressed by Adrian. Pat Boone was frankly enamored of his co-star:

> When she walked in, I was stunned, because I was expecting an older woman. And I was just enchanted because, man, if I hadn't been married, I might've wanted to date this woman! She just

Janet and her admirer, Pat Boone, in a still from *Bernadine*,
20th Century-Fox, 1957.

had a glow…she was like a combination of Shirley Temple, Brigitte Bardot and Grace Kelly. Very attractive, but perhaps protected by this tremendous ladylike quality she exuded, too. So you can't imagine truck drivers making a crude pass at her.[312]

Obviously marriage, motherhood and retirement agreed with Janet, and *Bernadine* was the last film she ever made. In the end, it was a light-hearted, fun role that netted Janet a tidy $50,000 and proved, once again, that she still had allure.

Janet then made her first foray into Broadway theatre, under Adrian's advice and support. She took the role of Julia Edmonds Tate, matriarch of a Midwestern family, in *The Midnight Sun*. She signed on for the part in July of 1959 and was set to go into rehearsals on October 12. Adrian signed on to do the costumes for the original Broadway production of *Camelot* at the same time so they could spend the winter in New York. In mid-September, Janet came to New York ahead of Adrian to start work on the play; it was the first time in their married life they had been apart. Robin and a college friend drove the Adrian car cross-country and arrived a few days before Adrian was set to join them; he was flying out within a few days for Switzerland. Robin stayed at the Adrians' tiny NYC apartment so he and Janet could have a good visit. At 6 a.m. the next morning, Janet received a phone call from a doctor in Los Angeles: Adrian had collapsed and was in critical condition. Robin remembers, as soon as Janet hung up the phone, she turned to him and said, "You'd better bring a dark suit if you don't have one there."[313] She knew—they knew—that Adrian was dying. He never fully recovered from his 1942 heart attack or the low-grade fever he contracted in Brazil. By the time they arrived in Los Angeles, it was too late. Adrian had died of a cerebral hemorrhage on September 13, 1959.

Convinced that work would be the only remedy for her grief, Janet continued rehearsals for *The Midnight Sun*. In an interview a month after his death, Janet said, "sometimes the grief washes up and overwhelms, but I am telling myself I am not the first widow and I will not be the last."[314] Friends like Irene Selznick (who was now a Broadway producer) and Mary Martin stayed close to Janet, trying to help as much as they could. The play opened in New Haven on November 4, and Janet was onstage wearing the costumes Adrian designed for her just before he died. The play was not a success, and closed in Boston on November 28 before ever making it to Broadway. In her grief, Janet gave away all the clothes Adrian had ever made for her. Decades later, when asked about Adrian, Janet still wept.

Over the years, the Adrians' marriage has been examined by several writers, many of whom conclude that it was nothing more than a "lavender cover-up." This is based on the supposition that Janet, because of her friendships with Margaret Lindsay and Mary Martin, was a lesbian, and that Adrian, because he was a fashion designer, was therefore (and stereotypically) gay. The assumption that Janet and Adrian's marriage was simply an arrangement to hide their own supposed sexual proclivities pointedly ignores all that Adrian and Janet did and were to each other throughout their married lives. Their child, their homes together in New York, Hollywood, and Brazil, their mutual support for each others' endeavors: these are the marks of a true marriage.

Janet's relationship with Adrian was "close, engrossing, and private":[315] the single-most selfish thing she ever did. She left films because she desired a life beyond the camera; she found that life with Adrian. Janet could have continued in motion pictures, especially after her alliance with Selznick International brought about a career renaissance that could have propelled her well into the 1940s, but she chose instead to leave her career and devote herself to being a wife and mother. While Laura had been a permanent fixture in Janet's first marriage to Lydell Peck, Janet left Laura behind when she married Adrian. Laura stayed in a comfortable beach house in Santa Monica, staffed with servants and paid for by her daughter. When Laura died in 1969, her passing was peaceful and quiet, thanks to the luxury and care Janet had always provided for her. Paul Gregory remembered, "she had her two martinis and succumbed. [She was] 94. And she was a wild, wonderful gal."[316]

Janet left that incredibly comfortable, secure lifestyle to live with Adrian on a remote plantation in Brazil, which, for the first year they lived there, had no electricity or running water. Most marriages would have been tested under such primitive conditions, but Janet and Adrian thrived. In Adrian, Janet found her soul mate, someone who shared her sense of adventure, her artistic ambitions, her need to live in the present, and her desire for privacy. They shared an intellectual curiosity and a drive for perfection. Their marriage lasted twenty years, during which Janet and Adrian lived together and traveled together constantly. They wanted to be alone, together. Their romance ended only with Adrian's death, which, as Robin said, "knocked her flat. It took her a very, very long time to get over it."[317]

Chapter Thirteen
Pristine Lives

"I can tell you that the reason why they have not been the subject of books and all this stuff is because their lives were so pristine. They had pristine lives."

– Paul Gregory

The remains of The Racquet Club stand shuttered behind a construction fence, mute and still. The wreckage tells nothing of the glamorous parties, the must-see fashion shows, the star-spangled radio broadcasts, the royalty and ex-presidents who lunched, or the celebrities that strolled under its latticed archway. The fate of the Racquet Club was the same for decades after Charlie left: every few years, a new company bought the Club with pie-in-the-sky plans of making it great again. At one point, it was going to be a gay and lesbian retirement community; a few years later, luxury condominiums. For years, whatever the plans, the end result was the same: the buyer went bankrupt, the fences went up, and the Racquet Club settled back to its silence and its memories. In 2009 the buildings were partially razed to make way for more lavish townhomes and condos. When that buyer went bankrupt, the demolition work halted in mid-destruction, leaving the lush and tranquil Racquet Club as cratered and marred as London after the Blitz. What is left barely warrants a stop on the star-seeking bus tours that wind through the village. The Racquet Club merited no plaque from the Historic Preservation Board of Palm Springs, marking it as historically significant; a designation that might have prevented its ultimate annihilation. All this, though one could argue it was Charlie Farrell and his Racquet Club that put Palm Springs on the map in the first place.

The Racquet Club was never the same after Charlie sold it in 1959; that much everyone can agree upon. It changed ownership three times in the ten years that Charlie was kept on as business manager. Howard Lapham, a modernist architect who designed homes in the Thunderbird Country Club and the Chi-Chi nightclub in Palm Springs, met Charlie at a party in 1961. His memory of the event was as sparkling as the champagne that was served. "Everyone was just bubbling over," he kept repeating as he recalled that informal meeting around the Racquet Club pool. Everyone cracked jokes, everyone had a few drinks. He recalled Charlie as "happy-go-lucky, likeable, the kind of guy who likes to mingle." Lapham also recalled that from the moment Charlie sold the Racquet Club and it went public, "it was all downhill from there."[318]

In 1930 when Charlie played Liliom, his co-star Rose Hobart characterized him as "this All-American boy who played a ukulele between takes."[319] Over time, however, the carousel of the play and the Racquet Club in Charlie's life evolved into uncanny parallels. When Liliom left the carousel, his former employer, Mme. Muskat, tried to lure him back. "The carousel is crowded just the same…without me?" Liliom asked, to which Mme. Muskat replied, "Crowded—yes. But not the same." Her response echoes how everyone felt when Charlie sold the club: it was still crowded, but never the same. Charlie's dynamic personality was behind the Club's success. "Out there is your art," Mme. Muskat urges Liliom, "the only thing you are fit for…You've always been happy at the carousel. It's a great life—pretty girls and beer and cigars and music—a great life and an easy one."[320] That too was the siren song of the Club: pretty women, music, and drinks. Charlie was lured back, time after time.

The Club had become so important, so integral to social life in Palm Springs that the social sea-

Cover of luncheon menu from the Racquet Club.

son did not officially begin until the ceremonial bell was rung at its grand opening every fall. Newspaper editors and all important press contacts were given special memberships to the Club. Vicki McDermott, who was Miss Palm Springs of 1961, still remembers the thrill when Charlie gave her classmates permission to use the Racquet Club's Olympic-sized pool for her senior class party. Even though Charlie no longer officially owned the Club, he came there every day, commandeering a corner booth in the bar, where people would stop and say hello, and even ask for his autograph. At that time, Charlie Farrell's identity was so synonymous with Palm Springs that he was known as Mister Palm Springs. Frank Bogert, who became mayor of Palm Springs in 1958, went to a mayoral conference in Hawaii only to be scolded by one of the others in attendance. "You are not the mayor of Palm Springs," the man chided Bogert. "There will only ever be one mayor of Palm Springs, and he is Charlie Farrell."[321]

Charlie's success in television and his freedom from business responsibilities at the Club revitalized him. Now in his late fifties, still handsome, distinguished, and sportive, he began a long-term affair with Diana Lewis Powell, known as "Mousie" because of her diminutive stature. Diana was pretty and blonde, nearly twenty years his junior, and twenty-seven years younger than her husband, the actor William Powell. Diana came

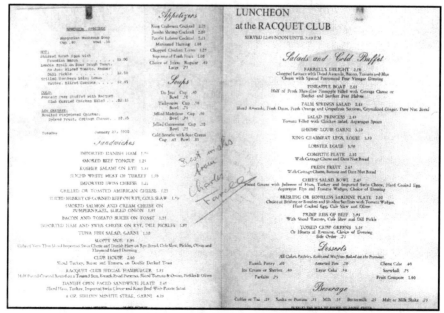

Inside sections of the luncheon menu, autographed by Charlie Farrell.

William and Mousie Powell talk with friends at the Racquet Club.

from a vaudeville background and entered films in the mid-1930s; she is best remembered today for her role as Daphne Fowler (the debutante) in *Andy Hardy Meets Debutante* (1940). Diana met Powell when she was on a photo shoot for MGM: the publicity department used Powell's pool for the shoot, and Diana was the bathing suit model. After the shoot ended, Powell asked Diana to dinner. After a lightning-quick courtship that lasted all of three weeks, they were married in Warm Springs, Nevada, on January 6, 1940. "He was mad about her," Powell's frequent co-star and movie wife, Myrna Loy, recalled. "We were all properly skeptical, predicting that a marriage would never last. Well, it did last, until his death, and she was a wonderful wife to him."[322]

Diana continued to work in films for a few more years, until she had an honest discussion with Powell about the roles she was being given. "I'll tell you frankly," Powell said, "they will never make you a star."[323] With that, Diana renounced her career to focus on her marriage, telling the press, "My marriage means all the world to me. It means much more than a career. I've been in show business all my life, but this is more important to me than anything else."[324] In time, Mousie Powell became a popular hostess and famed sportswoman, enjoying a whirlwind lifestyle of tennis games, golfing and bowling tournaments. The Powells moved to Palm Springs in the mid-1940s, settling in a Spanish Revival-style home at 383 Vereda Norte. The Powells naturally migrated to the Racquet Club to socialize and play—everyone did. Indeed, Charlie and Mousie probably fell in love over tennis.

Charlie and Mousie, together at the Racquet Club.

Their affair was public knowledge and lasted for at least two decades, a relationship that was the closest thing Charlie ever had to a second marriage. One Palm Springs matron recalled, with a hint of jealousy, Diana's enviable routine of spending her days with Charlie Farrell, and her nights with William Powell. Powell had battled colo-rectal cancer in 1938, enduring a primitive and embarrassing treatment that eradicated the cancer; however, he suffered from ill health and struggled with prostate issues for the rest of his life. Powell took a pragmatic view of Mousie's affair with Charlie: he was happy that she found someone he trusted and liked, who could be both sexual partner and tennis partner for his beloved Mousie. Virginia Valli did not take the same view of the affair: she was angered and hurt, but still inexplicably, stayed in the marriage. Surely by now, Virginia understood that Charlie was unfulfilled in their marriage. Why she never granted him the divorce he sought remains a mystery.

Mysterious, too, was the sale of the Racquet Club in 1959, an announcement that "was like Queen Elizabeth telling the Cockneys she was renting out Buckingham Palace."[325] True, it freed Charlie and Virginia from endless business responsibilities. It gave Charlie enough capital to invest in resort properties in Jamaica: along with Prince Rainier and Princess Grace of Monaco, Charlie backed the newly built Reef Hotel. But when Charlie was deprived of his art, whatever the medium—be it film, television, or the Club—he became despondent. Just like Liliom, who listened to the far-off music of the carousel and grew "gentle...he gets thoughtful and very quiet, and his big eyes stare straight ahead...he's unhappy because he isn't working. It preys on his mind."[326] An intriguing piece of the puzzle emerged in a 1960 interview with Ralph Bellamy:

> Farrell, always a "Good-time Charlie," took a drink any time a member invited him. In time, he turned into an alcoholic. But there is a happy ending. Farrell, one-time screen lover of Janet Gaynor, joined Alcoholics Anonymous and is now one of its most ardent crusaders in Palm Springs. He never takes a drink. He also sold the Racquet Club for a million dollars cash plus a ten-year contract at $10,000 a year to continue as its manager.[327]

Charlie had started, as many people do, as a social drinker, imbibing only at parties. Of course, every day was a party at the Racquet Club and as its host, Charlie felt the pressure to keep up with his guests. After the war, in an attempt to establish sanity and privacy, Charlie and Virginia moved out of Farrell House at the Club and built a home at the corner of Via Miraleste and Tachevah, over a mile away. According to legend, Charlie had the stoplight on the corner installed when he was on the city council, so he would know where to turn when walking home drunk. Frank Bogert recalled that Charlie would get so plastered that he

Good time Charlie: Off the wagon, in a whiskey advertisement, circa 1971.

would peer in windows, trying to figure out which house was his. As a joke, Bogert began having Charlie tailed by a detective, as though he were a peeping tom, which drove Charlie mad. Finally, Virginia took Frank aside and asked him to call off the joke, saying, "Charlie can't figure out what he's done, and he's afraid he murdered someone or something."[328] When Charlie sold the Racquet Club, it may have been part of a serious, thoughtful effort at sobriety. How long Charlie remained sober is, unfortunately, questionable.

During the 1960s, Charlie lost, in quick succession, his father, his sister, and his wife. David died in 1965, and Ruth in 1966, which was the same year Virginia suffered a stroke that left her housebound and dependent. She died on September 24, 1968, of the lingering effects of the stroke. Watching Virginia struggle for those last two years and then watching her die left Charlie with an overwhelming sense of guilt and remorse. Their marriage had never exactly been happy, but it had endured. Later, he confessed to a reporter, "Eight years ago she died. I never realized how much she'd done for me until she was gone."[329] The pressure of still trying to remain, on the surface at least, a "Good-time Charlie" for his guests and for Mousie, while also dealing with the losses of his family and his wife brought Charlie back to the bottle. When his contract as manager of the Racquet Club ended, he retreated to his home on Tachevah, to the air-conditioned hermitage he rarely left, save for a public appearance with Janet Gaynor.

After Adrian died, Janet struggled for some time, trying to find happiness and meaning in her life once more. She attended the opening night of *Camelot* and wept as she saw Adrian's glorious costumes realized. She found a new designer, California sportswear designer Jo Lathwood, whose clean lines and unexpected use of textiles echoed Adrian's style, but she still wore a neckerchief of cotton gingham her husband designed for her. She attended art openings and spent time with Robin, who left his studies in Paris and pursued a bachelor's degree in History from Stanford. After a while, she was wooed by long-time friend Paul Gregory, a theatrical producer who had purchased the Hawaiian house to which Janet and Laura retreated often in the 1930s. Gregory had gained fame throughout the 1950s for revitalizing the career of Charles Laughton, with a series of "readings" that toured the country. These readings were brilliantly simple, featuring Laughton with a cast of other renowned actors, including Charles Boyer, Cedric Hardwicke, and Agnes Moorehead (*Don Juan In Hell*), or Tyrone Power, Dame Judith Anderson, and Raymond Massey (*John Brown's Body*). It was the vanguard of minimalist theatre, featuring no sets or costumes, just fine actors reading magnificent words in stripped-down auditoriums. Gregory also produced Laughton's directorial film debut, *The Night of the Hunter* (1955) and the film adaptation of Norman Mailer's novel *The Naked and the Dead* (1958). While on location in Panama for *The Naked and the Dead*, Gregory visited the Adrians' farm in Brazil, "but I had no idea at that time that I would ever marry Janet. It was just that they were just my good friends."[330]

A few years after Adrian's death, Paul invited Janet back to her old Hawaiian home. Adrian had never visited Janet's home in Hawaii, so Paul "suggested that Janet come over and that she wouldn't be seeing [Adrian] every place she looked. So she did and it just so happened that we stayed six months. We fell in love and got married and it's as simple as that."[331] They were married in a ceremony the press called "rapid even by Hollywood standards," flying into Las Vegas on December 24, 1964. They obtained a license, had the ceremony performed at the county courthouse, and left for Los Angeles all within an hour.[332] Robin, who had known Paul since he was a child, thought the marriage "was terrific. I was happy that she had found somebody that she was happy with and I always thought he was a terrific guy so it worked out great."[333] Of his new family, Paul recalled, "Robin is my dearest friend and [so were] Adrian and Janet. Robin has both of their most sterling qualities and Adrian was an absolute angel of a man. I just loved Adrian. And he was talented to the point of exasperation. I've never seen such talent."[334]

Paul called his wife "an astonishing human being, self-fulfilled," and together they embarked on a life that embraced change, exciting new opportunities, and travel. They kept the fazenda in Brazil and the beach house in Hawaii, and added a working ranch in Palm Springs, "complete with cattle, burros, geese, ducks...four dogs, a parrot, and a macaw."[335] While at the ranch, Janet indulged her passion for painting, often working for six or seven hours a day. She painted impressionistic still life works, in which she tried to capture "the blues and greens of a cauliflower leaf, the ruffled edge of a lettuce, the sheer voluptuousness of a cabbage—and flowers, the subtlety of them, the light on them, around them and through them."[336] Her dedication paid off in a series of five exhibitions with the Wally Findlay Galleries in New York, Palm Springs, and Chicago. Such luminaries as Andy Warhol, Heller Halliday DeMerritt, former co-star Paulette Goddard, Lillian Gish, Betty Furness, Sylvia Miles, and Slim Keith, snapped up paintings at $450 to $1,000 each. Janet

Glory of Summer, Janet Gaynor, 1970s.

delved further into her artistic side after her success in art, branching into gourmet cooking. Her cuisine was such a hit that she marketed oven-ready stuffed squab and boneless chicken under the "Janet Gaynor Singing Trees Ranch" brand of gourmet frozen foods.

Throughout the 1970s, Janet received renewed attention and accolades. She appeared in Kevin Brownlow's documentary series *Hollywood* to discuss her work with F. W. Murnau. She was a presenter at the 1971 Academy Awards for Best Director, and at the 1978 Academy Awards for Best Actress. In 1979, she and Mary Martin were awarded the Brazilian National Order of the Southern Cross, for promoting friendship between the United States and Brazil.

Janet's life expanded during the 1970s and 1980s, embracing and charming an entirely new generation of fans. Her status as the first Best Actress Academy Award winner firmly established her place in film history. But Janet also guarded her rank closely, just as she had at Fox in 1930. She refused to dwell on the past and often said, "I can't think of anything more boring than sitting around showing my old movies to friends after dinner,"[337] but staunchly defended all her years of work by standing up for herself and her career. When she was approached to present an Oscar at the Fiftieth Annual Academy Awards, she was offered to present the Oscar for Best Costume Design. "I will present the Oscar for Best Actress, or none at all," Janet replied, and the Academy surrendered. Janet gracefully bestowed Diane Keaton with the Best Actress Oscar for *Annie Hall*. In 1980, she appeared in the Broadway production of *Harold and Maude*, the darkly humorous existentialist romance between the 79-year-old Maude and the suicidal 19-year-old Harold. Maude's character resonated with Janet: echoing her toughness, feistiness, and her celebration of life. As Janet explained, "Maude brings this young boy who's caught in his own personal kind of prison and helps him learn to enjoy and appreciate life, rather than throw it all away."[338]   Unfortunately, the play folded after only thirteen previews and four performances. Critics praised Janet's performance as "charming and creditable" but derided the play's "laboriously cutesy" style. Unfazed,

Candid snapshot of Janet and Paul Gregory together, early 1980s.
Courtesy of Gina LoBiondo.

Janet made a guest appearance on *The Love Boat* with former co-star Lew Ayres as "The Frugal Pair," and then delved back into theatre, appearing as Ethel Thayer in *On Golden Pond* at the World Playhouse in Chicago.

While Janet's life widened, Charlie's contracted until only a close circle of friends, a live-in maid named Mildred Gamache, and a companion named Yvonne Welles remained. For a while, he still went up to the Racquet Club but in time, those visits ended. He made a few appearances at benefit screenings of his films, but only if Janet shared the stage. In time, those public appearances ceased. He spoke to Janet over the phone quite often, but hardly ever saw her. As in *7th Heaven*, when Chico draws his strength from Diane, Charlie drew from Janet's strength and vitality. In his last public interview, Charlie recalled Janet with his usual tenderness, saying, "She was lovely. She *is* lovely." Then, perhaps remembering *Liliom* and Rose Hobart, he added, "I can't say that about all the leading ladies. Some of them were bitches."[339]

Charlie's decline could be blamed on a relapse into alcoholism, which started anew after Virginia's death. Paul Gregory put it bluntly but not unkindly when he said, "[Charlie's] seclusion was his drink." His depression was certainly not helped by an unflattering *Los Angeles Times* profile that appeared in 1977. Using the "hipper-than-thou" vernacular that many 1970s journalists adopted towards fading film stars, the reporter characterized Charlie:

> He has more time than ever before in his memory. He twitches his toothbrush mustache and speaks with reverence about sleeping, reading, and watching copious amounts of television. Farrell is still a tall cuss, broader at the shoulder than at the beam and not bent by the years. His calves are stringy and bone-thin, forcing a shuffle out of the same legs that once Sturm and Dranged all over the silver screen. His shock of pure white hair shows no sign of receding irreparably, but his eyes are rimmed in liquid these days and don't pierce like a sheik's anymore.[340]

Then, driving a final nail into the coffin, the interview concludes with Charlie looking over a picture book that featured his films:

> [The stills] show the sneers and leers that made him a ladies' man before sound tracks ran his dashing voice up an octave higher than the female imagination.[341]

Charlie in the late 1970s. Photograph by H. Robert Case.

Of course, Charlie's career did not end because of his voice, but unlike Janet, Charlie was unwilling to fight for his place in film history. He was even reluctant to defend his place in Palm Springs history. His last public interview was with the *Desert Sun* (no more Norma Desmond-esque exposes in the *Los Angeles Times*, thank you very much), in which he was asked what he felt he had done for Palm Springs. Bruce Fessier, who conducted the interview, remembered Charlie's modesty and embarrassment, as he turned to Yvonne Welles and told her, "I can't blow my own horn. You'll have to tell them for me."[342]

Within the next four years, Charlie's isolation deepened, shutting out his two closest friends: Mousie Powell and Frank Bogert. Frank remembered going to see Charlie often, only to be ignored as Charlie watched television. During his last visit, Charlie turned the TV set up so loud, Frank could not talk over it. After a few choice words, Frank left, never seeing Charlie again. Mousie Powell held out even longer, but after being constantly rebuffed, she too got the message. Charlie finalized their breakup by significantly cutting her share of his estate. In his original will, signed March 9, 1982, Charlie intended to leave Mousie $50,000. In a codicil to the will, added October 17, 1984, this amount was reduced to $5,000. (A few months prior to that, William Powell had died of a heart attack.) Someone, possibly Yvonne Welles, sent occasional bulletins to Charlie's family back East, informing them of his deteriorating condition. After 1984, Charlie became bedridden. He rarely left the house and saw only his handful of faithful retainers.

Over the Labor Day weekend in 1982, Janet and Paul traveled to Jonesy's town, San Francisco, to appear on the PBS television show, *Over Easy*. The show featured such famous guest stars as Cyd Charisse, Patti Page, and Vivian Vance; the topics covered included aging and the plights and rights of senior citizens. Mary Martin was hosting the show that season. Though Martin had a home in Rancho Mirage, the Gregorys rarely saw her: as always, Mary had a busy schedule of performances and lived a jet-setting lifestyle. *Over Easy* was an excuse for a happy reunion of close friends.

The reunion quickly became a nightmare when Janet, Mary, Paul, and Mary's manager and companion Ben Washer,[343] piled into a taxicab for a quick trip to Chinatown for Sunday night dinner. Paul sat in front next to the driver, and Mary, Janet, and Ben sat in the backseat. No one buckled their seat belts. At the intersection of California and Franklin, the taxi was violently broadsided by a van that ran the red light. The impact spun the cab around and hurled it against a tree. Ben Washer was killed almost instantly. Both of Paul's legs were broken and two of his ribs were fractured. Mary suffered a punctured right lung, two fractured ribs, pelvic fractures, and a bruised kidney. Ronald Drury, the cab driver, suffered minor injuries. Of the survivors, Janet's injuries were by far the worst. She caught most of Ben Washer's weight in the crash (his knee actually hit her abdomen) and suffered from 11 fractured ribs, a broken collar bone, multiple pelvic fractures, a perforated bladder, and extensive internal bleeding. The driver of the van, Robert Cato, had a blood alcohol limit exceeding .10, the legal limit in California at the time. Cato and his passenger, John McCue, were treated for minor injuries before Cato was taken away in handcuffs from the hospital. He was charged with vehicular manslaughter, felony reckless driving, speeding, felony drunken driving, and running a red light. Audaciously, he entered a "not guilty" plea and was held on $3,500 bail.

Robin, who was on a camping trip over the Labor Day holiday, had no idea that the accident had occurred. He was listening to a book on tape and heard none of the news updates on his drive home. When Robin pulled into the driveway, he was met by his mother-in-law:

> I thought "That's kind of strange. I wonder what she's doing here." And she of course knew about what had happened, also realized that we may not have heard about it so she reserved us plane tickets and all that to go up to San Francisco. That's how I heard about it. She heard about it through the news like everybody else did.[344]

Fortunately, Robin was spared the sight of the accident scene, which was broadcast in ghastly detail on every news network. Reporters and cameramen crowded around the mangled cab, its back windshield blown out, and in some reports, the back of Janet's tiny, vulnerable blonde head could be seen through its broken glass. Sirens wailed in the distance, and passersby gawked at the gruesome tableau. Charlie, who kept his television on round-the-clock, surely saw the entire event unfold while he was bedridden and unable to do anything. While Janet underwent five hours of lifesaving surgery at San Francisco General, requiring ten pints of blood, Robin and his wife endured the agonizing plane ride, not sure if Janet would make it through.

She did, with her usual blend of toughness and optimism. She remained at San Francisco General for four months (Martin and Gregory were discharged after ten days), endearing herself to the astonished physicians and nurses who cared for her. "I am grateful for all the prayers and thousands of letters, cards, and wires I have received during my convalescence," Janet said as she left the hospital. "The outpouring of concern from around the world has been overwhelming." Although Janet was well enough to go home to Singing Trees, she endured six more operations between 1982 and 1984.

In March 1983, Robert Cato stood trial for vehicular manslaughter in the death of Ben Washer. Cato's attorney, Thomas Horne, argued that Cato had not been drinking heavily but had been distraught over a business deal and temporarily lost his reason. After deliberating for six hours, the jury returned a "guilty" verdict. In sentencing Cato, Judge Raymond Arata accused him of "real callousness," adding, "It was as if you took a gun and shot it down Franklin Street." Arata then sentenced Cato to three years in prison which, unfortunately, was the maximum penalty he could receive at the time.[345]

Even though Janet grew progressively weaker as the surgeries took a toll on her body, she graciously attended the American Cinema Awards tribute in her honor in 1983, and the San Diego Festival of the Arts tribute in March 1984. Janet finally succumbed to pneumonia on September 14, 1984, an illness that was directly linked to the trauma she suffered in the 1982 car crash. Her attending physician, Dr. Bart Apfelbaum, told the press, "All through her illness, she maintained a wonderful attitude and was truly loved by everyone who helped take care of her." As Janet had requested, there was no public memorial service. She was buried in the Hollywood Forever cemetery in Los Angeles, next to Adrian. In loving homage to Paul, her simple tombstone reads "Janet Gaynor Gregory, 1906-1984."

Charlie died on May 6, 1990 after a long battle with arteriosclerosis, which culminated in a heart attack. So complete was his isolation that, when interviewed for this book, Paul Gregory insisted Charlie had died before Janet. In some ways, he had. No accolades or warm remembrances followed Charlie's death; indeed, following his dying wish, Charlie's caretakers buried him next to Virginia Valli in the Welwood Murray Cemetery in Palm Springs and then, a week later, notified the press that he was gone. His tombstone, as simple as Janet's, reads "Charles D. Farrell, 1990"—no allusions to his film or television career, or his heritage as Mr. Palm Springs. His entire estate, minus a few stipends for Mousie, Mildred Gamache, and a few close friends, was left to his caretaker, Yvonne Welles. Charlie's extended family back East received no share of his wealth.

Janet always regarded her career as secondary to her life, but also fiercely protected her legacy. She answered her copious amounts of fan mail personally and by hand. In 1982, just prior to that fatal accident, she wrote to a young fan who was an aspiring actress:

It is wonderful that you have definite goals to work toward. You should spend your energy and time working towards them and let the frustrations go. There is a lot of wonderful life to be had out there so relax and go get it. Know that you have every good wish of mine.[346]

Janet imparted that radiant *joie de vivre* to her friends, family and admirers throughout her life. It was the same energy she had tried to share with Charlie in 1938, when she scolded him for being a playboy and told him to find another artistic outlet. Janet discerned in Charlie that weakness that was always braced by hard work or artistic achievement; perhaps this weakness, plus his womanizing reputation were the flaws that prevented her from marrying him back in 1929. She foresaw that the Racquet Club could not remain his only purpose in life, without grave consequences—and she was right.

Janet was, as Daniel Selznick recalled, "Someone who one imagined had to fight all her life to be taken seriously,"[347] and she did. Her fight started when she changed her name from Lolly to Janet, and continued through her legal stand-offs with all of her studios and even her refusal to present the Best Costume Design Oscar at the 1978 Academy Awards. She was an iron fist in a velvet glove, the "Original Platinum Butterfly" as Paul called her. She was also, as Daniel Selznick remembered, "a natural beauty, considerate, genuinely interested in thoughts and ideas of others, sweet but not sickly sweet: in short, a woman of intelligence and character."[348]

Charlie accomplished remarkable things when he knew he was working towards something worthwhile or good. He knew it when he worked with directors like James Cruze, Victor Fleming, and especially Frank Borzage, and when making *My Little Margie*. He knew it throughout his selfless wartime service. He knew it when he was working for the betterment of his adopted hometown. There was a sweetness and an affability about Charlie that endeared him to almost everyone he encountered. It was his charm that set the Racquet Club's tone and made it a world-famous resort. William Powell even entrusted him with his darling Mousie: that's how downright likable Charlie was. At the same time, Charlie was too humble to make a stand for himself in a world that pivots on self-promotion and aggrandizement. Tragically, Charlie died believing he was alone and forgotten.

But he wasn't. In the 1990s, a committee that included Diana Lewis Powell commissioned a bronze statue of Charlie from artist George Montgomery. The statue, which shows Charlie playing tennis, now greets arriving visitors at the Palm Springs airport. In 1992, Charlie was one of the first VIPs to receive a star on the Palm Springs Walk of Stars. This complements, of course, the two stars he received on the Hollywood Walk of Fame, one for his work in films, the other for his work in television. His final, and most valuable tribute, came from his former best friend, Frank Bogert. He had not seen or spoken to Charlie in years, but when asked by the author in 2006 to describe Charlie in one word, his eyes suddenly filled with tears. "*Simpático*," he replied. "Do you know what that word means? In Spanish, it is the nicest thing you can say about a person. Charlie was *simpático*."

Together, the girl who didn't want fame but was forced into the spotlight, and the boy who sought fame but never had enough, made screen history. Starting with that fateful pairing in *7th Heaven*, their chemistry dazzled film audiences around the world, in a dozen different pictures. It weathered lovers' trysts, the advent of sound, broken contracts, broken engagements, creative differences, studio takeovers, marriages, and divorce. As one journalist put it, "They set a new standard for screen romance, gave us love scenes which for sincerity and spirituality have never been equaled." Though both feared that their screen work lost its relevance over time, they were wrong. Time has not dimmed the radiant light they project onscreen.

Their off-screen romance evolved from idealistic first love to an enduring friendship that lasted for decades—a friendship which they both needed and cultivated. Their private lives "finished the unfinished romance on-screen," and gave audiences, admirers, and friends the vicarious pleasure of watching both unfold. "Long may it last, this delightful double life," proclaimed one fan magazine, an affirmation which all Gaynor-Farrell fans, past and present, answer with an amen.

Walking away from it all: Janet and Charlie together on the Fox lot, circa 1932.

Janet Gaynor Filmography

Because the complete extent of Janet Gaynor's unbilled or extra parts may never be fully determined, this filmography lists her billed roles, beginning in 1926. Whenever possible, both premiere and release dates are given. Film length is given in either reels or minutes, according to the information available at this time.

The Johnstown Flood, directed by Irving Cummings. Starring George O'Brien, Florence Gilbert, Janet Gaynor, Paul Panzer, George Harris, Paul Nicholson, Anders Randolph, Max Davidson, Walter Perry, and Sid Jordan. Clark Gable, Carole Lombard, and Florence Lawrence appear as unbilled extras. Scenario by Edfrid Bingham and Robert Lloyd. Camera by George Schneiderman. Produced by William Fox, Fox Films. Released February 28, 1926. 6 reels.

The Shamrock Handicap, directed by John Ford. Starring Janet Gaynor, Leslie Fenton, J. Farrell MacDonald, Louis Payne, Claire McDowell, Willard Louis, Andy Clark, Georgie Harris, and Ely Reynolds. Scenario by John Stone from a story by Peter B. Kyne. Camera by George Schneidermann. Produced by William Fox, Fox Films. Released May 2, 1926. 6 reels.

The Blue Eagle, directed by John Ford. Starring George O'Brien, Janet Gaynor, William Russell, Margaret Livingston, Robert Edeson, Philip Ford, David Butler, Lew Short, Ralph Sipperly, and Jerry Madden. Scenario by L.G. Rigby from the story *The Lord's Referee* by Gerald Beaumont. Camera by George Schneidermann. Produced by William Fox, Fox Films. Released September 12, 1926. 7 reels.

The Midnight Kiss, directed by Irving Cummings. Starring Richard Walling, Janet Gaynor, George Irving, Doris Lloyd, Gene Cameron, Gladys McConnell, Herbert Prior, and Tempe Piggott. Scenario by Alfred A. Cohn from the play *Pigs* by Ann Morrison, Patterson McNutt, and John Golden. Camera by Abe Fried. Produced by William Fox, Fox Films. Released October 10, 1926. 5 reels.

The Return of Peter Grimm, directed by Victor Schertzinger. Starring Alec B. Francis, John Roche, Janet Gaynor, Richard Walling, John St. Polis, Lionel Belmore, Elizabeth Patterson, Bodil Rosing, Mickey McBan, Florence Gilbert, and Sammy Cohen. Scenario by Bradley King from the play by David Belasco. Camera by Glenn MacWilliams. Produced by William Fox, Fox Films. Released November 7, 1926. 7 reels.

7th Heaven (see combined filmography).

Two Girls Wanted, directed by Alfred E. Green. Starring Janet Gaynor, Glenn Tryon, Ben Bard, Joseph Cawthorn, Billy Bletcher, Doris Lloyd, Pauline Neff, and C.L. Sherwood. Scenario by Randall Faye and Seton I. Miller from the play by Gladys Unger. Camera by George Schneidermann. Produced by William Fox, Fox Films. Released September 11, 1927. 7 reels.

Sunrise: a Song of Two Humans, directed by F.W. Murnau. Starring George O'Brien, Janet Gaynor, Margaret Livingston, Bodil Rosing, Ralph Sipperly, Jane Winton, Arthur Housman, and Eddie Boland. Scenario by Carl Mayer from the story *Die Reise nach Tilsit* by Hermann Sudermann. Camera by Karl Struss and Charles Rosher. Produced by William Fox, Fox Films. Premiered September 23, 1927, released November 4, 1927. 9 reels.

Street Angel (see combined filmography).

4 Devils, directed by F.W. Murnau. Starring Janet Gaynor, Charles Morton, Barry Norton, Anders Randolph, Nancy Drexel, Mary Duncan, Philippe de Lacy, Anita Louise, Anne Shirley (as Dawn O'Day), Jack Parker, J. Farrell MacDonald, Claire McDowell,

Andre Cheron, George Davis, and Wesley Lake. Scenario by Carl Mayer, Marion Orth, and Berthold Viertel from the story *De Fire Djaevle* by Herman Bing. Camera by Ernest Palmer, L. William O'Connell. Art direction by William S. Darling. Produced by William Fox, Fox Films. Released October 3, 1928. 120 minutes.

Lucky Star (see combined filmography).

Christina, directed by William K. Howard. Starring Janet Gaynor, Charles Morton, Rudolph Schildkraut, Harry Cording, and Lucy Dorraine. Scenario by Marion Orth from the story by Tristram Tupper. Camera by Lucien N. Andriot. Produced by William Fox, Fox Films. Released December 15, 1929. 73 minutes.

Sunny Side Up (see combined filmography).

Happy Days (see combined filmography).

High Society Blues (see combined filmography).

The Man Who Came Back (see combined filmography).

Daddy Long Legs, directed by Alfred Santell. Starring Janet Gaynor, Warner Baxter, Una Merkel, John Arledge, Claude Gillingwater, Kathlyn Williams, Effie Ellsler, Kendall McComas, Elizabeth Patterson, Louise Closser Hale, and Sheila Bromley. Scenario by S.N. Behrman and Sonya Levien, from the novel by Jean Webster. Camera by Lucien N. Andriot. Produced by Fox Film Corporation. Released June 5, 1931. 9 reels.

Merely Mary Ann (see combined filmography).

Delicious (see combined filmography).

The First Year (see combined filmography).

Tess of the Storm Country (see combined filmography).

State Fair, directed by Henry King. Starring Janet Gaynor, Will Rogers, Lew Ayres, Louise Dresser, Sally Eilers, Norman Foster, Frank Craven, Victor Jory, and Frank Melton. Scenario by Sonya Levien and Paul Green, from the novel by Philip Stong. Camera by Hal Mohr. Set decoration by Duncan Cramer. Produced by Fox Films Corporation. Premiered January 26, 1933, released February 10, 1933. 10 reels.

Adorable, directed by William Dieterle. Starring Janet Gaynor, Henri Garat, C. Aubrey Smith, Herbert Mundin, Blanche Friderici, Hans Heinrich von Twardowski, and James A. Marcus. Scenario by George Marion, Jr. and Jane Storm, from the story *Ihre Hoheit Befiehlt* by Robert Liebmann, Paul Frank, and Billy Wilder. Camera by John F. Seitz. Art direction by Gordon Wiles. Produced by Fox Films Corporation. Released May 19, 1933. 87 minutes.

Paddy, the Next Best Thing, directed by Harry Lachman. Starring Janet Gaynor, Warner Baxter, Walter Connolly, Harvey Stephens, Margaret Lindsay, J. M. Kerrigan, Fiske O'Hara, Merle Tottenham, and Roger Imhof. Scenario by Edwin J. Burke and Gertrude Paige. Camera by John F. Seitz. Art direction by Gordon Wiles. Produced by Fox Films Corporation. Premiered August 25, 1933, released September 1, 1933. 8 reels.

Carolina, directed by Henry King. Starring Janet Gaynor, Lionel Barrymore, Robert Young, Henrietta Crosman, Richard Cromwell, Mona Barrie, Stepin Fetchit, Russell Simpson, Ronnie Cosby, Jackie Cosbey, Almeda Fowler, Alden 'Stephen' Chase, and Shirley Temple. Scenario by Reginald Berkeley, from the play *The House of Connelly* by Paul Green. Camera by Hal Mohr. Produced by Fox Films Corporation. Released February 2, 1934. 85 minutes.

Change of Heart (see combined filmography).

Servants' Entrance, directed by Frank Lloyd, animated sequence directed by Walt Disney. Starring Janet Gaynor, Lew Ayres, Ned Sparks, Walter Connolly, Louise Dresser, G. P. Huntley, Astrid Allwyn, Sig Ruman, John Qualen, Catherine Doucet, Greta Meyer, Dorothy Christy, Josephine Whittell, Jerry Stewart, Ruth Marion, Harold

Minjir, Anne Gibbons, and Buster Phelps. Scenario by Samson Raphaelson, from the novel by Sigrid Boo. Camera by Hal Mohr. Produced by Winfield R. Sheehan, Fox Film Corporation. Released September 24, 1934. 10 reels.

One More Spring, directed by Henry King. Starring Janet Gaynor, Warner Baxter, Walter King, Jane Darwell, Roger Imhof, Grant Mitchell, Rosemary Ames, John Qualen, Dick Foran, Astrid Allwyn, Lee Kohlmar, and Stepin Fetchit. Scenario by Edwin J. Burke, from the novel by Robert Nathan. Camera by John F. Seitz. Art direction by Jack Otterson. Produced by Winfield R. Sheehan, Fox Film Corporation. Premiered February 12, 1935, released February 15, 1935. 9 reels.

The Farmer Takes a Wife, directed by Victor Fleming. Starring Janet Gaynor, Henry Fonda, Charles Bickford, Slim Summerville, Jane Withers, Andy Devine, Roger Imhof, Margaret Hamilton, Siegfried Rumann, John Qualen, Kitty Kelly, and Robert Gleckler. Scenario by Edwin J. Burke, from the play *Rome Haul* by Marc Connelly and Frank B. Elser, from the novel *Rome Haul* by Walter D. Edmonds. Camera by John F. Seitz. Produced by Winfield R. Sheehan, Fox Film Corporation. Released June 11, 1935. 94 minutes.

Small Town Girl, directed by William A. Wellman. Starring Janet Gaynor, Robert Taylor, Binnie Barnes, Andy Devine, Lewis Stone, Elizabeth Patterson, Frank Craven, James Stewart, Isabel Jewell, Charley Grapewin, Nella Walker, Robert Greig, Edgar Kennedy, Willie Fung. Scenario by John Lee Mahin, Frances Goodrich, Albert Hackett, and Edith Fitzgerald, from the novel by Ben Ames Williams. Camera by Oliver T. Marsh and Charles Rosher. Art direction by Cedric Gibbons. Produced by Hunt Stromberg, Metro-Goldwyn-Mayer (MGM). Released April 10, 1936. 11 reels.

Ladies in Love, directed by Edward H. Griffith. Starring Janet Gaynor, Loretta Young, Constance Bennett, Simone Simon, Don Ameche, Paul Lukas, Tyrone Power, Alan Mowbray, Wilfrid Lawson, J. Edward Bromberg, Virginia Field, Frank Dawson, Egon Brecher, Vesey O'Davoren, John Bleifer, and Eleanor Wesselhoeft. Scenario by Melville Baker, from the play by Ladislaus Bus-Fekete. Camera by

Hal Mohr. Art direction by William S. Darling. Premiered October 9, 1936, released October 28, 1936. 10 reels.

A Star Is Born, directed by William A. Wellman. Starring Janet Gaynor, Frederic March, Adolphe Menjou, May Robson, Andy Devine, Lionel Stander, Owen Moore, Peggy Wood, Elizabeth Jenns, Edgar Kennedy, J. C. Nugent, and Guinn 'Big Boy' Williams. Scenario by Dorothy Parker, Alan Campbell, and Robert Carson, from a story by Robert Carson and William A. Wellman. Camera by W. Howard Greene. Art direction by Lyle Wheeler. Premiered April 20, 1937 (Los Angeles) and April 22, 1937 (New York), and released April 27, 1937. 12 reels.

Three Loves Has Nancy, directed by Richard Thorpe. Starring Janet Gaynor, Robert Montgomery, Franchot Tone, Guy Kibbee, Claire Dodd, Reginald Owen, Cora Witherspoon, Emma Dunn, Charley Grapewin, Lester Matthews, Grady Sutton, Mary Forbes, and Grant Withers. Scenario by David Hertz, George Oppenheimer, Bella Spewack, and Samuel Spewack, from a story by Mort Braus. Camera by William Daniels. Art direction by Cedric Gibbons. Produced by Norman Krasna, Metro-Goldwyn-Mayer (MGM). Released September 1, 1938. 70 minutes.

The Young at Heart, directed by Richard Wallace. Starring Janet Gaynor, Douglas Fairbanks, Jr., Paulette Goddard, Roland Young, Billie Burke, Minnie Dupree, Henry Stephenson, Richard Carlson, Lawrence Grant, Walter Kingsford, Eily Malyon, Tom Ricketts, Irvin S. Cobb, Lucile Watson, and Margaret Early. Scenario by Paul Osborn, adapted by Charles Bennett from the story *The Gay Banditti* by I.A.R. Wylie. Camera by Leon Shamroy. Art direction by Lyle R. Wheeler. Produced by David O. Selznick, Selznick International Pictures. Released November 3, 1938. 10 reels.

Bernadine, directed by Henry Levin. Starring Pat Boone, Terry Moore, Janet Gaynor, Dean Jagger, Dick Sargent, James Drury, Ronnie Burns, Walter Abel, Natalie Schafer, Isabel Jewell, and Jack Constanzo. Scenario by Theodore Reeves from the play by Mary Chase. Camera by Paul Vogel. Produced by Samuel G. Engel, 20th Century-Fox Corporation. Released July 24, 1957. 94 minutes.

Charles Farrell Filmography

Because the complete extent of Charles Farrell's unbilled or extra parts may never be fully determined, this filmography lists his billed roles, beginning in 1925. Whenever possible, both premiere and release dates are given. Film length is given in either reels or minutes, according to the information available at this time.

Wings of Youth, directed by Emmett J. Flynn. Starring Ethel Clayton, Madge Bellamy, Katherine Perry, Marion Harlan, Charles Farrell, Robert Cain, Freeman Wood, George Stewart, Douglas Gerard. Scenario by Bernard McConville, from the novel *Sisters of Jezebel* by Harold P. Montayne. Camera by Ernest Palmer. Produced by William Fox for Fox Film Corporation. Released May 21, 1925. 6 reels.

The Love Hour, directed by Herman Raymaker. Starring Huntley Gordon, Louise Fazenda, Willard Louis, Ruth Clifford, John Roche, Charles Farrell, Gayne Whitman. Scenario by Gregory Rogers (aka Darryl Zanuck). Camera by E. B. DuPar. Produced by Vitagraph Company of America, distributed by Warner Bros. Released August 1925. 7 reels.

Clash of the Wolves, directed by Noel M. Smith. Starring Rin-Tin-Tin, Nanette, Charles Farrell, June Marlowe, Heinie Conklin, Will Walling, Pat Hartigan. Scenario by Charles A. Logue. Camera by E.B. DuPar and Allen Q. Thompson. Art direction by Lewis Geib and Esdras Hartley. Produced by Warner Bros. Released November 28, 1925. 7 reels.

The Gosh-Darn Mortgage, directed by Edward Cline. Starring Charles Farrell, Douglas Gerrard, William McCall, Peggy O'Neill, Thelma Parr, Edna Tichenor. Scenario by Mack Sennett. Produced by Mack Sennett, Mack Sennett Comedies, distributed by Pathé Exchange. Released January 3, 1926. 2 reels.

Sandy, directed by Harry Beaumont. Starring Madge Bellamy, Leslie Fenton, Harrison Ford, Gloria Hope, Bardson Bard, David Torrence, Lillian Leighton, Charles Farrell. Scenario by Eve Unsell, from a novel by Elenore Meherin. Camera by Rudolph Bergquist. Produced by William Fox, Fox Film Corporation. Released April 11, 1926. 8 reels.

A Trip to Chinatown, directed by Robert P. Kerr. Starring Margaret Livingston, Earl Foxe, J. Farrell MacDonald, Anna May Wong, Harry Woods, Marie Astaire, Gladys McConnell, Charles Farrell. Scenario by Beatrice Van, from the play by Charles Hale Hoyt. Camera by Barney McGill. Produced by William Fox, Fox Film Corporation. Released June 6, 1926. 6 reels.

Old Ironsides, directed by James Cruze. Starring Charles Farrell, Esther Ralston, Wallace Beery, George Bancroft, Charles Hill Mailes, George Godfrey, Johnnie Walker. Scenario by Dorothy Arzner, Harry Carr, and Walter Woods from a story by Laurence Stallings. Camera by Charles P. Boyle and Alfred Gilks. Produced by James Cruze and B. P. Schulberg, Famous Players-Lasky-Paramount. Released December 6, 1926. 12 reels.

The Rough Riders, directed by Victor Fleming. Starring Charles Farrell, Mary Astor, Charles Emmett Mack, Noah Beery, George Bancroft, Frank Hopper. Scenario by Robert N. Lee and Keene Thompson, adapted by John F. Goodrich from a story by Hermann Hagedorn. Camera by James Wong Howe and E. Burton Steene. Produced by Lucien Hubbard and B. P. Schulberg, Famous Players-Lasky-Paramount. Premiered June 1927, released October 1, 1927. 10 reels.

7th Heaven (see combined filmography).

Fazil, directed by Howard Hawks. Starring Charles Farrell, Greta Nissen, Mae Busch, Tyler Brooke, Vadim Uraneff, John Boles. Scenario by Seton I. Miller, adapted by Philip Klein from the play *L'Insoumise* by Pierre Frondaie. Camera by L. William O'Connell. Produced by William Fox, Fox Film Corporation. Released June 4, 1928. 7 reels.

Street Angel (see combined filmography).

The Red Dance (a.k.a. *The Red Dancer of Moscow*), directed by Raoul Walsh. Starring Charles Farrell, Dolores Del Rio, Ivan Linow, Dorothy Revier, Demetrius Alexis, Andres de Segurola. Scenario by James Ashmore Creelman, adapted by Pierre Collings and Philip Klein from a story by Eleanor Browne. Camera by Charles Clarke and John Marta. Produced by William Fox, Fox Film Corporation. Premiered June 25, 1928, released December 2, 1928. 10 reels.

The River, directed by Frank Borzage. Starring Charles Farrell, Mary Duncan, Ivan Linow, Margaret Mann, Bert Woodruff, Alfred Sabato. Story by Tristram Tupper, screenplay by Philip Klein, Dwight Cummins, and John Hopper Booth. Camera by Ernest Palmer. Art direction by Harry Oliver. Produced by William Fox for Fox Film Corporation. Premiered December 22, 1928, pulled from circulation April 1929, re-released as *Song of the River* October 6, 1929. 7,704 feet (silent) or 6,536 feet (sound).

City Girl (aka *Our Daily Bread*), directed by F. W. Murnau. Starring Charles Farrell, Mary Duncan, David Torrence, Edith Yorke, Anne Shirley (Dawn O'Day), Tom McGuire, Richard Alexander. Scenario by Marion Orth and Berthold Viertel, with dialogue from the play, *The Mud* Turtle, by Elliott Lester. Camera by Ernest Palmer. Art direction by Harry Oliver. Produced by William Fox, Fox Film Corporation. Released February 16, 1930. 8,215 feet (silent) or 6,171 feet (sound).

Lucky Star (see combined filmography).

Sunny Side Up (see combined filmography).

High Society Blues (see combined filmography).

Liliom, directed by Frank Borzage. Starring Charles Farrell, Rose Hobart, Estelle Taylor, H. B. Warner, Lee Tracy, Walter Abel, Mildred Van Dorn, Lillian Elliott, Guinn 'Big Boy' Williams, Anne Shirley (as Dawn O'Day), Bert Roach. Screenplay by S. N. Behrman and Sonya Levien, from the play *Liliom* by Ferenc Molnar. Camera by Chester A. Lyons. Art direction by Harry Oliver. Produced by William Fox, Fox Film Corporation. Released October 15, 1930. 90 minutes.

The Princess and the Plumber, directed by Alexander Korda. Starring Charles Farrell, Maureen O'Sullivan, H. B. Warner, Joseph Cawthorn, Bert Roach, Lucien Prival, Murray Kinnell, Louise Closser Hale. Scenario by Howard J. Green from a story by Alice Duer Miller. Camera by L. William O'Connell and Dave Ragin. Art direction by Stephen Goosson. Produced by Fox Films. Released December 21, 1930. 7 reels.

Body and Soul, directed by Alfred Santell. Starring Charles Farrell, Elissa Landi, Humphrey Bogart, Myrna Loy, Don Dillaway, Crauford Kent, Pat Somerset, Ian Maclaren, David Cavendish. Screenplay by Jules Furthman, adapted from the story *Big Eyes and Little Mouth* by Elliott White Springs, and the play *Squadrons* by from A. E. Thomas. Camera by Glenn MacWilliams. Art direction by Anton Grot. Produced by Fox Film Corporation. Released February 22, 1931. 70 minutes.

Merely Mary Ann (see combined filmography).

Heartbreak, directed by Alfred L. Werker. Starring Charles Farrell, Madge Evans, Hardie Albright, Paul Cavanagh, John Arledge, Claude King, John St. Polis, Albert Conti, and Theodore von Eltz. Screenplay by William Conselman and Leon Gordon. Camera by Joseph H. August. Produced by Fox Film Corporation. Released November 8, 1931. 60 minutes.

After Tomorrow, directed by Frank Borzage. Starring Charles Farrell, Marian Nixon, Minna Gombell, William Collier, Sr., Josephine Hull, William Pawley, Greta Granstedt, Ferdinand Munier, Nora Lane. Screenplay by Sonya Levien, from the play *After Tomorrow* by Hugh S. Stange and John Golden. Camera by James Wong Howe. Art direction by William S. Darling. Produced by Fox Film Corporation. Released March 6, 1932. 79 minutes.

The First Year (see combined filmography).

Tess of the Storm Country (see combined filmography).

Wild Girl, (AKA *Salomy Jane*), directed by Raoul Walsh. Starring Charles Farrell, Joan Bennett, Ralph Bellamy, Eugene Pallette, Minna Gombell, Irving Pichell, Sarah Padden, Willard Robertson, Louise Beavers. Scenario by Doris Anderson and Edwin Justus Mayer, adapted from the play by Paul Armstrong and the story *Salomy Jane's Kiss* by Bret Harte. Camera by Norbert Brodine. Produced by Fox Film Corporation. Released October 9, 1932. 79 minutes.

Aggie Appleby, Maker of Men, directed by Mark Sandrich. Starring Charles Farrell, Wynne Gibson, William Gargan, Zasu Pitts, Betty Furness, and Blanche Friderici. Scenario by Humphrey Pearson and Edward Kaufman from the play by Joseph Kesselring. Camera by J. Roy Hunt. Art direction by Carol Clark and Van Nest Polglase. Produced by Merian C. Cooper and Pandro S. Berman, RKO Radio Pictures. Premiered October 19, 1933, released November 3, 1933. 8 reels.

Girl without a Room, directed by Ralph Murphy. Starring Charles Farrell, Charles Ruggles, Marguerite Churchill, Gregory Ratoff, Grace Bradley, Walter Woolf, Leonid Snegoff, Leonid Kinsky, Mischa Auer, and Alexander Mellish. Scenario by Claude Binyon and Frank Butler from the novel by Jack Lait. Camera by Leo Tover. Art direction by David S. Garber. Produced by Charles R. Rogers and Harry Joe Brown, Paramount Pictures. Released December 8, 1933. 75 minutes.

The Big Shakedown, directed by John Francis Dillon. Starring Charles Farrell, Bette Davis, Ricardo Cortez, Glenda Farrell, Allen Jenkins, Henry O'Neill, Dewey Robinson, and John Wray. Scenario by Rian James and Niven Busch, from the story *Cut Rate* by S. Engels. Camera by Sid Hickox. Produced by Warner Bros. Released January 6, 1934. 64 minutes.

Change of Heart (see combined filmography).

Falling in Love (AKA *Trouble Ahead*), directed by Monty Banks. Starring Charles Farrell, Margot Grahame, Mary Lawson, Gregory Ratoff, H.F. Maltby, Diana Napier, Cathleen Nesbit, and Patrick Aherne. Scenario by Fred Thompson, Miles Malleson, and John Paddy Carstairs, from the story by Allan Hyman and Lee Loeb. Camera by Geoffrey Faithfull. Produced by Howard Welsch, Vogue Pictures, Inc. Released February 4, 1935 (UK), September 23, 1936 (USA). 8 reels.

Forbidden Heaven, directed by Reginald Barker. Starring Charles Farrell, Charlotte Henry, Beryl Mercer, Fred Walton, Eric Wilton, and Phyllis Barry. Scenario by Sada Cowan and Jefferson Parker, from a story by Christine Jope-Slade. Camera by Milton R. Krasner. Produced by Trem Carr, Republic Pictures. Released October 5, 1935. 79 minutes.

Fighting Youth, directed by Hamilton McFadden. Starring Charles Farrell, June Martel, Andy Devine, J. Farrell MacDonald, Ann Sheridan, and Edward J. Nugent. Scenario by Hamilton McFadden, Henry Johnson, and Florabel Muir, from an idea by Stanley Meyer. Camera by Edward Snyder. Art direction by Ralph Berger. Produced by Fred S. Meyer and Ansel Friedberger, Universal Pictures. Released November 1, 1935. 78 minutes.

The Flying Doctor, directed by Miles Mander. Starring Charles Farrell, Mary Maguire, James Raglan, Joe Valli, Margaret Vyner, Eric Colman, Tom Lurich, Maudie Edwards, Katie Towers, Phillip Lytton, Andrew Beresford, Jack Clarke, and Phil Smith. Scenario by Miles Mander and J.O.C. Orton, from a story by Robert

Waldron. Camera by Errol Hinds and Derick Williams. Produced by Miles Mander, National Pictures. Released August 21, 1936 (Australia), September 1937 (UK). 68 minutes.

Moonlight Sonata, directed by Lothar Mendes. Starring Ignace Jan Paderewski, Charles Farrell, Marie Tempest, Barbara Greene, Eric Portman, W. Graham Brown, Queenie Leonard, Laurence Hanray, and Binkie Stuart. Scenario by E.M. Delafield and Edward Knoblock, from a story by Hans Rameau. Camera by Jan Stallich. Set decoration by Laurence Irving. Produced by Lothar Mendes, Pall Mall Productions, Ltd. Released February 11, 1937 (UK), May 9, 1938 (USA). 90 minutes.

Midnight Menace (AKA *Bombs Over London*), directed by Sinclair Hill. Starring Charles Farrell, Margaret Vyner, Fritz Kortner, Danny Green, Wallace Evennett, Monte De Lyle, Dino Galvani, Arthur Finn, Laurence Hanray, and Arthur Gomez. Adapted by G.H. Moresby-White, from the story by D.B. Wyndham-Lewis. Camera by Cyril Bristow. Set decoration by C. Wilfred Arnold. Produced by Harcourt Templeman and Angus MacLeod, Grosvenor Films, Ltd. Released July 1, 1937 (UK), 1939 (USA). 7,122 feet.

Flight to Fame, directed by Charles C. Coleman. Starring Charles Farrell, Jacqueline Wells, Hugh Sothern, Alexander D'Arcy, Jason Robards, Sr., Charles D. Brown, Addison Richards, Frederick Burton, Selmer Jackson, and Reed Howes. Scenario by Michael L. Simmons. Camera by Lucien Ballard. Art direction by Stephen Goosoon. Produced by Columbia Pictures Corp. Released October 12, 1938. 5,158 feet.

Just Around the Corner (a.k.a. *Lucky Penny* or *Sunnyside Up*), directed by Irving Cummings. Starring Shirley Temple, Joan Davis, Charles Farrell, Amanda Duff, Bill Robinson, Bert Lahr, Franklin Pangborn, Cora Witherspoon, Claude Gillingwater, and Bennie Bartlett. Scenario by Ethel Hill, J.P. McEvoy, and Darrell Ware, from the story *Lucky Penny* by Paul Girard Smith. Camera by Arthur C. Miller. Art direction by Boris Leven and Bernard Herzbrun. Produced by Darryl F. Zanuck and David Hempstead, 20th Century-Fox Film Corporation. Released November 11, 1938. 8 reels.

Tail Spin, directed by Roy del Ruth. Starring Alice Faye, Constance Bennett, Nancy Kelly, Joan Davis, Charles Farrell, Jane Wyman, Kane Richmond, Wally Vernon, Joan Valerie, Edward Norris, J. Anthony Hughes, Harry Davenport, and Mary Gordon. Scenario by Frank Wead. Camera by Karl Freund. Art direction by Bernard Herzbrun and Rudolph Sternad. Produced by Darryl F. Zanuck and Harry Joe Brown, 20th Century-Fox Film Corporation. Released February 19, 1939. 9 reels.

The Deadly Game, directed by Phil Rosen. Starring Charles Farrell, June Lang, John Miljan, Bernadene Hayes, J. Arthur Young, Dave Clarke, Dave O'Brien, and John Dilson. Scenario by Wellyn Totman. Camera by Arthur Martinelli. Art direction by Charles Clague. Produced by Dixon R. Harwin and Barney Sarecky, Monogram Pictures Corporation. Released August 8, 1941. 7 reels.

Combined Filmography

Whenever possible, both premiere and release dates are given. Film length is given in either reels or minutes, according to the information available at this time.

7th Heaven, directed by Frank Borzage. Starring Janet Gaynor, Charles Farrell, Ben Bard, David Butler, Marie Mosquini, Albert Gran, Gladys Brockwell, Emile Chautard, George Stone, Jessie Haslett, Brandon Hurst, and Lillian West. Scenario by Benjamin Glazer, from the play by Austin Strong. Camera by Ernest Palmer and Joseph A. Valentine. Art direction by Harry Oliver. Produced by William Fox and Sol M. Wurtzel, Fox Film Corporation. Premiered May 6, 1927 (Los Angeles), released May 25, 1927. 12 reels. Nominated for Best Art Direction and Best Picture Academy Award. Won Best Director and Best Writing (Adaptation) Academy Awards. Janet Gaynor won Best Actress for her performances in *7th Heaven*, *Street Angel*, and *Sunrise*. Won Photoplay Medal of Honor, 1927. Won Best Foreign Language Film, 1928, Kinema Junpo Awards. Awarded to the National Film Registry, 1995.

Street Angel, directed by Frank Borzage. Starring Janet Gaynor, Charles Farrell, Alberto Rabagliati, Cino Conti, Guido Trento, Henry Armetta, Louis Liggett, Milton Dickinson, Helena Herman, Natalie Kingston, Dave Kashner, and Jennie Bruno. Scenario by Marion Orth, adapted by Philip Klein and Henry Roberts Symonds, from the novel *Lady Cristilinda* by Monckton Hoffe. Camera by Ernest Palmer. Art direction by Harry Oliver. Produced by William Fox, Fox Film Corporation. Released April 9, 1928. 10 reels. Nominated for Best Art Direction and Best Cinematography Academy Awards.

Lucky Star, directed by Frank Borzage. Starring Janet Gaynor, Charles Farrell, Guinn 'Big Boy' Williams, Hedwig Reicher, Paul Fix, Gloria Grey, Hector Sarno. Scenario by Sonya Levien, from the story *Three Episodes in the Life of Timothy Osborne* by Tristram Tupper. Camera by Chester A. Lyons and William Cooper Smith. Art direction by Harry Oliver. Produced by William Fox, Fox Film Corporation. Premiered July 21, 1929, released August 18, 1929. 10 reels. Released as both a talkie and a silent film; only the silent print has survived.

Sunny Side Up, directed by David Butler. Starring Janet Gaynor, Charles Farrell, Marjorie White, El Brendel, Frank Richardson, Mary Forbes, Sharon Lynn, Joe Brown, Peter Gawthorne, Jackie Cooper (uncredited). Scenario by Buddy G. DeSylva and Ray Henderson. Camera by Ernest Palmer and John Schmitz. Art direction by Harry Oliver. Songs by DeSylva, Brown and Henderson, Inc. Produced by David Butler and Buddy G. DeSylva, Fox Film Corporation. Released October 3, 1929. 80 minutes.

Happy Days, directed by Benjamin Stoloff. Starring Marjorie White, Charles E. Evans, Richard Keene, Stuart Erwin, Martha Lee Sparks, James J. Corbett, George MacFarlane, Janet Gaynor, Charles Farrell, Victor McLaglen, El Brendel, Frank Richardson, William Collier, Sr., George Jessel, Dixie Lee, Ann Pennington, Warner Baxter, Nick Stuart, Rex Bell, Sharon Lynn, Will Rogers, 'Whispering' Jack Smith, Lew Brice, J. Farrell MacDonald, Edmund Lowe. Scenario by Sidney Lanfield with dialogue by Edwin J. Burke. Camera by Lucien N. Andriot, John Schmitz, and J.O. Taylor. Songs by Joseph McCarthy, James F. Hanley, James Brockman of Red Star Music Co. and DeSylva, Brown, and Henderson, Inc. Produced by William Fox, Fox Film Corporation. Premiered September 17, 1929 (New York), released February 13, 1930. 86 minutes.

High Society Blues, directed by David Butler. Starring Janet Gaynor, Charles Farrell, William Collier, Sr., Hedda Hopper, Joyce Compton, Lucien Littlefield, Louise Fazenda, Brandon Hurst, Gregory Gaye. Scenario by Howard J. Green, from the story *Those High Society Blues* by Dana Burnet. Camera by Charles Van Enger. Songs by Joseph McCarthy and James F. Hanley. Produced by William Fox and Al Rockett, Fox Film Corporation. Premiered March 23, 1930, released April 18, 1930. 98 minutes. Only the soundtrack is known to exist at this time.

The Man Who Came Back, directed by Raoul Walsh. Starring Janet Gaynor, Charles Farrell, Kenneth MacKenna, William Holden, Mary Forbes, Ullrich Haupt, William Worthington, Peter Gawthorne, Leslie Fenton. Scenario by Edwin J. Burke, from the play by Jules Eckert Goodman, and the novel by John Fleming Wilson. Camera by Arthur Edeson. Art direction by Joseph Urban. Produced by Raoul Walsh, Fox Film Corporation. Premiered January 3, 1931, released Janaury 11, 1931. 85 minutes.

Merely Mary Ann, directed by Henry King. Starring Janet Gaynor, Charles Farrell, Beryl Mercer, G.P. Huntley, Jr., J.M. Kerrigan, Tom Whiteley, Lorna Balfour, Arnold Lucy. Scenario by Jules Furthman from the play by Israel Zangwill. Camera by Arthur E. Arling and John F. Seitz. Produced by Fox Film Corporation. Premiered September 6, 1931, released September 11, 1931. 74 minutes.

Delicious, directed by David Butler. Starring Janet Gaynor, Charles Farrell, El Brendel, Raoul Roulien, Lawrence O'Sullivan, Manya Roberti, Virginia Cherrill, Olive Tell, Mischa Auer, Marvine Maazel. Scenario by Sonya Levien from Guy Bolton's story *Skyline*. Camera by Ernest Palmer. Art direction by Joseph C. Wright. Music and lyrics by George and Ira Gershwin. Produced by Fox Film Corporation. Released December 25, 1931. 71 minutes.

The First Year, directed by William K. Howard. Starring Janet Gaynor, Charles Farrell, Minna Gombell, Dudley Digges, Leila Bennett, Robert McWade, George Meeker, Maude Eburne, Henry Kolker, Edna Voelkel. Scenario by Lynn Starling from the play by Frank Craven. Camera by Hal Mohr. Produced by Fox Film Corporation. Premiered July 31, 1932, released August 20, 1932. 80 minutes.

Tess of the Storm Country, directed by Alfred Santell. Starring Janet Gaynor, Charles Farrell, Dudley Digges, June Clyde, Claude Gillingwater, George Meeker, Sarah Padden, Edward Pawley, Professor Peppy

(Peppy the Monkey). Scenario by Rupert Hughes, Sonya Levien, and S.N. Behrman, based on Rupert Hughes' play of the novel by Grace Miller White. Camera by Hal Mohr. Premiered November 18, 1932, released November 19, 1932. 75 minutes.

Change of Heart, directed by John G. Blystone. Starring Janet Gaynor, Charles Farrell, Ginger Rogers, James Dunn, Nick Foran, Beryl Mercer, Gustav von Seyffertitz, Kenneth Thomson, Theodore von Eltz, Drue Leyton, Nella Walker, Shirley Temple, Barbara Barondess, Fiske O'Hara, Jane Darwell, Mary Carr. Scenario by Sonya Levien and James Gleason from the story *Manhattan Love Song* by Kathleen Norris. Camera by Hal Mohr. Set decoration by Jack Otterson. Produced by Winfield R. Sheehan, Fox Film Corporation. Premiered May 10, 1934 (New York), released May 18, 1934. 76 minutes.

Endnotes

Introduction

1.   Opening title card from *Street Angel*, 1928.

Chapter One: A Very Remarkable Fellow

1.   Details of the Farrell family history provided by Belle Lundstedt and Shirley Seaward. Information on Walpole and Onset Bay at the turn of the century provided by Betty Cottrell and Lynda Ames, historians. Charles Farrell's birth story provided by Betty Cottrell.

2.   David M. Katzman and William M. Tuttle, Jr., eds. "Experiences of a Street Car Conductor," *Plain Folk*.   Chicago: University of Illinois Press, 1983, 15-21.

3.   Brian Burns, "Remembering Walpole Actor Charles Farrell," *Walpole Times*, September 2002.

4.   Betty Cottrell, letter to author, February 11, 2006.

5.   Interview with Pat Houde, conducted by Cheryl MacDonald, August 14, 2008.

6.   Mary Pickford. *Sunshine and Shadow*. New York: Doubleday, 1955, 65.

7.   Henry M. Fine, "Through College Days with Charles Farrell," *New Movie Magazine*, November 1932, 100.

8.   Henry M. Fine, "Through College Days with Charles Farrell," 100.

9.   Henry M. Fine, "Through College Days with Charles Farrell," 51.

10.   Henry M. Fine, "Through College Days with Charles Farrell," 102.

11.   Gene A. Plunka, *The Black Comedy of John Guare*, Newark: University of Delaware Press, 2002, 23-24.

12.   William Malin, unpublished interview with Charles Farrell, April 14, 1976.

13.   Anthony Slide, *The Encyclopedia of Vaudeville*, Westport: Greenwood Press, 1994, pp. 259-260, 280, 381.

14.   Jan L. Jones, *Renegades, Showmen & Angels: A Theatrical History of Fort Worth from 1873-2001*, Fort Worth: Texas Christian University Press, 2006, 109.

15.   Bruce Fessier, "Question and Answer with Charles Farrell," *The Desert Sun*, October 27, 1980, A1-A6.

279

16. William Malin, unpublished interview with Charles Farrell, April 14, 1976.

17. William Malin, unpublished interview with Charles Farrell, April 14, 1976.

18. William Malin, unpublished interview with Charles Farrell, April 14, 1976.

19. DeWitt Bodeen, "Charles Farrell," *Films in Review*, October 1976, 451.

Chapter Two: Lolly

20. Unidentified newspaper clipping, circa 1928.

21. Anita Loos, *The Talmadge Girls*, New York: Viking Press, 1978, 7.

22. Lucy Perkins Carner, *The First One Hundred Years of the Young Women's Christian Association of Germantown, 1870-1970*, 9.

23. Lucy Perkins Carner, *The First One Hundred Years...*12.

24. Thomas E. Lewis, "Janet's Dad," *The New Movie Magazine*, February 1931, 112-113.

25. Thomas E. Lewis, "Janet's Dad,"... 112-113.

26. Janet Gaynor and Dorothy Spensley, "My Life So Far," *Photoplay*, December, 1928, 35.

27. John Dos Passos, *The 42nd Parallel: Volume One of the U.S.A. Trilogy*, New York, Mariner Books, 2000, 199-120.

28. Glenda Riley, *Divorce: An American Tradition*, University of Nebraska Press, 1997.

29. Janet Gaynor and Dorothy Spensley, "My Life So Far,"..., 107.

30. Janet Gaynor and Dorothy Spensley, "My Life So Far, ... 35.

31. Janet Gaynor and Dorothy Spensley, "My Life So Far,"..., 35.

32. Irene Mayer Selznick, *A Private View*, New York: Knopf, 1983, 137.

33. Janet Gaynor and Dorothy Spensley, "My Life So Far,"..., 35, 105.

34. Weona Cleveland, unidentified newspaper article, Melbourne newspaper, circa 1980s.

35. Janet Gaynor and Dorothy Spensley, "My Life So Far,"... 106.

36. Janet Gaynor and Dorothy Spensley, "My Life So Far,"..., 107.

37. Janet Gaynor and Dorothy Spensley, "My Life So Far,"... 107.

38. Janet Gaynor and Dorothy Spensley, "My Life So Far,"... 50.

39. Janet Gaynor and Dorothy Spensley, "My Life So Far,"...50.

40. Janet Gaynor and Dorothy Spensley, "My Life So Far,"...50.

Chapter Three: Lucky Breaks

41. Fay Wray, *On the Other Hand*, St. Martin's Press, 1989, 54.

42. Janet Gaynor, "My Life So Far," *Photoplay*, January 1929, 94.

43. Janet Gaynor, "My Life So Far,"...94.

44. Fay Wray, *On the Other Hand*...54-55.

45. William Foster Elliot, "The Soul of the Violin," *Los Angeles Times*, July 2, 1922, 23.

46. Jeanine Basinger, *Silent Stars*, New York: Knopf, 1999, 456.

47. Fay Wray, *On the Other Hand...*56.
48. Janet Gaynor, "My Life So Far," ... 94.
49. "Pick WAMPAS Ball Gowns," *Los Angeles Times,* January 24, 1926, B5.
50. Isabel Stuyvesant, "Society of Cinemaland," February 7, 1926, 30.
51. Fay Wray, *On the Other Hand...* 57.
52. "WAMPAS Ready for Big Frolic," *Los Angeles Times,* January 31, 1926, B6.
53. Madge Bellamy, *A Darling of the Twenties,* Vestal Press, 1989, 71.
54. "'Sandy' Reaches Artistic Heights," *Los Angeles Times,* April 12, 1926.
55. Esther Ralston, *Some Day We'll Laugh: an Autobiography,* Metuchen, NJ: Scarecrow Press, 1985, 95.
56. Esther Ralston, *Some Day We'll Laugh* ...97-98.
57. American Cinematographer 8/87 p. 39.
58. "The Shadow Stage," *Photoplay,* February 1927, 58.
59. Henry M. Fine, "Through College Days with Charles Farrell," *New Movie Magazine,* November 1932, 102.
60. Whitney Williams, "Under the Lights," *Los Angeles Times,* August 15, 1926.
61. Madge Bellamy, *A Darling of the Twenties,* Vestal Press, 1989, 73.
62. Janet Gaynor, unpublished interview transcript, Columbia University Oral History Research Project, November 1958, 26-27.
63. Janet Gaynor, unpublished interview transcript, Columbia University Oral History Research Project...5.
64. Marquis Busby, "The Return of Peter Grimm," *Los Angeles Times,* October 24, 1926, H6.

Chapter Four: *7ᵗʰ Heaven*

65. John Golden, *7th Heaven,* New York: Grosset and Dunlap, 1924, 16.
66. Madge Bellamy, *A Darling of the Twenties,* Vestal Press, 1989, 66-67.
67. Janet Gaynor, unpublished interview transcript, Columbia University Oral History Research Project, November 1958, 6.
68. "Favored Player Arrives at Cinema Heights after Only Two Years in Film Roles," *Los Angeles Times,* October 17, 1926, C24.
69. Janet Gaynor, unpublished interview transcript, Columbia University Oral History Research Project...6.
70. William Malin, unpublished interview with Charles Farrell, April 14, 1976.
71. John Golden, *7th Heaven*...1924, 35.
72. William Malin...April 14, 1976.
73. Mary Astor, *My Story: An Autobiography,* New York: Doubleday, 1959, 101.
74. William Wellman, Jr. *The Man and His Wings,* Westport, Conn: Praeger, 2006, 114.
75. William Malin...April 14, 1976.
76. Roy Newquist, "Interview with Janet Gaynor," *Showcase,* 1966, 124-125.

77. Jean Loup Bourget, "Seventh Heaven," *Monogram*, 4, 1972, 24-25.

78. John Belton. *The Hollywood Professionals: Howard Hawks, Frank Borzage, Edward G. Ulmer*, New York: A.S. Barnes, 1974, 79.

79. Carli Elinor, letter to Charles Farrell, April 8, 1953.

80. *Hollywood: The Man with the Megaphone*. Directed by Kevin Brownlow and David Gill. New York: Thames Television Ltd., HBO Video, 1980.

81. Rex Reed, "Janet Gaynor: From film queen to stage doyenne," *Chicago Tribune*, 1976.

82. Myra Nye, "Society of Cinemaland," *Los Angeles Times*, May 8, 1927, 32.

83. Mayme Ober Peak, "*7th Heaven* Assures Charles Farrell of Fame," *Boston Globe*, May 17, 1927.

84. "Film Pair's Altar Pact Rescinded." *Los Angeles Times*, October 1, 1927, A1.

85. Myra Nye, "Society of Cinemaland," *Los Angeles Times*, May 8, 1927, 32.

86. Alfred B. Kuttner, *National Board of Review*, 1927.

87. Connie Billips, *Janet Gaynor: A Bio-Bibliography*, New York: Greenwood Press, 1992, 14.

88. Marquis Busby, "*Rough Riders* Splendid Film," *Los Angeles Times*, June 26, 1927, A7.

89. Letter from Milton Cohen to Alfred Wright, 20th Century-Fox Legal Files, Performing Arts Special Collections, UCLA.

90. According to California law, the age of majority was 18 when Janet signed her contract. This was amended in 1927, when the age of majority was changed to 21. However, this change was not retroactive and therefore did not have any bearing on Janet's original contract.

91. Muriel Babcock. "Hilarious Comedy Offered in *Two Girls Wanted*," *Los Angeles Times*, September 18, 1927, I4.

92. Todd MCarthy, *William Wellman: The Grey Fox of Hollywood*, New York: Grove Press, 1997, 85.

93. Janet Gaynor, unpublished interview transcript, Columbia University Oral History Research Project... 12-13.

94. John Belton. *The Hollywood Professionals*.81.

95. David Menefee. *The First Female Stars: Women of the Silent Era*, Westport, Conn: Praeger, 89.

96. Norbert Lusk, "*Sunrise* Is Much Praised," *Los Angeles Times*, October 2, 1927, 17.

Chapter Five: Fame

97. Anita Loos, *A Girl Like I*, New York: Viking, 1979, .

98. Diana Serra Cary, *What Ever Happened to Baby Peggy?*, New York: St. Martin's Press, 1996, 124.

99. Paul Gregory, interview with author, April 2006.

100. Irene Mayer Selznick, *A Private View*, New York: Knopf, 1983, 119.

101. Irene Mayer Selznick, *A Private View*...119.

102. Fay Wray, *On the Other Hand*, New York: St. Martin's Press, 1989, 53-54.

103. Douglas Fairbanks, Jr., *The Salad Days,* New York: Doubleday, 1988, 116.

104. DeWitt Bodeen, "Charles Farrell," *Films in Review*, October 1976, 455.

105. Laurence Reid, "Laurence Reid Reviews the New Photoplays," *Motion Picture Classic*, September 1928, 52.

106. "The 'Red Dance' of Revolution Gyrates Madly," *Davenport Democrat and Leader,* December 12, 1928, 25.

107. Janet Gaynor, unpublished interview transcript, Columbia University Oral History Research Project, November 1958, 17.

108. Janet Gaynor, unpublished interview transcript, Columbia University Oral History Research Project...19.

109. "Janet Gaynor Denies Troth," *Los Angeles Times*, June 28, 1928, 2.

110. Janet Gaynor, unpublished interview transcript, Columbia University Oral History Research Project... 13-15.

111. Mordaunt Hall, "Four Devils," *New York Times*, October 4, 1928.

112. P.K.S. "Naturalness Chief Asset of *Christina*," *The Los Angeles Times*, December 20, 1929, A11.

113. Information and quotations about the filming of *The River* from Herve Dumont's book, *Frank Borzage: the Life and Times of a Hollywood Romantic,* North Carolina: MacFarland, 2006, 134-144.

114. Herve Dumont, *Frank Borzage: the Life and Times of a Hollywood Romantic,* North Carolina: McFarland, 2006, 144.

115. "Community Development," *Los Angeles Times,* November 25, 1928, E4.

116. *Screen Secrets* magazine, circa 1928.

117. Details about Fred Thomson's death and funeral are from Cari Beauchamp's book, *Without Lying Down: Frances Marion and the Powerful Women of Early Hollywood,* Los Angeles: University of California Press, 1997.

118. William Malin, unpublished interview with Charles Farrell, April 14, 1976.

Chapter Six: Lucky Star

119. Telegram from George Bagnall to Sol Wurtzel, January 8, 1929.

120. Herve Dumont, *Frank Borzage: the Life and Times of a Hollywood Romantic,* North Carolina: McFarland, 2006, 145.

121. Herve Dumont, *Frank Borzage: the Life and Times*...145.

122. Herve Dumont, *Frank Borzage: the Life and Times* ... 146.

123. Herve Dumont, *Frank Borzage: the Life and Times* ... 153.

124. Herve Dumont, *Frank Borzage: the Life and Times* ...154.

125. "Transformation of player seen in 'Lucky Star'," *Los Angeles Times*, September 2, 1929, 9.

126. Paul Gregory, "A Star Was Born," A&E *Biography*.

127. Rex Reed, "Janet Gaynor: From Film Queen to Stage Doyenne," *Chicago Tribune*, circa 1979.

128. Anita Loos, *A Girl Like I*, New York: Viking, 1966, 171.

129. David Butler and Irene Kahn Atkins, *David Butler*, Hollywood, CA: Directors' Guild of America, 1993.

130. Mordaunt Hall, "Sunny Side Up," *New York Times*, October 4, 1929.

131. Mordaunt Hall, "Sunny Side Up," *New York Times*, October 4, 1929.

132. Rex Reed, "Janet Gaynor: From Film Queen to Stage Doyenne," *Chicago Tribune*, circa 1979.

133. Robin Gaynor Adrian, interview with author, May 2006.

134. "Noted Film Love Scene Team Split," *Los Angeles Times*, September 10, 1929, A2.

135. Robin Gaynor Adrian, interview with author, May 2006.

136. Paul Gregory, interview with author, April 2006.

137. "Big Money," *Time Magazine*, April 21, 1930.

138. Mordaunt Hall, "High Society Blues," *New York Times*, April 19, 1930.

139. Janet Gaynor, letter to Win Sheehan, February 1930, 20th Century-Fox Legal Files, Performing Arts Special Collections, UCLA.

140. Janet Gaynor, letter to Win Sheehan, February 1930, 20th Century-Fox Legal Files, Performing Arts Special Collections, UCLA.

Chapter Seven: Strike and Depression

141. Paul Gregory, interview with author, April 2006.

142. Janet Gaynor, letter to Win Sheehan, February 1930, 20th Century-Fox Legal Files, Performing Arts Special Collections, UCLA.

143. *Liliom* was filmed three other times: in 1919, directed by Michael Curtiz; in 1934, directed by Fritz Lang; and in 1956, as the Rodgers and Hammerstein musical *Carousel*.

144. Win Sheehan, telegram to Sol Wurtzel, March 8, 1930, 20th Century-Fox Legal Files, Performing Arts Special Collections, UCLA.

145. Irene Mayer Selznick, *A Private View*. New York: Knopf, 1983, 137.

146. Rose Hobart, *A Steady Digression to a Fixed Point*, Metchuchen, NJ: Scarecrow Press, 1994, 68-69.

147. Rose Hobart, *A Steady Digression to a Fixed Point...* 68-69.

148. "Liliom," *Theatre Magazine*, December 1930, 50.

149. F. Scott Fitzgerald, *Tender Is the Night*, New York: Scribner's and Sons, 1934, 3-4.

150. Richard Bueller, *A Beautiful Fairy Tale: The Life of Actress Lois Moran*, Pompton Plains, NJ: Limelight Editions, 2005, 237.

151. Micheal G. Ankerich, *The Sound of Silence: Conversations with 16 Film and Stage Personalities who Bridged the Gap between Silents and Talkies*, North Carolina: McFarland, 1998, 189.

152. Frank Bogert, interview with author, October 2004.

153. Paul Gregory, interview with author, April 2006.

154. $30,000 in 1930 is the equivalent of $369,000 in 2007.

155. Barbara Leaming, *Bette Davis: A Biography*, New York: Simon and Schuster, 1992, 99.

156. Digest of Demands of Janet Gaynor, June 26, 1930, 20th Century-Fox Legal Files, Performing Arts Special Collections, UCLA.

157. Thomas E. Lewis, "Janet's Dad," *The New Movie Magazine*, February 1931, 112-113.

158. Mollie Merrick, "Janet Gaynor Punished Because of Her Tantrum," unknown newspaper clipping, circa 1930.

159. Paul Tabori, *Alexander Korda*, London: Oldbourne, 1959, 108.

160. Peter Buckley, "Janet Gaynor: At 74, A Star Reborn," publication unknown, circa 1980.

161. Janet Gaynor, unpublished interview transcript, Columbia University Oral History Research Project, November 1958, 27.

162. "The Man Who Came Back," *Film Daily*, January 4, 1931.

163. Winifred Aydelotte, "The Man Who Came Back," *Los Angeles Record*, January 8, 1931.

164. Harrison Carroll, "Body and Soul," *Los Angeles Evening Herald Express*, March 13, 1931.

165. Louella Parsons' column, *Los Angeles Times*, January 2, 1931.

166. "Farrell and Miss Valli Wed In East," *Los Angeles Times*, February 17, 1931.

Chapter Eight: Heartbreak

167. Katherine Albert, "Janet Is Back on the Job," *Photoplay*, November 1930, 144.

168. Mordaunt Hall, "Daddy Long Legs," *New York Times*, June 6, 1931.

169. Paul Gregory, interview with author, April 2006.

170. Mordaunt Hall, "Merely Mary Ann," *New York Times*, September 12, 1931.

171. Information on *Swenson vs. Delicious* from 20th Century-Fox Legal Files, Performing Arts Special Collections, UCLA.

172. Mordaunt Hall, "After Tomorrow," *New York Times*, March 7, 1932.

173. "After Tomorrow," *LaCrosse Tribune and Leader-Press*, March 20, 1932, 12.

174. "After Tomorrow," *Lima News*, March 31, 1932, 3.

175. Barry Paris, *Louise Brooks*, New York: Knopf, 1989, 237.

176. John Kobal, interview with Joel McCrea, *People Will Talk*, New York: Knopf, 1986, 308.

178. Mordaunt Hall, "The First Year," *New York Times*, August 22, 1932.

179. Phillip K. Scheuer, "The First Year," *Los Angeles Times*, August 1, 1932.

180. Letter from Edwin P. Kilroe to John Tracy, Fox Legal Department, August 1,

1932, 20th Century-Fox Legal Files, Performing Arts Special Collections, UCLA.

181. "Tess of the Storm Country," *Film Daily*, November 19, 1932.

182. Mordaunt Hall, "Tess of the Storm Country," *New York Times*, November 19, 1932.

183. Memo from Fox Studio to Charles Farrell, November 12, 1932, 20th Century-Fox Legal Files, Performing Arts Special Collections, UCLA.

184. Memo from Alfred Wright to George Bagnall, November 14, 1932, 20th Century-Fox Legal Files, Performing Arts Special Collections, UCLA.

Chapter Nine: Change of Heart

185. AKA the "Hays Code," the Production Code was the first industry-regulated censorship of motion pictures, which imposed a moral code of "dos and don'ts." This was later replaced by the MPAA motion picture rating system now in place.

186. Elizabeth Yeaman, HCN, July 7, 1934.

187. DeWitt Bodeen, "Charles Farrell," *Films in Review*, October, 1976, 460.

188. Dennis McDougal, "Palm Springs Squire Remembers 'A Helluva Career,'" *Los Angeles Times*, January 23, 1977.

189. William Malin, unpublished interview with Charles Farrell, April 14, 1976.

190. The author did find very specific evidence of one movie star being fired for his voice—or lack thereof. In December 1929, Rin-Tin-Tin was fired from Warner Bros., because his talents were not "in keeping with the policy that has been adopted by us for talking pictures, very obviously, of course, because dogs don't talk." Warner Bros. Interoffice Memo, dated December 6, 1929.

191. Janet Gaynor, unpublished interview transcript, Columbia University Oral History Research Project, November 1958, 12.

192. Rex Reed, "Janet Gaynor: From Film Queen to Stage Doyenne," *Chicago Tribune*, circa 1979.

193. Belle Lundstedt, interview with Cheryl MacDonald, August 12, 2008.

194. DeWitt Bodeen, "Charles Farrell," *Films in Review*, October, 1976, 460.

195. "Romantic actress and husband part," *Los Angeles Times*, December 21, 1932.

196. Lydell Peck went back to Oakland to practice law and became active in local politics. He was State Fire Marshal from 1939-1941. He married San Francisco socialite Ruthmarie Laumeister in 1941. They had two daughters. Ruthmarie and Lydell were divorced in 1956. Later that year, Peck attempted suicide by locking himself in a closet and setting off four gopher bombs. He died January 24, 1957. The cause of his death was not listed in the newspaper, but he may have made a final, successful suicide attempt. In his obituaries, no mention was made of his second marriage; just his first, and most infamous, marriage to Janet Gaynor.

197. *State Fair* has been remade in 1945 as a Rogers and Hammerstein musical, and in 1962 as a musical starring Pat Boone, Ann-Margaret, and Bobby Darin.

198. Mordaunt Hall, "State Fair," *New York Times*, January 27, 1933.

199. Mordaunt Hall, "Adorable," *New York Times*, May 19, 1933.

200. Mordaunt Hall, "Adorable," *New York Times*, May 19, 1933.

201. Mordaunt Hall, "Aggie Appleby," *New York Times*, October 20, 1933.

202. A.D.S., "The Big Shakedown," *New York Times*, February 12, 1934.

203. Alice Tidelsley, "Business Sense Comes to Hollywood," *Sunday Journal and Star*, January 24, 1937.

204. Paul Gregory, interview with author, April 2006.

205. *Carolina* is considered a lost film. The plot summary comes from the *New York Times* review of the film, February 16, 1934.

206. Mordaunt Hall, "Girl without a Room," *New York Times*, December 11, 1933.

207. Mordaunt Hall, "Change of Heart," *New York Times*, May 11, 1934.

208. "Change of Heart," *Monassen Daily Independent*, May 19, 1934.

209. Louella Parsons news item in the *Fresno Bee*, September 16, 1934.

210. "Servants' Entrance," *Motion Picture Magazine*, September 1934.

211. Mordaunt Hall, "Servants' Entrance," *New York Times*, September 27, 1934.

212. Robert Nathan was a highly successful and esteemed novelist of the 1930s and 1940s. His other works include *Portrait of Jennie* and *The Bishop's Wife*, both of which were adapted as films in the 1940s. Nathan worked as a screenwriter for MGM in the 1940s, and his projects there included *The White Cliffs of Dover* (1943) and *The Clock* (1945).

213. Andre Sennwald, "One More Spring," *New York Times*, February 22, 1935.

214. Andre Sennwald, "One More Spring," *New York Times*, February 22, 1935.

215. "Charles Farrell, Wife Deny Divorce," *Oakland Tribune*, October 10, 1934.

216. *The Zanesville Signal*, November 17, 1935.

217. "Amicable Settlement," *Time Magazine*, July 29, 1935.

Chapter Ten: A Star Is Born

218. Janet Gaynor, unpublished interview transcript, Columbia University Oral History Research Project, November 1958, 23-24.

219. Henry Fonda with Howard Teichmann, *Fonda: My Life*, New York: New American Library, 1981, 97.

220. Andre Sennwald, "The Farmer Takes a Wife," *New York Times*, August 9, 1935.

221. It is unclear when Hilary actually passed away but Paul Gregory was sure it was prior to Laura Gaynor's death in 1969. According to Paul, "she was driving one day and dropped dead at the wheel of her car, at the stop sign."

222. Kent Bailey, "A Star Is Born Again," *Photoplay*, July 1937, 96.

223. Telegram from Jack Gain to Janet Gaynor, July 24, 1935, 20th Century-Fox Legal Files, Performing Arts Special Collections, UCLA.

224. Telegram from Darryl Zanuck to Janet Gaynor, October 29, 1935, 20th Century-Fox Legal Files, Performing Arts Special Collections, UCLA.

225. Frank S. Nugent, "Small Town Girl," *New York Times*, April 11, 1936.

226. Frank S. Nugent, "Small Town Girl"...1936.

227. Frank S. Nugent, "Ladies in Love," *New York Times*, October 29, 1936.

228. Rudy Behlmer, *Memo from Darryl F. Zanuck,* New York: Grove Press, 1993, 11.

229. Tyrone Power, Sr., (1869-1931) was one of the most acclaimed actors of his time, widely respected for his interpretation of Brutus in *Julius Caesar.*

230. Barbara Hayes, "How Tyrone Power Stole the Lonely Heart of Janet Gaynor," *Photoplay*, January 1938.

231. Statement to the press by 20th Century-Fox, issued September 25, 1936, 20th Century-Fox Legal Files, Performing Arts Special Collections, UCLA.

232. Statement to the press by Janet Gaynor, issued September 26, 1936 20th Century-Fox Legal Files, Performing Arts Special Collections, UCLA.

233. Paul Gregory, interview with author, April 2006.

234. Statement to the press by 20th Century-Fox, issued September 27, 1936.

235. Alice L. Tildesley, "Business Sense Comes to Hollywood," *Sunday Journal and Star*, January 24, 1937.

236. T.M.P., "Fighting Youth," *New York Times*, November 2, 1935.

237. William Malin, unpublished interview with Charles Farrell, April 14, 1976.

238. A style of trick horseback riding, in which one rider stands on top of a pair of horses, one foot on each horse.

239. William Malin, unpublished interview with Charles Farrell, April 14, 1976.

240. *The Movie Fan*, August 19, 1936.

241. Paul Harrison, "Australia's 'Spoiled Child' Is Here to Win Film Fame—And May Do It," *Syracuse Herald*, February 2, 1937.

242. Email from Charles Farrell historian Stephen O'Brien to author, October 22, 2008.

243. Janet Gaynor, unpublished interview transcript, Columbia University ... 20.

244. Email from Daniel Selznick to author, July 28, 2008.

245. Irene Mayer Selznick, *A Private View*, New York: Knopf, 1983, 208.

246. Janet Gaynor, unpublished interview transcript, Columbia University ... 20.

247. Telegram from David O. Selznick to Janet Gaynor, March 3, 1937, the David O. Selznick Collection, Harry Ransom Humanities Research Center, the University of Texas at Austin.

Chapter Eleven: Retirement

248. Kent Bailey, "A Star Is Born Again," *Photoplay*, July 1937, 98.

249. Maude Cheatham, "Now Back at the Head of the Class," *Motion Picture Magazine,* circa 1937.

250. Harry Lang, "Janet Gaynor's Amazing Coup," *Screen Book Magazine,* August 1937, 75.

251. Memo from David O. Selznick to Daniel O'Shea, April 23, 1937, the David O. Selznick Collection, Harry Ransom Humanities Research Center, the University

of Texas at Austin.

252. Kent Bailey, "A Star Is Born Again," *Photoplay*, July 1937, 36.

253. Maude Cheatham, "Now Back at the Head of the Class," *Motion Picture Magazine*, circa 1937.

254. Walter Winchell, March 17, 1937.

255. Jimmie Fiedler, "Jimmie Fiedler's Hollywood," March 15, 1937.

256. Harrison Carroll, "Behind the Scenes in Hollywood," *Evening Independent*, February 22, 1938.

257. William Drew, "Annabella," *At the Center of the Frame*, Vestal Press, 1999, 135.

258. Mayme Ober Peak, "How Janet Gaynor Helped Charles Farrell Come Back," *Movie Mirror*, October 1938, 83.

259. Members of Charlie's polo team included Frank Borzage, Walter Wanger, champion Carl Crawford, and Dr. Walter Branch. Prior to his death in 1935, Will Rogers was also a member of the team.

260. "Movie actor Charles Farrell appearing at Lakewood this week," *The Independent Reporter*, August 5, 1937.

261. Greg Niemann, *Palm Springs Legends*, California: Sunbelt Books, 2006, 133.

262. Robert Hardy Andrews, "Gatekeeper of the World's Most Opulent Oasis," *Midweek*, circa 1960.

263. Mayme Ober Peak, "How Janet Gaynor Helped Charles Farrell Come Back," *Movie Mirror*, October 1938, 83.

264. Mayme Ober Peak, "How Janet Gaynor Helped Charles Farrell Come Back," *Movie Mirror*, October 1938, 83.

265. Edwin Schallert, "'Young in Heart' Exhibits Quality," *Los Angeles Times*, December 1, 1938.

266. Frank S. Nugent, "Tail Spin," *New York Times*, February 11, 1939.

267. Memo from Daniel O'Shea to Janet Gaynor, June 8, 1938, the David O. Selznick Collection, Harry Ransom Humanities Research Center, the University of Texas at Austin.

268. Philip K. Scheuer, "Janet Gaynor New Type in 'Three Loves Has Nancy," *Los Angeles Times*, August 26, 1938.

269. Colette, "Film and Fashion," *Colette at the Movies: Criticism and Screenplays*, edited by Alain and Odette Virmaux, Frederick Ungar Film Publishing Co., 1980, 31.

270. Some writers have indicated that Adrian was asked by Louis B. Mayer to change his last name to disguise his Jewish heritage; however, the name changed occurred before Adrian came to MGM. According to son Robin, "The only thing that I heard was at that time it was fashionable to go by one name like Erte and a number of others, that was kind of how you made your mark. You picked a thing. If you went by a single name, Picasso, Dali, that's kind of how you did it. That's how he wanted to make his mark." Since Mayer also kept his own Jewish last name, it seems unlikely that he would ask any employee to change theirs.

271. Email from Daniel Selznick to author, August 11, 2008.

272. Robert Riley, "Adrian," *American Fashion*, edited by Sarah Tomerlin Lee, New

York: Fashion Institute of Technology, 1975, 41. Much of the biographical information concerning Adrian in this chapter comes from Riley's work.

273. In fact, Capra and Riskin were afraid that Janet was too big a name to star in *You Can't Take It with You,* as they were unsure of the commercial appeal of the film and worried it would tank at the box office.

274. Memo from David O. Selznick to Daniel O'Shea, October 10, 1938, the David O. Selznick Collection, Harry Ransom Humanities Research Center, the University of Texas at Austin.

275. *Forever* was written by author Mildred Cram, whose stories were made into films throughout the 1930s-1940s. It does not appear that *Forever* was made into a film.

276. Janet Gaynor, unpublished interview transcript, Columbia University Oral History Research Project, November 1958, 25.

277. Irene Mayer Selznick, *A Private View,* New York: Knopf, 1983, 119-120.

278. Gladys Hall, "The Most Revealing Interview Janet Gaynor Ever Gave," *Modern Screen,* August 1934.

279. Howard Gutner, *Gowns by Adrian: The MGM Years, 1928-1941,* New York: Harry N. Abrams, Inc., 191.

280. Howard Gutner, *Gowns by Adrian...* 101.

281. Robin Gaynor Adrian, interview with author, May 2006.

282. Janet Gaynor, unpublished interview transcript, Columbia University Oral History Research Project, November 1958, 25.

283. Bettina Johnson, *The Oakland Tribune,* March 1, 1941. Faye was between marriages at the time.

284. Frederick Othman, "Grapefruit Outdraws Film Stars," *Wisconsin State Journal,* February 12, 1941.

285. Joe Fisher, "Thumbnail previews," *Big Spring Daily Herald,* August 15, 1941.

286. Louella Parsons news item, January 7, 1943.

287. Charlie's nephew and namesake, Charles Farrell Jelliff (1927-1978), also served in the Navy as a Seaman Second Class. He enlisted on August 4, 1944 and was honorably discharged on October 8, 1947.

Chapter Twelve: Comeback

288. Report on the Fitness of Officers, April 5, 1943.

289. Report on the Fitness of Officers, July 31, 1943.

290. Report on the Fitness of Officers, April 18, 1944.

291. The original VF-17, under the command of Lt. Commander Tom Blackburn was disestablished on April 10, 1944.The Jolly Rogers, as this group was known, reformed under the command of Roger Hedrick as VF-84. Lieutenant Commander Marshall Beebe (1913-1991) led two squadrons in WWII and commanded Air Group 5 in the Korean War. Retired from the Navy with rank of captain in 1963.

Author James Michener dedicated *The Bridges of Toko-Ri* to Beebe.

292. Report on the Fitness of Officers, March 29, 1945.

293. Information on the *Hornet's* battles and statistics comes from the *USS Hornet* website, at http://www.uss-hornet.org.

294. Report on the Fitness of Officers, July 8, 1945.

295. Bob Hope, "It Says Here," *Abilene Reporter News*, November 25, 1948.

296. Bob Thomas, "Former Film Star Charles Farrell Keeps Busy as Mayor, Club Operator at Resort," *Evening Journal*, January 31, 1951.

297. Bob Thomas, "Gaynor, Farrell Meet Again in 7th Heaven'," *Tri-City Herald*, March 21, 1951.

298. Inez Robb, "Top Moment in Radio," *Doylestown Daily Intelligencer*, March 15, 1951.

299. Gale Storm, *I Ain't Down Yet*, New York: Bobbs-Merrill Company, 1981, 65.

300. Gale Storm, *I Ain't Down Yet*...72.

301. Gale Storm, *I Ain't Down Yet*...73.

302. Gale Storm, *I Ain't Down Yet*...67.

303. Ellis Walker, "Video Notes," *Daily Review*, June 7, 1956.

304. Robin Adrian, interview with author, May 2006.

305. Connie Billips, *Janet Gaynor: A Bio-Bibliography*, Westport, CT: Greenwood Press, 1992, 36.

306. Bob Thomas, "Adrians Leave Hollywood for Home in Brazil," *Austin Daily Herald*, October 21, 1955.

307. Stacy Wolf, *A Problem Like Maria: Gender and Sexuality in the American Musical*, University of Michigan, 2002, 84.

308. Bea Traub (1901-1982) was a famous personal shopper for Bonwit Teller, who helped celebrities such as Gloria Swanson make purchases. Although Wolf calls Traub a "bra maker," Traub would have been the person to find the bra maker and place the order on Halliday's behalf.

309. Stacy Wolf, *A Problem Like Maria*...84.

310. Robin Adrian, interview with author, May 2006.

311. Janet has been included in several exposes of gay and lesbian Hollywood, including Boze Hadleigh's *Hollywood Babble On* and Axel Madsen's *The Sewing Circle*. In a 2006 letter to the author, Hadleigh offered as proof of Gaynor's sexuality several rumors and innuendoes that were riddled with inaccuracies, including his insistence that she and Adrian were divorced. Hadleigh also included Charlie Farrell in his book, offering as proof the frequently misquoted "confession" by Anita Page that Charlie wore makeup. Madsen, in a 2006 letter to the author, admitted he had no proof of Janet's supposed sexuality, other than "Boze Hadleigh's usually unreliable word" but included her in *The Sewing Circle* anyway.

312. Pat Boone, "A Star Was Born," A&E *Biography*.

313. Robin Adrian, interview with author, May 2006.

314. Gay Pauley, "Janet Gaynor Seeks Relief from Grief in Stage Role," *Simpson's Leader-*

Times, October 14, 1959.

315. Robert Riley, "Adrian," *American Fashion*, edited by Sarah Tomerlin Lee, New York: Fashion Institute of Technology, 1975, 44.

316. Paul Gregory, interview with author, April 2006.

317. Robin Adrian, interview with author, May 2006.

Chapter Thirteen: Pristine Lives

318. Howard Lapham, interview with author, October 2004.

319. Letter from Rose Hobart to Connie Billips, Woodland Hills, California, circa 1990s.

320. Ferenc Molnar, *Liliom: A Legend in Seven Scenes and a Prologue*, New York: Boni and Liverwright, 1921,

321. Frank Bogert, interview with author, October 2004.

322. Myrna Loy and James Kotsilibas-Davis, *Myrna Loy: Being and Becoming*, New York: Knopf, 1987, 264.

323. Charles Francisco, *Gentleman: The William Powell Story*. New York: St. Martin's Press, 1985, 211.

324. Charles Francisco, *Gentleman*...210.

325. Dennis McDougal, "Palm Springs Squire Remembers 'A Helluva Career,'" *Los Angeles Times*, January 23, 1977.

326. Ferenc Molnar, *Liliom*...57.

327. James Bacon, "Star Millionaire only on Screen," *Show Time*, June 19, 1960.

328. Frank Bogert, interview with author, October 2004.

329. Dennis McDougal, "Palm Springs Squire..." *Los Angeles Times*, January 23, 1977.

330. Paul Gregory, interview with author, April 2006.

331. Paul Gregory, interview with author, April 2006.

332. James Bacon, "Janet Gaynor Weds Producer 15 Yrs. Younger," *Philadelphia Inquirer*, December 25, 1964.

333. Robin Adrian, interview with author, May 2006.

334. Paul Gregory, interview with author, April 2006.

335. "Oscar Winner-Janet Gaynor-is Broadway's Newest Star," *After Dark*, February 1980.

336. Elmer Pasta, "Janet Gaynor Debuts Own Paintings," publication unknown, circa 1970s.

337. Rex Reed, "Janet Gaynor: From film queen to stage doyenne," *Chicago Tribune* (1976).

338. Oscar Winner-Janet Gaynor-is Broadway's Newest Star," *After Dark*, February 1980.

339. Bruce Fessier, "A Conversation with Charles Farrell," *The Desert Sun*, October 27, 1980, A-6.

340. Dennis McDougal, "Palm Springs Squire..." *Los Angeles Times*, January 23, 1977.

341. Dennis McDougal, "Palm Springs Squire..." *Los Angeles Times*, January 23, 1977.

342. Bruce Fessier, "A Conversation..." *The Desert Sun*, October 27, 1980, A-6.

343. Washer had been Martin's companion following Richard Halliday's death in 1973.

344. Robin Adrian, interview with author, May 2006.

345. "Driver Gets Three-Year Term in Martin-Gaynor Crash," Syracuse Herald-Journal, March 16, 1983.

346. Letter from Janet Gaynor Gregory to Gina LoBiondo, circa 1982.

347. Email from Daniel Selznick to author, July 27, 2008.

348. Email from Daniel Selznick to author, July 27, 2008.

Index

They say there's nothing like a good book...

We think that says quite a lot!

BearManorMedia